THE NOVELS OF ANTHONY POWELL

The Novels of
Anthony Powell

James Tucker

Columbia University Press

New York   1976

77–10146

Published in Great Britain in 1976 by
THE MACMILLAN PRESS LTD

Printed in Great Britain

Library of Congress Cataloging in Publication Data

Tucker, Allan James, 1929–
    The novels of Anthony Powell.

    Bibliography: p.
    Includes index.
    1. Powell, Anthony, 1905–   —Criticism and
interpretation.   I.   Title.

PR6031.074Z94   823'.9'12   76–15201
ISBN 0–231–04150–0

Contents

Preface

The form of this book gave me some problems. In one sense it seemed wrong not to start with Powell's main achievement, the *Music of Time* sequence. Yet it was necessary to show how the early, pre-war novels pointed towards this later work. I decided to take the early novels first (several deserve full consideration on their own account, anyway, not just for what they promised) and try to correct any consequent loss of proportion by attempting early a general picture in the Introduction. It is an Introduction which, I suppose, might almost just as appositely have come as a conclusion; though in a section headed Conclusion there would be pretensions to a certainty and definiteness which I am happy to avoid.

How to treat the *Music of Time* sequence itself also raised some questions. I wanted to look overall at the work, to try to draw its general qualities together for discussion, but was also aware that many readers might know only some of the twelve books. My compromise, not altogether satisfactory, is to give first a simplified route through the twelve volumes by means of a *Who's Who* of characters; then to examine certain important features of the sequence; and lastly – this being the most difficult – to take the books in chronological order of publication, say briefly what each is about, while treating also what seem to me the most interesting critical aspects raised: some of my choices may seem arbitrary, but I could think of no other way of tackling such varied yet unified subject matter.

Throughout discussion of *A Dance to the Music of Time* I have been inclined to use the word 'novel' for the whole sequence and 'book' or 'volume' for its separate parts. If there are inconsistencies I hope the reader will be able to deduce from the context which is meant.

I would like to thank Professor Gwyn Jones of University College, Cardiff, for reading much of the text and for making a great number of helpful suggestions. John Grigg, also of the college, and a Powell devotee, read the draft and donated some excellent insights, as well as proposing a beneficial cut or two. My wife, Marian, helped considerably with the checking of names, but any errors are mine.

Some of the abbreviated titles look formidable, but I think the reader will get used to them. I am grateful to William Heinemann Ltd, Powell's publishers, for allowing me to quote extensively. The *Who's Who* appeared slightly shortened in *The New Review*.

J.T.

Biographical Note

Anthony Powell was born in 1905, the son of a regular army officer in the Welch Regiment. He was educated at Eton and Oxford. He now lives in Somerset.

After Oxford he worked for Duckworth, the publishers, who brought out his first four novels. He left publishing to become a film scriptwriter for a short time and has also worked in literary journalism. From 1952 to 1958 he was literary editor of *Punch*. At present he reviews regularly for the *Daily Telegraph*.

During the war he served in the Welch Regiment and the Intelligence Corps, becoming a major. He was awarded several foreign decorations. In 1956 he was made a C.B.E. He is a Trustee of the National Portrait Gallery.

At Lady Molly's (1957) won the James Tait Black prize; and *Temporary Kings* (1973) the W. H. Smith fiction award. He is a D.Litt. of the University of Sussex (1971).

In 1934 he married Lady Violet Pakenham and has two sons. Besides the works dealt with here he has written *John Aubrey and His Friends* (London, 1948) and two plays, *The Garden God* and *The Rest I'll Whistle* (London, 1971). He has edited *Novels of High Society from the Victorian Age* (London, 1947) and *Brief Lives and Other Selected Writings of John Aubrey* (London, 1949). He has contributed 'This Wat'ry Glade' [Eton] to *The Old School. Essays by Divers Hands*, edited by Graham Greene (London, 1934); 'Proust as a Soldier' to *Marcel Proust 1871–1922, A Centenary Volume*, edited by Peter Quennell (London, 1971); 'A Memoir' to *Constant Lambert*, by Richard Shead (London, 1973).

Abbreviations

Introduction

Anyone wanting to give a general idea of Anthony Powell's novels will find himself talking pretty soon about an easily recognised prose style and a steady concern with the well-born, well-off and well-educated. As it happens, the writing changes sharply between the early books and *ADTTMOT*; for that matter, there are changes within *ADTTMOT*. But a distinctive polish, restraint and wit do run through all, and touches of learning are fairly regular. As to class, a few books may glance at lowish, or even low, life but this is not typical and usually signals a trip to bohemia, a barracks or – in *HSH* – to Cultsville.

One further common quality needs to be mentioned early: a constant aim to be readable, to entertain, for the most part wonderfully realised. To draw the three elements together, one can say that much of this readability in *ADTTMOT* and in several of the earlier books comes from the elegantly deadpan treatment of liberated upper-class behaviour, and especially sexual behaviour: the lowdown on high life in charming undemonstrative prose.

If Powell's work went only this far it would be slight: no more than a slick and funny exposé of the privileged. That is not how it turns out. Certainly the novels occupy themselves at some length with shallow, possibly effete, lives and skilfully create the right drifting, inconstant, often anarchic tone of the society they inhabit. What seems to give the books their substance is this unflurried willingness to see high life as it is and accept its rough edges; while suggesting in a moderate, not too convinced manner that it is better on the whole to do things in a humane, temperate way free from self-obsession and from cruelty. About this light-hearted compliance with the world's uneven style is something of what Orwell saw and liked in Henry Miller, though Powell and Miller are, of course, looking at very different pictures. Tolerance, humanity, decency attend Powell's heroes and narrators and come through to the reader as the qualities most worth bothering about.

That sounds a modest proposition. All the same, the three qualities demand, an immediate word of reservation. The tolerance is very open-eyed – it would not be needed otherwise – and mixed with irony; sometimes temporarily swamped by it. The humanity can be disturbingly selective and, notably in the early books, seems to stop short of waiters, doormen and the sick: bronchitis rates as a joke in early Powell. The decency has limits, too, and occasionally dwindles into respect for mere *savoir faire* and clique loyalties: it is often from the standpoint that Widmerpool, the *Music of Time's* abiding villain, is seen as an oddity.

A strong, practical and wholesome gospel comes over, none the less. Calculated or careless harshness to others is what the books brand as most odious. Three examples will do here. Sexual philanderers qualify for amused, entirely uncensorious treatment unless, like Odo Stevens, they flaunt their adultery and cause extra pain to the cuckold. Such a thesis may look facile since any broken marriage can bring distress, whether or not the adultery is discreet. Powell, though, starts from the assumption that love and sex will go their own way and that we had better recognise it; tact marks the difference between the inevitable and the thoughtless – not all-important, but important.

Second: Widmerpool's basic evil is callousness; lacking humanity he cannot reach to tolerance or decency, only to humbug. At first his faults reveal themselves in the small-scale, almost permissible – almost inculcated – savageries of those starting disadvantaged and frantic for career advancement; laughing matters. Later, though, from the same roots they blossom to a murderous disregard – literally that – for others.

Lastly, Mr Passenger in *FAVTAD* has a similar cold, deadly wilfulness and this, coupled with the fierce self-centredness of the hero, Zouch, gives the book its sombre note of comprehensive disapproval.

One feels, then, a plea throughout Powell's books for the natural warmth and vitality of life to be allowed their expression. Bores and monsters get in the way. It is this belief which gives the platform on which Powell's humour, elegance and *épatant* disclosures rest, and which provide the books with the solid ground to support their charm. A reservation must be made here too, though. In many ways, Powell, like the narrator of *ADTTMOT*, has a classical mind and terms like warmth and vitality may sound purple; after all, the standard description of his style is cool. In addition, a conservative, if not Conservative, rationality pervades the books: the temporary Leftist excesses of Erridge and St John Clarke in *ADTTMOT* are sent up with protracted relish; and Uncle Giles takes a constant drubbing for falling short of accepted values and for trying to make a creed of disorderliness. Yet, for all their attention to control, and their regard for decorum and what is proper (for what Stephen Potter would have termed OK) the books see further. We sympathis, for instance, with the desperately contorted feelings between Pamela and Trapnel. Men of the imagination, like Barnby, Moreland and Trapnel, whose lives are none too well organised, come over as 'better' than figures of power and wealth like Donners; though it is true that novels traditionally take more kindly to men of the imagination than to the other sort, and not only because fiction gets written by men of the imagination. Part-ruined figures such as Jeavons, Stringham, Maclintick – the last not even passably good-natured – are presented as more worthwhile than, say, Buster Foxe or Widmerpool, both of whom for long periods seem to have the world cut and dried.

The distinction of Powell's novels is that they engagingly look at surfaces and, at the same time, suggest that this is by no means enough. They will continually disturb the surface to show us much more. In their quiet way they direct us towards a good, practical, unextreme general philosophy of life. Where very specific admirable behaviour is implied by the irony the books are less assured: Nicholas Jenkin's radiantly unexceptionable marriage comes to seem freakish, given the surrounding sexual restlessness; what St John Clarke, during his Marxist days, would have called bourgeois. The assertions which really count in the book, though, are made through an overall generosity of outlook and a consistent advocacy of sound sense.

What, then, is Powell's stature? It can be unfair and dangerous to blame novelists for what they have left out: the critical focus has slipped on to infinity. All the same, one does feel conscious of large gaps in Powell's work. Without joining such of Powell's justifiably guyed figures as Guggenbühl – who heavily demands social commitment in literature ('No mere entertainment, please') – one would like to glimpse the presence now and then, or even the shadow, of that duller, poorer, grubbier world most of us inhabit. It seems something of a dodge that when, in *HSH*, we do make a peacetime excursion from high society and bohemia it has to be into the world of dropout cranks; and the occupations which the two principals have quit – antiques and art-dealing – are no doubt tough but not particularly commonplace. Again, though Powell believes in and extols feelings he is not good at igniting them on the page so that the reader feels the heat; it does happen, but the moments are exceptional. The books fall particularly short on the emotional lives of women, and a disproportionate number of his females seem brassy, shallow, restless. When, during the later books of *ADTTMOT*, he attempts something more in Pamela Flitton he resorts to over-colouring. Yet Ortrud Mavrin, portrayed by Powell with such delightful warmth in what was only his second novel, *V*, showed a genuine understanding of women, and it is hard to know why he discarded it.

Possibly related to his failure to involve us in feelings is an inability, or disinclination, to deal with action as if it were taking place while we watch; the reader tends to view from afar, with the aid of first-class field-glasses, it is true, and an amusing commentary, but we are at times conscious of the distance. In Powell's work there is a general flight from immediacy, and notably in *ADTTMOT* where the narrative method is allowed to fuzz incident and situation. Often this is essential to Powell's intent, but the lack of definition and energy which can result is a disturbing weakness, just the same.

There are the standard comparisons to be considered. I do not think very much can be learned from putting *ADTTMOT* alongside Proust's *A la Recherche de Temps Perdu*. Proust's eye is on his narrator's development ('the goal is in my heart', as *Swann's Way* has it); Powell's is not: the goal is in social patterns. Proust is 'Far more subjective', as Powell put it in a BBC television interview on 8 September 1975. Waugh? Powell does better at keeping comic matter credible and naturalistic. He can be more facetious but is less enslaved by formula understatement; is less dutifully clipped and more various and bold in style. Waugh is superior – enormously – at suggesting emotion. Powell has greater skill than Waugh's in tracing political and social shifts and, at least until *HSH*, remains free from the lumpy transcendentalism which buckles the structure of *Brideshead Revisited*.

What Powell has is a powerful sense of life through character, caricature and period; fine humour and invention; a largely humane point of view; and unequalled competence at setting down the ways of a small, deeply interesting class of English society. Technically, he has remarkably extended what can be done through the first-person narrative; and he has the control to mix comfortably within one volume very different modes of novel writing: naturalism, fantasy, comedy, farce, occasional tragedy.

EARLY NOVELS

Afternoon Men

'I'm not a religious sort of chap. I don't know anything about
that sort of thing. But there must be something beyond all this
sex business.'
'Yes.'
'You think so?'
'Oh yes. Quite likely. Why not?'
'But what?'
'I can't help.'
'You can't.'

Much of the matter and method of Anthony Powell's first novel
Afternoon Men (1931), is caught in this comically becalmed exchange between Fotheringham, a struggling, drink-hazed journalist,
here blindly seeking deeper truths, and William Atwater, the book's
hero, who so blankly refuses guidance. This is a book of continuously
mannered style whose entertaining surface is broken now and then
by the brief but clear sight of some enormously important theme; it
is the early form of a method which Powell will follow throughout
his work. Like leaping fish, big topics may glint for a second in *AM*
before sinking again beneath the sea of inarticulate if not opaque
dialogue. Fotheringham's insight that 'there must be something beyond this sex business' is central to the novel. But it must be spoken
by a lightweight, hilariously disorganised character so that the
book's sustained tone of farce and inconsequence will not be ruptured by *prêchi-prêcha*.

Yet the theme is constantly present and *AM*'s apparent shallow-
ness may at any time be touched by sadness and, to risk a more
ponderous term, significance. The novel shows a group of mainly
young people at a fairly undistinguished level of London society between the wars. Although we do see and hear something of their
work, the book is preoccupied with their social and sexual lives. The
picture is not without affection – possibly, at times, complicity –

but Powell's purpose is mainly satiric. His title comes from Burton's *The Anatomy of Melancholy*: 'they are a company of giddy-heads, afternoon men.' In its understated, elusive way the novel is asking what place genuine feelings can have in the empty world under examination. With regret, it answers, none.

William Atwater's experiences reveal this sombre truth. Although physically not striking – 'a weedy-looking young man with straw-coloured hair and rather long legs' – he finds himself involved with a series of women. Of these, Susan Nunnery, a beauty, affects him powerfully. More so than Atwater she is very much a part of the rootless, wilfully superficial life that he would like to leave. They come together briefly and almost at once she begins to draw away. From the start we know she is changeable: apparently she has just given up living with a man called Gilbert.

Eventually, she and Atwater go out to dinner together, but the meeting turns to fiasco because the restaurant is full of people they know who join them from time to time, talking banalities, preventing any real intimacy. It is one of the book's funniest scenes and looks forward to a technique that Powell will often employ in *ADTTMOT*: his insistence that members of such London social groups lived almost ludicrously confined, interdependent lives. Atwater does attempt to woo Susan during dinner, all the same.

'You're so lovely.'
She smiled at him.
He said it again that he thought her lovely and he was trying to think of a less pedestrian formula when . . .

There is another interruption. What Powell wants to say here is what he tells us throughout the novel: the relentless trivia of social life may kill any deeper relationship, probably before it starts. Prufrock longed to break out from the cocktail party chatter about Michelangelo to something larger. Though several of them are painters, the members of Atwater's circle do not reach even that level of small talk.

At first, it is only comic accident which gives Atwater such a rough time. Then Susan begins to demonstrate a second and more pointed stage of Powell's case: if emotion is outlawed in favour of pleasure and excitement, emotion finally becomes impossible. 'No, don't be a bore. I'm tired,' she says, fending off Atwater in the taxi after dinner. A bore: it is the rebuke for off-colour social behaviour, not for the over eagerness of a would-be lover.

And Susan continues to drift from him. It is not that she is simply an empty creature incapable of feeling. She has taken a decision to live only on the surface, and hints that she has been in love, found it painful and now intends to run from seriousness, much as Atwater wants to run from superficiality.

> She said: 'What's the good of our going out together?'
> 'Well, I like it.'
> 'But I'm not in love with you. I tell you I hate being in love. I don't want to be in love.'

And, after they have been to a boxing match, she tells Atwater, 'It is always rather a business. Our meetings.' It is 'rather a business' because Atwater is looking for the real thing, and this she finds tiresome.

Finally, Susan leaves London – and the novel – with Verelst, a Jew, apparently of independent means. Bereft, Atwater is seen at the end of this book dismally about to take up where Chapter 1 began, preparing for another party. (A similar circular construction will be found in *AQOU*.) Atwater's search for something deeper has failed and, we gather, will go on failing. The warmth, vitality and feelings prized in Powell's novels are rarely suggested in *AM*. And, in its offhand way, the book mourns their absence from the characters' lives.

The message is reinforced by Atwater's inability to find love with another woman. He pursues a model named Lola, though in spectacularly uncommitted fashion. The sex is flat, meaningless and – in the author's view rather than Atwater's – absurd. The scene I quote below looks forward to the dismal sex between Nicholas and Gypsy Jones in *ABM*. (We may notice that the passage following the dialogue – often cited approvingly as an example of Powell's early style – shows the casual way with metaphor which will occasionally turn up later in his work: an edifice which broods and creaks and changes into a mechanism which can lumber.)

> 'Don't,' she said. 'You're not allowed to do that.'
> 'Why not?'
> 'Because you're not.'
> 'I shall.''
> 'She said: 'I'm glad we met. But you must behave.'
> Slowly, but very deliberately, the brooding edifice of seduction, creaking and incongruous, came into being, a vast Heath

Robinson mechanism, dually controlled by them and lumbering gloomily down vistas of triteness. With a sort of heavy-fisted dexterity the mutually adapted emotions of each of them became synchronised, until the unavoidable anticlimax was at hand. Later they dined at a restaurant quite near the flat.

It is sometimes said of *AM* that Powell, unlike Waugh, offers no comment on his characters. True, explicit comment is rare, though strongly and unambiguously suggested throughout. And occasionally, as in this last extract, Powell could scarcely be more direct in giving us his view of characters and, at the same time, in stating his theme: the aridity of 'this sex business'. Atwater's affair with Lola ends untouched by feeling. 'So it was all over', he reflects, reading her letter of dismissal.

Atwater has also a fleeting, though consummated, affair with Harriet Twining, the mistress of his friend Raymond Pringle, an artist. Farce, or very heavy irony, predominates. They make love in a wood, having just watched unwittingly what the reader takes to be Pringle's suicide by drowning. Again there are the deadening, impersonal, mechanical preliminaries. Harriet says:

'This is silly.'
'Not at all.'
'Wait a moment.'
'That's better.'

And once more Atwater is disappointed. 'Curse you for giggling,' he tells her. Irritability and paralysingly banal conversation about the weather close their afternoon together.

The lives of others beside William are filled, as it were, with sexual emptiness. Barlow, the painter, debates amusingly about which of several girls he should marry, never citing love as a factor. It is very nearly true to say that no settled sexual relationship is shown anywhere in the book. There are characters who are, or have been, married, but their spouses are missing. Susan lives with her father, and we meet no Mrs Nunnery. A Mrs Race has 'a late Race'. Shattering impermanence prevails. One of Atwater's contemporaries, Undershaft, has seemingly found contentment with a coloured woman in New York: only far away and through what, by this group's standards, constitutes outlandish behaviour is such magical stability possible; New York is wonderland. In any case, as soon as Undershaft returns to Britain he takes up with a new girl; new to him, at least, since it is Lola. One apparently permanent relationship is seen in *AM*. This is between Mr and Mrs Chalk, parents of the maid who cleans Pringle's country cottage. But they are of a different class from the chief characters and their inclusion only strengthens the generalisation that *AM* is a touching though consistently funny account of the trivialisation of life by a set with some social privilege.

How much? Social classification is made a little difficult by the bohemian personnel, the painters and models. And, although it is continually implied that some people and behaviour are unarguably all right, while others and their behaviour are unarguably not, no very consistent standard of social judgements is obvious; about such standards as we do see there is something exceedingly frail.

It can be said definitely enough, though, that we are among, at the lowest, middle-class people and possibly something higher. Between Atwater's set and the few working-class characters seen a brutally emphatic demarcation exists. This great gulf is typical of Powell's early novels. Most of the working-class characters in these books are flunkeys and they come in for very rough handling. They may be repulsively ill (like the doorman in *V*, who has a birthmark on his face and suffers a 'bronchial upheaval like a tornado'); or ugly and ill (like Ethel Chalk in *AM*, who looks anaemic; or the boy in Atwater's museum, who is ill-conditioned, overgrown, with a cauliflower ear and freckles); or ugly and stupid (like the 'ape-faced dotard' who is on the door at Pringle's art exhibition, and who is also 'a senile cretin'); or physically flawed and stupid (like the porter at the country station near Pringle's cottage who is 'deaf and partly mad'); or disreputable in some not too specific way (like the waiter at Atwater's dinner with Susan, whose face was 'furrowed with the minor dishonesties of uncounted years'; or the commissionaires outside the club where we first meet Atwater, who look like 'two Shakespearian murderers, minor thugs from one of the doubtfully ascribed plays'). Whether these cheap, savage views of people are the hero's or the author's is not clear. We must hope, I think, though without very convincing evidence, that in this early work Powell had not completely learned how to tell a story; how to ensure that his central figure's opinions are not attributable to the novelist. When, in *ADTTMOT*, we come to the death of Moreland, illness and ill-breeding are no longer equated for a giggle.

More subtle than the blazing distinction between middle and working classes are the suggestions that not everyone who strays into the same social scene as *AM*'s main group of characters may be altogether acceptable. The treatment of Verelst is worrying. Once more we are not sure whether the description comes from Powell or Atwater, but once more one hopes from Atwater: Verelst has 'bags under the eyes and rather a thick nose, but the general effect was not bad and he hardly looked like a Jew at all.' Classic manipulation of smear operates here. It is taken for granted that Jewish appearance is intolerable, and Verelst obviously has just enough of it to be off-putting. He may come very near to some standard of social excellence, but only very near: 'His moustache was arranged so that it made him look as if he might be in the Brigade of Guards, but although it was plausible it was not really convincing.' Or: 'He looked rather distinguished, but his clothes fitted him too well in the wrong way.' Everyone knows which is the wrong way, of course.

Yet Powell shows Verelst as having fought in the war and as being worldly, knowing and impressively cool. Further, he does get the girl, though that may be in part a comment on Susan and her flight from love. It looks as if Powell is saying something that will appear in *ADTTMOT* through the character of Kenneth Widmerpool: that social acceptability may comfort those who confer it upon each other but some outsiders may do pretty well without it. Powell is concerned in *AM* not only with the set's sexual emptiness, but also with the dire frailty of social assumptions after the First War, at least in this *demi-monde*. Perhaps it is only through caustic treatment of doormen that superiority can be asserted. As to money, few of the principal characters seem to have enough, though Pringle lives on a private income. They argue about small sums and, in Fotheringham's case, struggle along in dismal jobs. Of course, some of the stinginess could be simply part of an upper-class attitude to the lower orders, and this is probably how we are to take the long, extremely funny argument about the size of the tip for the man who saves Pringle from drowning. Overall, though, there seems little real money about, and much of the satire lies in this conjunction of pretension and poverty, attitude and emptiness.

AM's construction and style catch admirably the mood of drifting inconsequence seen in its characters' lives. Two brilliant set-pieces carry much of the book: the opening party which, in preparation and immediate aftermath, occupies almost a fifth of the novel; and the excursion to Pringle's cottage, the supposed suicide and marvellously matter-of-fact debate among the guests about what action should be taken. Between these come smaller set-pieces. Atwater and Susan at dinner; Atwater at work; Atwater and Susan at a boxing match. Links between these scenes are minimal; cause and effect do not obtrude; minor characters (such as the comic nuisance Dr J. Crutch) and background incident (such as the boxing) are given sizeable space, without having too much bearing on the book's main theme. Characters like the American publisher Scheigan, always searching for some epic party, come and go, providing comic adornment. Undershaft, frequently the subject of conversation – sometimes almost reverential conversation – does not appear. Consistently Powell avoids neatness, symmetry and well-fashioned motivation because these would clamp on to his glimpse of this social group an inappropriate system and order.

Many chapters end in farce or banality, particularly chapters where some deep, possibly poignant, matter has been hinted at. The technique is deliberate and, for the most part, highly effective. Powell is, of course, writing here and in most of his work about a group which conceals, plays down and even avoids feelings. But feelings cannot be entirely excluded from life, nor are they from the novel. In the world that Atwater inhabits, though, they must be spoken of only obliquely and briefly, then buried. Powell will glance into the depths but make sure that the final view is of anticlimax: let not the sun go down upon your emotion. And so, at the party (the novel's second) where Susan tells Atwater that she is going away, we are briskly led from this mood of sadness to drunken ramblings about clean glasses and germs from the book's stand-by clown, Fotheringham. Similarly, when Susan has failed to turn up for a meeting with Atwater – an unmistakable signal to the reader that graver disappointments lie ahead – Atwater finishes the chapter with Nosworth, a museum colleague, at The Plumbers' Arms. Here Nosworth contributes several halfpennies to a busker's bag and we feel the scale of things coming down sharply. Then: ' "I must be going," Norworth said. They went out and Atwater made his way home through the rain.' There is similar deflation in the account of lovemaking with Lola already mentioned, with its final throwaway sentence embodying the sexual anticlimax: 'Later they dined at a restaurant quite near the flat.' Most of the damage is done by the banal exactitude of that 'quite'.

Possibly the closing letdown is overused in *AM* and becomes something of a routine. This is a young man's book and Powell was not yet ruthless enough in rationing and varying his techniques. As Jenkins decides, while reflecting about writing methods in *TAW*, understatement has its own hazards. All the same, the overall impact in *AM* is right: to make us see the flatness of life when feelings are kept out.

A discussion of style in *AM* must be mainly to do with dialogue. Powell abandons the heavy reliance on speech after this novel and in *ADTTMOT* conversation is comparatively sparing. *AM*'s dialogue is almost always laconic and, by intent, generally trite and laborious. Through it Powell conveys much of his amused criticism of this aimless and silly group. Lola explains to Atwater how she spilled her drink over Pringle:

> 'Is your friend angry?'
> 'Yes.'
> 'I was looking for my bag.'
> 'Were you?'
> 'It was suddenly knocked out of my hand all over him.'

A contrived slowness is operating. It would be clearly wasteful for a novelist interested in pace and economy of expression – and novelists are generally interested in both – to follow an unmesmeric remark like 'I was looking for my bag' with the stagnant line 'Were you?' On many other occasions throughout the book Powell's object is to hold back the narrative, stretch the emptiness, often by repetition:

> 'What would you like to eat?'
> 'Anything.'
> 'Anything?'
> 'Oh, yes, anything.'

These sluggish, formula conversations excellently catch the pattern of such lives. Effects vary: sometimes world-weariness; sometimes slow-wittedness, the result, we infer, of late nights and/or drink; and sometimes we feel the vain effort to reach deeper significance despite inadequate vocabulary and traditional reticence. Nor, in most cases, do these conversations defy belief. Like Pinter, Powell was able to spot and reproduce in entertaining form the stunted nature of so much speech.

Frequently, too, he can use monosyllabic, repetitious conversation to say far more than appears, a skill crucial in realistic fiction. Susan telephones to say she is not coming to meet Atwater:

> 'So sorry I shalln't be able to see you tonight. I'm in the country.'
> 'I see.'

'I can't get away.'
'Can't you?'
'You don't mind, do you?'
'Yes.'
She laughed.
'No, you don't really.'
'All right, I don't.'

Those words, seemingly at the rock-bottom of communication, in fact manage to say everything about this hopeless affair.

At time, perhaps, the technique becomes a little too obvious and insistent, a little too systematic: once more the fault seems to be that of a young writer fascinated by his skills.

Barlow said: 'Susan Nunnery.'
Atwater said: 'That's Susan Nunnery, is it?'
'That,' said Pringle, 'is Susan Nunnery.'

Irrelevant, inane background conversation is allowed to drag on now and then, as if Powell cannot let the joke die. Authors wanting to portray vacuousness ought to guard against seeming vacuous.

There would be little point in simplifying speech in *AM* if literary graces were apparent outside the quotation marks. An obvious pointer to Powell's wish to avoid undue faciliness in the prose in his continual introduction by dialogue by 'said'; hardly ever does he resort to those novelist's synonyms like 'went on' or 'added' or even 'asked', useful in preventing monotony: the practice is on view in the three lines of speech just quoted but can be spread over much longer conversations in *AM*. Life, as shaped by this group, is casual and down-beat; the writing must be, too. Only very occasionally in the search for extreme simplicity does Powell slip into the *faux-naïf*: the first sentence of Chapter 2, with its harping on 'was' and awkward second use of 'party' reads a little too much like the writing of a child, though it may conceivably be meant as pastiche Hemingway: 'The party had begun by the time they arrived and was a good one, except that the flat it was being given in was not big enough to hold all the people who had decided to come to the party.'

It would be untrue to say that all the writing of *AM* is pared down and simple. Once or twice Powell turns to a very complicated, parenthetic style, rich in multisyllable words; in fact, a style which foreshadows the prose of *ADTTMOT*. Atwater's seduction of Lola is in that sort of language: double-barrelled epithets such as 'heavy-fisted' and 'mutually-adapted'; asides like 'creaking and incongruous'; an image like 'vistas of triteness' – all these leave behind the fiercely restrained prose usual in *AM*. Occasionally, too, convoluted language will be used to carry some facetiousness, a mannerism familiar to readers of Fielding, Dickens or Wodehouse: first the high-sounding verbosity, then the abrupt fall: 'It was at that moment of time, when Pringle was speculating as to the probability of his comparative success or the reverse with Harriet, that a glass of beer was upset over his legs.' Novelists are, of course, at liberty to vary their style within a book, or within a paragraph. In *AM*, though, these sudden and rare changes from the established tone of voice do produce slightly uncomfortable moments. Significantly, the style is generally used here for direct address by Powell to the reader and, as I have already suggested, he is sometimes confused in *AM* about how the story is to be told, whether via Atwater's or the author's eye. In this novel, Latinate style generally signals that Powell is elbowing his way forward to pitch some message or joke or interpretation at us. It is this clash with his customary obliqueness, subtlety and detachment which unsettles the reader. By the time he reaches *ADTTMOT* he will have evolved a more sophisticated and adaptable narrative method which permits at least two, and sometimes more, simultaneous viewpoints and which works very well.

AM remains a book of remarkable qualities, despite signs of immaturity. Characterisation is not yet highly developed, but Atwater and Susan have their intricacies of personality, as we have seen, and even comic figures like Pringle and Fotheringham are liable to flashes of individuality and dignity. Above all, the novel is very funny, combining understated wit, farce and what might be called comedy of mannerisms. It also sounds a gentle but clearly heard note of sadness that things should be as they are. We are given a credible portrait of a social group whose failings are special to them, yet which, because they are to do with the trivialiation of life, hint at the failings of men everywhere. As Walter Allen puts it in *Tradition And Dream* (London, 1964) Powell opposes the 'messiness' of these particular lives with 'what might be called an aesthetic disdain expressed in the austerity, the formal order, of the novel itself.' That order is functioning even when *AM* seems to drift and sprawl.

Venusberg

Like *AM*, Powell's second novel *Venusberg* (1932), also moves in something of an ironic, deflationary circle, its end similar in mood to its opening. Although *V*, too, is almost continuously funny, the flavour has become more subtle; and the novel's world is wider and harsher, its personnel socially more various, their lives less confined and less protected.

In a superficial sense the book may be seen as a love story. More conventionally plotted than *AM*, it contains no elaborate comic set-pieces and skilfully uses several minor characters in linking roles. A general article on Powell in the *TLS* (16 February 1951) found *V* an advance on *AM* because of 'symmetry of form'.

Lushington, the hero of *V*, does get the girl finally, as well as another with whom he occupies the waiting time. Yet the novel's happy ending – a colourful phrase in the circumstances – springs out of sad, farcical accident, and amounts to no rhapsody of fulfilment. The avowals pulsate with compromise. Lucy says:

> 'I suppose I'm more or less yours now.'
> 'Yes.'
> 'If you still want me.'

Lushington does not reply. Another affirmative would presumably make matters too emphatic, even passionate.

The book's irony is remarkably complicated, beginning with the basic agonies of those who yearn only for the lover they cannot have, and developing towards vast strokes of luck – good or bad, depending on who you are – in the conclusion. Lushington loves Lucy. But Lucy loves Lushington's friend, Da Costa. He does not love her. Lushington's pain is further sharpened when he goes as foreign correspondent to a Baltic city where Da Costa is a diplomat, and is thus constantly reminded of his failure with Lucy. On the boat out Lushington starts an affair with Ortrud Mavrin, and this continues when they arrive. Ortrud's husband, a professor of psychology, comes to suspect that she is unfaithful and asks for a talk with Lushington on the subject. He is duly fearful, but it turns out to be Da Costa whom this world expert on human behaviour suspects. He also believes that Ortrud actively dislikes Lushington, regarding him as a rival for Da Costa's affection. After a ball, Da Costa and Ortrud share a cab home and are shot dead by assassins aiming at the local police chief. Da Costa is thus removed as a rival and, we are to infer, Professor Mavrin will assume that, since the two were together, his suspicions were correct. Lushington returns to Britain and Lucy. She also suspects an affair between Da Costa and Ortrud. Lushington's involvement remains secret and he is thus able to take over Lucy.

The point Powell is making does not become entirely clear. One must beware of sounding like Professor Mavrin and imposing weightily obtuse interpretations on a book where charm and delicacy of touch are so important. *V* does seem to say that life may at any time become violently random and that when it does there will be winners and losers. Those who win may find that the way they do so is not what they intended or wanted and that, as a result, the prize is less spectacularly desirable than they had hoped. But all should make the best of things as they are.

This is not, of course, a notably original outlook. 'Life's a funny business,' people say, and 'what's the use of worrying?' In *V* there are touches of Candide, of fatalism, even of cynicism. It could be to the point that Professor Mavrin, in his magnificently ponderous way, suggests that he and Lushington discuss 'the novels of Thomas Hardy and his belief in the inevitability of circumstances'. In *V* there are several hints of such determinism: Baroness Puckler who, like Mrs Erdleigh in *ADTTMOT*, does a little clairvoyance, can forecast much of Lushington's life and the death of Count Scherbatcheff, even though he jauntily chooses to regard the message in the ace of spades as directed at his grandmother. Fatalism in *V* is, in fact, nothing like as pervasively dark as Hardy's, yet the implications are there. And the affectionate debunking of Mavrin's subject by showing him hugely wrong in most major judgements of people suggests that life as Powell sees it here cannot be staked out by study. It is an acceptably realistic comment on the way things may happen.

May . . . Perhaps *V* can be criticised for overdoing the irony and becoming a little glib. It is worrying to see the regularity with which incident is shaped towards wryness; at times this seems as much a

simplification as would be thraldom to romantic cliché. We know
that life can be arbitrary and that novelists are entitled to treat their
characters and plots arbitrarily, since life is their subject. Where an
ironic pattern becomes unduly insistent, though, we come to feel
here and there that it is not much more than an affectation, a styl-
istic pose; the writing takes on a wearily amused arch to the eye-
brows, which may do very well for revue but can cause suspicion of
a novel. We do not like to feel that the *deus ex machina* is on hand
for a cue; and there is something of this about the resolution of *V*.
By the time he reaches *ADTTMOT* Powell will be using irony with
more restraint and subtlety.

AM showed the chassis of upper-middle-class English society to
be at least twisted, and possibly rusted through. In *V* things
are worse. Many of its characters have been touched in some way by
the Russian Revolution: Count Scherbatcheff, for instance, talks of
the lost luxuries once enjoyed by his family. We are among
the wrecks of a massive social collapse. Much of the irony and
humour come from contrasting the chaos of reality with the fixed
protocol and arrogance of those who believe themselves still socially
eminent. It is much the same method as in *AM*, but intensified. *V*
seems to me both funnier and darker.

Count Bobel illustrates Powell's technique. Above all Michel
Bobel is a magnificently comic creation. Of much disputed Russian
lineage he now operates as a commercial traveller, selling face-cream.
He womanises tirelessly and indiscriminately, boasts endlessly and is
endlessly snubbed. He is present at the killings and is actually arrested as a suspect. It turns out that he was drunk and waving a
cardboard pistol given away by a nightclub.

This culminating incident is social disruption mirrored in a clown;
but Powell uses Bobel to make perhaps more serious points, too. In
a choppy world he has learned how to keep afloat. By necessity he
is shady and tough: we are left to deduce that he lies not only about
his ancestry and status but perhaps even about his nationality; he
will cadge where he can and uses Lushington's name to secure a loan;
and he does not droop: when Lushington lies sea-sick Bobel is still
offering cigars. Should régimes fall, one must make oneself as comfortable as possible by wiliness and persistence. If Fate is random
one takes what one can at every chance.

It is Bobel who speaks what may be seen as *V*'s anarchic theme.
Offering consolation to Lushington at the time of his sea-sickness,
Bobel says: 'In Russia we have an expression – *nitchevo* . .

It means *nothing* or, more freely, *what does it matter?* . . . I tell you this because I think this is a moment when such a philosophy of life might be of value to you.' If we ask whether Bobel is entitled by nationality to lay claim to this Russian philosophy the answer is *nitchevo*.

Bobel represents vast social upsets and is himself an agent of disruption. There are two memorable expressions of this. First, in a fine scene, he arrives at Lushington's room with two nightclub hostesses (each claiming to be titled) when Bellamy, British chargé d'affaires and a stickler for decorum, is expected. Lushington is frantic to be rid of the three in time, and just manages it. We have seen the absurd conjunction, or near conjunction, of rigid, upper-crust British protocol with the sad facts of a scrambled existence in this city.

The second episode is connected and rather more sombre. The two nightclub girls understand little English and so Bobel, in his cheerfully insatiable way, can ask Lushington in their presence about a third woman, Flosshilde, the hotel receptionist. She is engaged to Pope, a British valet who works for Lushington and Da Costa. Pope – another wonderfully comic figure – seems to stand for some elements of British social stability among the *emigrés* and conspirators. In fact, all the British represent high and durable social standards: Lushington spends a good deal of time arguing with Pope about the correct clothes and fussing over his dress suits. Pope's very job suggests hierarchy. As an aside, almost, during Bobel's last appearance in the book he mentions that Flosshilde is pregnant by him. 'For my part I put such difficulties from my mind,' he says. Chaos – *nitchevo* – has reached out and shaken another and, until now, a seemingly secure pillar. In *V*, as in *AM*, marriage means next to nothing, an engagement less. It is, of course, important to novels that marital stability should not get out of hand or a good deal of subject matter would disappear. Powell's view of these frailties is exceptionally dark, all the same. Love seems often savage and irresponsible here, feelings almost absent and, in any case, not likely to find a response. Lushington, like Atwater, like Pamela Flitton, like Nicholas Jenkins, is looking for a real emotional experience, and we approve and sympathise. But only Nicholas seems successful, and we see little of this fulfilment actually taking place.

Unemphatic, oblique, deadpan, the narrative method of *V* looks forward to the way in which Powell will present *ADTTMOT*. Rarely does he seem interested in describing incident with force and immediacy; it is the results which concern him. On the boat out Lushington kisses Ortrud for the first time and their affair is under way. This is a significant moment; yet we are given no description of the contact, nor of Lushington's feelings at the time, only a retrospective mention by Ortrud:

> They leaned there together, looking out towards the sea.
> 'I was surprised when you kissed me,' she said.

Even when she goes to his cabin and they make love a deliberate abstractness in the few sentences of description ensures a lack of urgency and passion. We are told that Lushington felt as if 'he had been carried unexpectedly off his feet'. And we need to be told: we have seen no evidence of such turmoil for ourselves.

The book's climax – the shooting of Ortrud and Da Costa – is recounted to Lushington (and the reader) some time after the event by Pope and two other minor characters. It would not have been difficult – might even have been dramatic – for Powell to have let Lushington witness the shooting, and so provide an eye-witness account. But Powell does not seek such impact. Some might argue that his technique is self-protection only, enabling him to include the material of melodrama while disguising it with the soft pedal. The charge has some justice. Here and there throughout Powell's novels one feels an inability of the style to cope with action; as if events were regarded as disruptive to flow. But the flashback treatment of the killings in *V* does come off, I think. It has its own drama and suspense. Lushington is awoken out of a nightmare by a telephone call from Pope and told that there has been a serious, unspecified accident. We wait, curious to find out what. More important, the ironic character of the deaths themselves is extended in the absurd way that Lushington hears of them: through Pope, Waldemar – a pleasant but slightly comic army officer – and a doctor who can understand but not speak English. In tune with Powell's portraits of those who guard doors throughout his novels there are also two grotesque gendarmes doing sentry duty at the block of flats where Da Costa's body lies, 'stage policemen out of a knock-about farce'. Waldemar makes a ponderous, well-informed speech of condolence which concludes with a promise that when the guilty 'are apprehended the law will most surely exert its full rigour'. Just as Fotheringham's serious thoughts in *AM* have to be knocked on the head by the writing, so the sadness of these two deaths is deftly transformed into humour.

As a character Lushington has possibly even less definition than

B

Atwater. About his appearance we learn not much more than he has 'a pink and white face', Nor are we told much directly about his personality: the disclosure that he 'believed implicitly in eventual progress on a scientific basis, although he had had Anglo-Catholic leanings in his City days' has little to do with character portrayal but is a Powell joke: amused ominscience employed to throw in some disparate, slightly farcical item of information, like the aside about Da Costa's elder brother that he 'had once been called the most popular man in Throgmorton Street'. Of course, in a book whose theme is that we are creatures of circumstance there would be little place for a hero bursting with decisiveness. Lushington, on the whole, is someone to whom things happen, not who makes them happen; a character type common enough in twentieth-century fiction.

He is also, of course, an ironic observer and listener, something like Jenkins in *ADTTMOT*. Passive qualities are implied. Frequently there is not even need for Powell to describe Lushington's reactions: we sense them because we know what sophisticated and worldly values he stands for. We can fill in his scepticism and fatigue before the prosy ramblings of Cortney, an American, in Chapter 33. (Incidentally, Cortney, with his rooted innocence and sentimentality, confronted by European cool, seems to have come ready-packaged to Powell from James.) This is an admirably subtle technique but does require a central character here, as in *WBOW* and, above all, in *ADTTMOT*, with spectacular powers of self-effacement. Some readers find such shadowiness a let-down, particularly as it affects Jenkins.

Yet it is crucial to Powell's ironic campaign: an energetically intrusive central figure, seeking to set people and things to rights, would suggest more moral certainty than Powell wants to show. We are going to find throughout his novels a fascinating variety in his ways of presenting the narrative, and a thorough look at these methods will help us understand his aim, I think. For the moment, though, we may say that the unemphatic portrait of Lushington in *V* is well compensated for by the vividness and complexity of other characters. This novel provides a remarkable advance in Powell's creation of people. Even caricatures like Pope and Bobel have some stature, and some poignancy. Other minor figures – Waldemar, Scherbatcheff – are given convincing depth in fairly brief and very amusing treatments.

It is in Ortrud, though, that we may see the chief development. Sexuality, arrogance, coquettishness, vulnerability and a touch of doom combine marvellously in her, creating a far more credible, be-

guiling and complex woman than Susan Nunnery in *AM*. Her wilfulness produces one of the book's funniest scenes, when she takes
Lushington and others back to her apartment late after a nightclub
and persuades her husband, who has gamely risen from bed to greet
the guests and is in a dressing-gown, to put on full evening dress to
match that of her friends. By the time he has changed everyone is
leaving and Ortrud reproaches him for taking so long.

Yet it is her warmth and inner sadness which come over most
strongly, the kind of qualities which Powell is always interested in,
however much they may be overlaid. He is even able to contrive that
when Ortrud is at her most irritating she can cancel it by childlike
frankness and charm. She tells Lushington:

'You are treating me shamefully. I shall be annoying tonight. I
shall annoy you. There will be time to make it up before you go.'

A delightfully winning character, with a tangible physical presence, she
has no equal in Powell's other novels. Most of his women are elusive,
formidable or capricious, not sweet.

In general Powell keeps the style of *V* rigorously simple, sometimes to the point of flatness. As in *AM* we meet patterned dialogue,
though much less here; as suits a novel where more happens and has
to be described, there is, in fact, considerably less dialogue altogether.
The author is about more often to supply background and to evaluate.
Now and then in such passages we meet the kind of roundabout,
parenthetical prose, a bit coy about disclosing the main verb, which
will be a mark of *Music of Time*.

Coming of that professional stock who, like the Jews, live
secretly, holding at intervals well-attended family conclaves, remaining securely out of touch with life, Lushington had begun his
career in the City.

He had a way to go before mastering this style. Other uncertainties
include moments of competing banality and pretentiousness:

Among the beds without flowers and the chipped cupids, the
gnawings of actuality seemed for the moment silenced. In this
place which had been left without meaning it seemed easier to
feel meaning where there was perhaps none.

Overall, though, the prose is a controlled, sensitive instrument capable of holding tragedy and farce in a single grip. Powell shows, too,
the attractive gift of producing now and then some piece of wit
sparkling with insight:

Lushington noticed Count Bobel dancing with an elderly woman, who showed by her demeanour that she was paying for the evening's entertainment.

Happily, it is a skill that grows throughout his work.

From a View to a Death

Bare survival is a theme of both *AM* and *V*: Atwater will keep going through mere habit, Lushington through a patched-up unecstatic love affair. *From a View to a Death* (1933) concerns itself with durability in a more positive, though not exactly more pleasant, sense. Having shown social hierarchies shifting or already flat in the earlier books, Powell here demonstrates that there are also instances when those with position can look after themselves very capably, even when backed by little money. Between-wars London society may have begun to disintegrate in *AM*; European society may have been shaken up by the Russian Revolution in *V*; *FAVTAD*, though, deals with country-house society at a period (also between the wars) when class change had not reached out with anything like such force to rural England. Protected stability endured there. Some decline had begun and menace existed, yet menace could be sharply repelled and, in *FAVTAD*, is. Although sexual relationships are still generally unstable in this novel, the central propertied marriage and family remain secure: not happy or admirable or cheerful but lasting.

Arthur Zouch, embodying the threat from the jumped-up who mean to jump higher, seems a conscious attempt by Powell to move on from the passive, put-upon hero. Zouch thinks of himself as a 'superman' and seeks to marry into the socially established Passenger family of Passenger Court. The reverse of Lushington, he intends to make things happen, things favourable to himself. He is ruthless, amoral, brazen. Excluding Mary, the girl he hopes to marry, the whole of the Passenger family justly spot Zouch as a 'tuft hunter'. But the reader senses early on that his mission is terribly difficult and probably doomed. Zouch himself realises that Mr Passenger also is a 'superman'. And Mr Passenger has three advantages: he is entrenched; he is guarded by history and *savoir faire*; he knows horses. In the long run, despite his energy, Zouch has to be a loser, even more so than Atwater. Our recognition of this from near the beginning, coupled with some hints of courage and sensitivity in Zouch, do create a quota of sympathy for him. Otherwise the novel would have been considerably more bleak.

Zouch is not, though, central to *FAVTAD* as Atwater and Lushington are to the previous books, not the 'eye'. He represents only a partial turn towards the dynamic hero. Powell shifts the narrative between several groups of characters and Zouch and his viewpoint disappear for sizeable stretches. It is this loosening of allegiance to one character which enables Powell to make Zouch a more complicated hero than either of his predecessors, and to excite contradictory reactions to him in the reader: the kind of indecisive response that tallies with our judgement of some people in real life. True, we also have reservations about Atwater and Lushington, particularly Atwater. But there is not much doubt that they come out basically as endearing figures. Zouch baffles us, nauseates us with his brashness and calculation:

> He had no great objection to children and had often found that to spend a few minutes playing with them was an admirable method of convincing people that he had a heart, if not of gold, at least of some equally precious substitute.

Snobbish, casual to his women – to put it no worse – and disloyal to former friends, he frequently appears merely mean, not even resplendently evil. As Betty Passenger, Mary's sister, says, his past is full not of 'bad things' but 'just dreary things'. He is certainly no superman in the style of George Meredith's Alvan. He tortures a wasp. As a guest he fills his cigarette case from the family box.

Yet Zouch has about him the glint of low-level creative talent – he is a painter of 'bright, hopeless portraits' – and brings an occasional feel of intelligence to a milieu where craftiness and aggression are more customarily the chief product of male thought. In V. S. Pritchett's phrase he is 'the undesirable artist among the speechless fox-hunters' (*NS&N*, 28 June 1952). He is the despised repository of a special gift, though minor. We all recognise that he should be devoted more seriously to his work. But we know, too, that he has to live, artist or not; and if he seems to be aiming a little high and pushing a little hard and unscrupulously, that is human. The saving grace turns out to be warmth, vitality again. He has enough about him for the reader to believe that he would attract not only Mary but another local girl, Joanna. Good looking 'on a small scale', he occasionally seems genuinely inspired during a love affair, though these decent feelings are swiftly downed by self-interest. In later novels Powell gives several expert portraits of creative artists. Zouch must be the least magnetic (St John Clarke alone challenges), yet is not entirely lost: a subtle mix from a developing novelist.

By freeing himself from the single viewpoint Powell can also plump out the personalities of more supporting figures than in his previous books. Several of these stand for social class categories and *FAVTAD* is able to look further into such divisions than its predecessors, though not as far as the working class, of course. As Bernard Bergonzi says in *The Situation of the Novel* (London, 1970) this deeper examination of a social group foreshadows *ADTTMOT*. And, as in that work, there is some distaste for social barriers and some for those who wish to jump them. Among those guarding the barriers Vernon Passenger stands supreme and Powell is able to combine in him the qualities of class caricature and developed character. Although frequently not much more than a lampoon of the diminished gentry, prejudiced, irritable, dictatorial, Passenger will break clear now and then. Has he not edited, though catastrophically, the works of a seventeenth-century poet? His social position bores him and he wants to escape, though he has no idea to what. 'He knew only what he did not want to be. By allowing this to work on his mind he became every day more and more like what he wished most to differ from.' Megalomania eats him. Yet we are told that as a landlord he is easygoing and popular (though no evidence is produced.)

For another superman he is, then, a little irresolute behind the apparently egomaniac exterior; possibly more sensitive, in fact, than Zouch the artist. There is though the other side: it is Passenger's ruthlessness which defeats Zouch and brings about his accidental death. Passenger may be an unwilling country gentleman, but when threatened he will defend himself and his position furiously. Perhaps we are watching Powell draw a line between the man and his caste; we deduce that on all important matters caste will decide behaviour. Passenger links to the general thesis of Powell's novels that pretension, ambition, role-playing suppress the human essence of people, reduce them, and take away their natural decency and warmth. He is able to keep something of these at the edge of our feelings for Passenger, though it is often touch and go. Passenger defeats not only Zouch but Major Fosdick, a transvestite neighbour, who has been engaged in a niggling war with the Passengers, and who makes sharp reflections on the family's short lineage. It is Passenger who, in a memorably comic and desperately painful scene, inadvertently discovers the major dressed in his sequins and cherry-decked picture hat. This leads to Fosdick's capitulation over the disputed North Copse, and to his eventual complete breakdown. In an extravagant, baffling moment Passenger may claim to be a Communist, but his ways are those of a feudal lord. Chained by social obligations, he behaves like someone who will ultimately put up with restraints because they mean power. Powell has given a sad, complex, not unrelievedly hostile portrait which might have degenerated much further into cartoon if seen from an ironic standpoint only.

Yet Powell will revert to the single-view narrative for *ADTTMOT*. There are defects in *FAVTAD* which may show why. I shall want to look fully at Powell's narrative methods when discussing *ADTTMOT*, but a word or two here will be useful, and I would like to include, out of proper order, some remarks on *What's Become of Waring* (1939), whose narrative method so obviously looks forward to that of the *Music of Time*.

A good number of novelists have found that a reasonably sane, more or less passive 'eye' figures can give great help with the presentation of bizarre characters in a story: it is a question both of credibility and focus. If we believe in the mainstay of a book, we are some way towards accepting lesser figures; and it is fairly easy to believe in a hero who has no outrageous qualities: Atwater, Lushington and, above all, Jenkins in *ADTTMOT* can anchor for us a very mixed squadron of powerfully eccentric characters. Similarly, Nelly Dean gets a bluff grip on Heathcliff in *Wuthering Heights*, though one could hardly call her the mainstay of that novel, I know.

Lacking this consistent method of presentation, the opening chapters of *FAVTAD* work a little feverishly for comic effect. When confronted in a few pages with the deranged Major Fosdick, his two clownish sons, Jasper and Torquil, the blighted, unstable Orphans and Mrs Brandon, grandiosely self-obsessed, we may wonder if the author knows where he is going. And this doubt carries through until quite late, when Zouch's situation takes on a more urgent and compelling tone. The early sections seem designed more like clever, very sharp, witty sketches than the organised stages of a novel and may remind us of Powell's affection for the portraits, often of eccentrics, in John Aubrey's *Lives*.

A sensible narrator like the young man in *WBOW* might have held things together. Telling the story in the first person, he is a clear prototype for Nicholas Jenkins, the resemblances starting from occupation: both are in publishing, both are writing their own books.

The narrator of *WBOW* gets no name and is less involved in the action than either Lushington or Jenkins, though some who have read only part of *ADTTMOT* may find it hard to imagine anyone less implicated than Jenkins. Now and then the narrator of *WBOW* does have little surges of identity, even of spirit. Also he is an expert on Stendhal and thinks about money, being attracted back to advertising by the salary. These specks of personality apart, he remains simply a neutral guide, amiable, sane, calm and reasonably perceptive. Complicity with the reader and detachment are what Powell wants, both prerequisites for the irony present here and in the series.

Not everyone is much taken with the impassive 'eye' figure. Some readers find that Powell's books – and particularly *ADTTMOT* – have a central emptiness, coldness even, because they are relayed by someone who is so often a blank; a peep-hole instead of a man. Those bothered by the method argue that the narrator's detachment can easily dwindle into remoteness, and the eternally wry point of view drift towards preciousness. Does this middleman masquerade as a participant to conceal the author's lack of commitment to his creations?

Although I am going to argue later on in favour of Powell's narrative method for *ADTTMOT*; and although *FAVTAD* might have done better with some comparatively faceless unifying figure at the start, I do find myself when reading *WBOW* wanting to know why the story-teller does not drop his blandness and take some part in the action. There is a lack, a shadowed area. Preparing a critique on Stendhal has its points but does not add up to a full private life for a young man. Nor does Powell pretend that it does: on the last two pages he seems to recognise the deficiency and sends out in a rush for some characterisation, a little after the fashion that Hollywood has people 'find themselves' when a ship is sinking or a tower block has caught alight: death-bed maturings. Approaching sleep, the narrator has thoughts about power, France, money and, of course, Stendhal.

While it is fair to say that difficulties over the competing requirements of a narrator will dog Powell into *ADTTMOT* Jenkins will, I think, emerge as a highly developed if often muted character, here and there vigorously engaged in life. In any case, these central figures – even the poorly sketched ones – do have their own power, their special dynamism. It functions in transforming the luridly unusual into the feasible, and not merely because they themselves are so ordinary and credible. Because they possess ironic minds, the absurdities of those they describe are taken by the reader not as impartial observations, not the whole story; only as aspects of someone which amuse and fascinate the narrator. Detached is, in fact, not quite the word for him. One corrects his impressions. In *TAW* Jenkins will actually muse about the validity of the one-sided view to a novelist, its superiority to the fair, all-round picture: 'prejudice might prove the very element through which to capture and pin down unequivocally the otherwise elusive nature of what was of interest, discarding by its selective power the empty, unprofitable shell.' Truth through distortion, and funny with it. This sounds a convenient argument yet in practice it does come off more often than not.

That was a digression. I would like to return to a few general concluding remarks on *FAVTAD*. Style has become less mannered than in the first two books, a more straightforward instrument for telling a story: brisk, occasionally witty, still off-hand and anti-dramatic. As in *AM* there is some excellent terse conversation, but in this later book Powell manages now and then to touch surface ridiculousness with menace or sadness. After Zouch has been killed and Major Fosdick committed, his son, Jasper, and Captain McGurk talk at the Fox and Hounds, first about Zouch's death, then about other matters:

> 'A rotten thing,' said Jasper.
> 'And when are you getting spliced?' Captain McGurk said.
> 'The date's not fixed yet.'
> 'Looking forward to it?'
> 'And how.'
> 'And what?' said Captain McGurk.
> 'And how,' said Jasper. 'And how. It's an expression.'
> Captain McGurk grunted. He changed the subject.
> 'How's your governor?' he said.
> 'Getting on nicely. Say's he's very happy where he is and doesn't want to come back for a long time.'
> 'He needed the rest.'
> 'That's right. He did.'

Overall *FAVTAD* reveals a growing range of accomplishment but lacks – deliberately avoids for the sake of other intentions – the charm and carefully maintained single flavour of *AM* and *V*. Not only Zouch makes charm difficult to capture. Through the strange, slightly mysterious hiking journalist, Fischbein, a London acquaintance of Zouch, Powell seems to be reaching out to a grubbier English scene than he has so far shown. Perhaps Fischbein and his gang of noisy urban walkers, who trespass on Passenger's land, are meant to show how eventually the squires will be routed, even if they succeed in squashing people like Zouch who want to beat them by joining; regrettably, the Jewish name could have some point. In the scene from which I have just quoted, Fischbein and his girl, Hetty, are present and appear set on removing every inch of stature from Zouch's character. Useless on a horse, he also failed with women, they tell Jasper. As far as constituting a threat to the Passengers goes, it is as if Zouch had never existed. But Fischbein and Hetty are still there, full of intelligence and implied threat, forerunners of Gypsy Jones, perhaps. Passenger had better not relax.

It is not necessary to regard *ADTTMOT* as a kind of *Decline and Fall* of the English upper classes – as some do – to see these first three novels as early and variously emphatic treatments of disintegration, with *FAVTAD* the grimmest in tone and the most effectively ominous. The qualities which Powell prizes – tolerance, humanity, decency – have gone on leave for this novel, and he is showing us the dispiriting result.

Agents and Patients

As if to compensate for the sombreness of *FAVTAD* Powell gives each of his next two novels, *Agents and Patients* (1936) and *What's Become of Waring* (1939), a light, almost inconsequential surface. These last novels before *ADTTMOT* treat segments of English upper-middle-class and middle-class life with Powell's familiar wit and precision. *AAP* is often very funny; and *WBOW* has for at least three-quarters of the book a passably suspenseful and intricately shaped plot, something unique in Powell's novels. Having dealt in the last chapter with what I take to be the most interesting aspect of *WBOW* I would like to give most attention now to *AAP*.

Maltravers and Chipchase in this book recall Bobel : they, too, are preoccupied with survival in a rough and anarchic society, though at a rather higher level than Bobel's ,and largely in London once more. Like Zouch, they seek to advance themselves by feeding on the well-placed; or, more accurately now, the well-off. Maltravers and Chipchase do not strive to improve their rating in society: they already have style if not status. Cash is the problem and they conspire to lift some from a fool: their method – to involve a rich innocent in the mysteries of *outré* professions (psychiatry and film-making) – looks back to Jonson's predatory alchemists. Atwater was the suffering hero; Blore-Smith here is a victimised hero. Atwater missed the bus; Blore-Smith gets taken for a ride.

Although lacking the character development of Zouch, Maltravers and Chipchase are interesting outlines of a recognisable type: they have pretensions and *élan* but not much else; men with professional ambitions but no liking for hard graft. Money and the need for it press more in *AAP* than in any of Powell's previous books. Significantly, we hear explicit, though very brief, references to the depression. Motives centre on economics, for a change, not class.

As the title suggests, *AAP* is concerned, beneath its humour and extravagances, with freedom. Blore-Smith has a private income but feels desperately incapable of realising himself. During an early sequence he watches a street display in which a man tries to escape from fetters, and sees this as a symbol of his own life. 'He that is not free is not an Agent, but a Patient,' says the Wesley sermon. In *AAP* Blore-Smith tries to step out of the bonds of ignorance, inexperience and gaucheness, something like Jenkins in *ABM*. During a fine comic scene Blore-Smith does shed his innocence and wallet at a French brothel. Later he is more or less abducted by a worldly, beautiful woman, though she eventually leaves him. What Blore-Smith seems to have learned by the end is not so much style, confidence or flair but caginess. He has been systematically fleeced. He has not greatly liked his sexual awakening either. Invited in a late scene to spend the summer at St Tropez with the dubious Colonel Teape, Blore-Smith is apparently only just capable of refusing: ' "Saint-Tropez?" said Blore-Smith. "I – Look here, do you mind if I write to you about it? I think . . ." ' Blore-Smith also hesitated before committing himself to Maltravers and Chipchase. Do we infer that Blore-Smith might now be drawn into a relationship with Teape? After all, as terms agent and patient have their homosexual connotations. At any rate, Blore-Smith's nature has not dramatically changed. Does he ever cease to be a Patient? Although seeming to escape his inhibitions during the chaotic adventures abroad with Maltravers and Chipchase he is being used by them for most of the time. Even when he runs off with Mrs Mendoza – virtually stealing her from Maltravers and Chipchase – it is she who takes the decisions; Blore-Smith tags along.

Powell may mean that we are all prisoners of our personalities and will stay so, regardless of efforts to change. Blore-Smith will always be clumsy and dissatisfied; Maltravers and Chipchase will always be opportunists. In other words, there are no Agents, no freedom. Are we all fettered? Interestingly, the two escapologists in the opening sequence change their roles from day to day, one bound, the other collecting; and here the free one quietly berates the other for leaving him tied up too long in Piccadilly, and offers retaliation now. Freedom comes and goes.

It is a harsh message and may reach out towards Wesleyan predestination. In its brighter, more mannered way the book is as pessimistic as *FAVTAD*. The hunt for money comes over as more obnoxious than Zouch's hunt for position, as it is meant to. When, finally, Maltravers picks two knaves out of the pack of cards and throws them across the table Powell is, of course, offering a comment on his and Chipchase's roles. They represent those qualities which Powell consistently indicts and consistently depicts, shallow-ness, self-obsession, grab. Possibly they represent them too well and bring a degree of aridity to the book.

A gallery of fine eccentrics helps offset this feeling: Gaston de la Tour d'Espagne, Commander Venables, Schlumbermayer, Roth. Their mode of life – the socialising, general ruthlessness and lack of roots – looks back to *AM* and also points towards the crowded, changing tableaux of *ADTTMOT*. In *AAP* we are dealing almost entirely with caricatures, swiftly drawn, superficial, striking, often hilarious figures with little life implied beyond the restaurants, film-sets or bars where they perform; in *ADTTMOT* Powell will have the space, skill and wish to look further than comic exteriors, though without losing the exteriors.

AAP's frequent passages of short-line dialogue differs in essence from those in *AM*. In *AAP* the aim is pace, and the novel often does have the zest – as well as the ostentatious worldliness – of revue.

As they walked across the lawn Mrs Mendoza said:
'Who is the Frenchman?'
'Gaston de la Tour d'Espagne. You must have heard of him . . .'
'Is he married?'
'He's had at least three wives in his time. Whether or not he has one at the moment I can't say.'
'I'm mad about him.'
'I'm not surprised.'
'I suppose he has every vice?'
'Naturally.'

Occasionally the humour is stretched to the point of idiocy (a woman motoring correspondent talking about French car bodies is taken by Blore-Smith to be referring to his adventures with Parisian whores) and even some of the best comic pages can be infected by the type of waggish high-flown circumlocutions which so often do duty as humour in English, and which can disfigure the prose of the *Music of Time*.

At that moment, that is to say, the period of time coinciding with Blore-Smith's grasp of the identity of the scene's protagonist, the elderly man seemed to be in the act of threatening Maltravers with his hook. Immediately after this realisation Blore-Smith once more fell heavily to the ground, this time on account of a piece of camera apparatus that trailed in his path when he pressed forward to get a better view of the theatre of war.

What's Become of Waring

Although *WBOW* reveals an interest and cleverness in pure story-telling, it would be wrong to say that Powell follows the conventional requirements of a plotted novel. On the face of it, he has written a mystery story about an author who conceals his private life, and who turns out to have good reasons for his behaviour. But the mystery is cleared up about three-quarters of the way through (substantial hints having been given earlier), not as a climax on a late page. Powell interests himself as least as much in the effects of this revelation on his characters as in teasing and shocking the reader. I am not sure, in fact, whether the personnel of this book are developed enough to hold up the last quarter of the story once the suspense has been removed. We may take it as significant, though, in view of what was to come, that even in a novel where plot does count for something Powell will slip out of its confines and pursue his concern for people.

WBOW is a very capable lightweight exercise and represents a pause in Powell's progress: it contains few of those deeper implications which can be felt now and then in the earlier novels and throughout *ADTTMOT*. It would be twelve years before Powell published another novel. Without relegating all the pre-war books to roles as signposts, we can see now that they did give hints of what was ahead, particularly of course the social setting and a disinclination to look very much at people's work. Little is found on business or finance or politics before the *Music of Time*. Attention to social change, apparent in *V* and *FAVTAD*, will be carried over into *ADTTMOT*, and is especially noticeable in the first three or four books of that series. An apparent casualness in the construction of *AM* will be mirrored in the many coincidental meetings and chance relationships of *ADTTMOT*. And the harsh, recurrent problems of love found in the early books will also appear in the *Music of Time*, similarly presented in a climate of impermanent, shallow, frustrating relationships.

A DANCE TO THE MUSIC OF TIME

Who's Who

References are to volume and chapter. Each reference applies to the item immediately before it and then to the information which follows. The item immediately before the next reference is to be found at this location, and so on. For example: in the entry for Sergeant Ablett, the fact that he was with the Laundry is contained in *The Soldier's Art*, chapter 3, and so is the information that he does music-hall turns and is a good sergeant. His rescue at Singapore is disclosed in *Temporary Kings*, chapter 4, as is the information that he has become rich.

Most entries begin with some general information on a character, not attributed by volume.

ABERAVON, Lord. Dead five or six years before Nicholas born. First and last of line. Shipping magnate (*ABM* 1). Father of Lady Walpole-Wilson and Lady Goring. Family name Gwatkin; landed stock; peerage created by Victoria? First name, Rowland. Settled borders of Shropshire; house sold at death. Deputy-lieutenant (*TAW* 4). Was painted, badly, by Isbister. Related(?) to Captain Rowland Gwatkin (*TVOB* 4). Family goes back to Vortigern, fifth-century British prince.

ABLETT, Sgt. With Laundry (*TSA* 3). Does music-hall turns. Good sergeant. Rescued Singapore (*TK* 4). Rich.

AKWORTH, Bertram. Pupil older than Nicholas expelled for sending homosexual note to Templer (*AQOU* 1). Widmerpool intercepted and showed it to Le Bas. Descendant(?) at school after Second War (*BDFAR* 5). Grandfather of Clare (*HSH* 6). Now Sir. Company director. Ordinary-looking. Had Winderpool removed from bank board.

AKWORTH, Clare. See above. Marries Sebastian Cutts (*HSH* 6).

AKWORTH, Rupert. Uncle of Clare (*HSH* 6). Rival firm to Jonathan Cutts. Gives away Clare.

ALBERT. See Creech.

ALDREDGE. Quarry director (*HSH* 5).

ALFORD. See Erridge.

ALFORD-GREEN, Col., Gerald. Friend of Flavia (*HSH* 6).

ALFORD-GREEN, Rosamund. Wife of above.

AL SHARQUI, Major. Military attaché from Arab State (*TMP* 4).

AMESBURY, Lord. Garter (*ALM* 4). Friend of Lady Molly.

AMESBURY, Sybil, Lady. Related to Mrs Conyers, who looked after her (*ALM* 1). Intractable. Took Lady Molly about. Published allegedly scurrilous memoirs, disappointing to young Nicholas. Anecdote recorded about Lord Vowchurch releasing monkeys at ambassadorial ball.

ANDERS, General, G.O.C. Polish troops, Russia (*TMP* 1).

ANDRIADIS, Mrs Milly. Living Hill Street (*ABM* 1). Deplorable influence, says Deacon. Party-giver. About thirty-five (*ABM* 2). House rented from Duports. Involved with Stringham. Has lived Paris. Once mistress of royalty? Small, powder-grey hair, cockney. Several times married. Current husband well-off businessman, possibly from Manchester. Park Lane flat (*TAW* 4). Was in Havana same time as Umfraville, who owes her money. Sued by Duports over house. Off-colour. Maid, Ethel. Affair in progress, Guggenbühl. Still pretty. Military garb. Living alone, single room, Bloomsbury (*TMP* 1). Much drink, drugs. Second Front propagandist? Dies Paris, late 1950s (*TK* 3).

ARDGLASS, Countess of. Second wife of Earl of Ardglass, Lord Kilkeel (Jumbo), brother of Molly Jeavons. Mannequin pre-marriage. Tried stage, failed. Spent Ardglass money. Divorced by Ardglass. Promiscuous. Ardglass title and remaining money went to distant cousin. Mistress Prince Theodoric(?) (*ABM* 3). Mistress Duport (*TAW* 2). Ageing. Driver in war for Belgians or Poles under Lady McReith (*TSA* 2). Killed by bomb at the Madrid during fortieth birthday party. Father played Abanazar in *Aladdin* when Pilgrim's mother principal boy.

ARDGLASS, Earl of. See above.

ASBJØRNSEN, General. Military attaché (Norway?) (*TMP* 1 and 4).

BAGSHAW, Lindsay. Known as Books-do-furnish-a-room, reason uncertain. Worked for BBC. Little older than Nicholas. Missed university. Drinking companion of Moreland. All-round journalist. Squadron-Leader during war, RAF public relations in India (*BDFAR* 1). Revolutionary. Was engaged to Gypsy? Communist? Spanish war experience changed him politically. Switches jobs a good deal. Fascinated by revolutionary techniques. Facile writer. Knows and admires Trapnel. Has been married twice at least and marries again. Has been near D.Ts. Erridge was to put up money for *Fission*, paper Bagshaw edits.

Unpublished novel (*BDFAR* 3). No longer politically committed. TV on collapse of *Fission* (*TK* 1). Wanted Trapnel for TV, but no. Lives near Primrose Hill (*TK* 4). Not drinking. Own children plus three stepdaughters. Avril – bit subnormal; pregnant? – Felicity, Stella. Gwinnett lodges with them. Wife, May, in forties, lame. Wife dead (*HSH* 4). Spending time in turn with daughters. To do TV programme on Murtlock?

BAGSHAW, senior. Father of above. Formerly in insurance, now retired (*TK* 4). Short-sighted. Sees Pamela naked in house.

BARKER-SHAW. Field Security Officer (*TSA* 1). Professor philosophy?

BARNBY, Ralph. Artist. Womaniser. Older than Nicholas, about twenty-six or seven (*ABM* 3). Lives above Deacon's shop. Dark, thick-set, hostile to Nicholas at first. Affair with Baby Wentworth, supposed mistress Donners, whom he fears as rival, but who has bought one of his pictures and may commission mural. Father successful though not rich sculptor, at Slade with Deacon; grandfather book-illustrator. Dislikes Gypsy. Moves Camden Town, then Fitzroy Square area (*TAW* 1). Murals for Donners–Brebner building improve reputation. Involved with Lady Anne Stepney (*TAW* 4). Affair ends (*TAW* 5). Affair with Norma, waitress-model (*CCR* 1). Keeps on good terms with former mistresses. War Job as RAF artist, commissioned (*TVOB* 3). Works on camouflage; has new girl. Mural, direct hit (*TSA* 1). Shot down (*TSA* 3). Dead (*TMP* 3).

BASSET, Sgt. Replaces Pendry (*TVOB* 4).

BELKIN, Dr. Friend Ferrand-Sénéschal. Leftist contact man; executed for Stalinist sympathies(?) (*TK* 2). Friend Tokenhouse (*TK* 3).

BIGGS, Staff Officer Physical Training. Captain. Was in 1914–18 War. Bald. Persecution mania. Former sports organiser at seaside resort (*TSA* 1). Divorcing. Hangs himself in cricket pavilion (*TSA* 3).

BILLSON. Parlourmaid with Jenkins family at Stonehurst (*TKO* 1). Allegedly sees ghost. Late thirties. Loved by Bracey. Loves Creech, who secretly calls her Silly Suffolk. Appears at drawing-room door naked. Sent to Suffolk to recover. Works for Manasch, now called Doreen, nearly seventy? (flash-forward in *TKO* 1).

BITHEL, Lieut. Territorial Army Reserve. Alleged brother of V.C. and said to have played rugby for Wales. Age thirty-seven(?) (*TVOB* 1). Eccentric. Drinks. Ragged moustache, large pasty face. Scruffy. Missed university. Did not complete training as auctioneer. Worked in cinema. Interested theatre, had walk-on parts. Unmarried. Short of money. Confesses not V.C.'s brother, nor rugby international – never played rugby at all. Anti-gas course (*TVOB* 4). To command Mobile Laundry? Hated by Gwatkin. Arrested after Mess fracas. Widmerpool gets him out of army following drunken scene (*TSA* 3). Cries. In cult community (*HSH* 6). Drunk again. Good relationship Murtlock (*HSH* 7). Drinking on quiet. Used as messenger. Other duties, some unspeakable. In seventies. Has left Murtlock? Brings Modigliani for Henderson (*HSH* 7).

BLACKHEAD. Civil servant of supreme obstructive flair (*TMP* 1).

BLAIDES, (The Hon.) Mildred. Youngest sister Mrs Conyers. V.A.D. Daughter
Lord Vowchurch. Dashing, not handsome. Age about twenty 1916, about twenty
years younger than Mrs Conyers (*ALM* 1). Nursing at Dogdene First War.
Married M'Cracken, Flying Corps officer, killed over Germany soon after wedding. Flighty widowhood. Remarries, Haycock, retired Australian businessman,
fairly rich, villa South France; travels. Marriage a success. Two sons. Haycock
dies. Engaged Widmerpool. About forty. Was left money by Haycock (*ALM* 2).
Extravagant (*ALM* 4). Lives South France. Affair Buster Foxe? Spent leave
Jeavons, 1917. Not quite sane? Has jettisoned most signs of upper-class background. Sons fourteen and fifteen, at school. Stays at Jules's when in London.
Baby Wentworth cousin: her father succeeded Mildred's, who had only
daughters. Met Umfraville in Cannes about 1923 at Andriadis party. Father
rode horse upstairs. Stays on at Umfraville's club with Jeavons. Promiscuous,
says Lovell (*ALM* 5). Engagement off – sex failure by Widmerpool. Returns
France.

BOBROWSKI, General. Polish military attaché. Brought about two brigades of
Poles from France (*TMP* 1). Began career Russian rifle regiment. Killed by taxi
in exile (*HSH* 1).

BORDA. French officer, Kernével's assistant, marries English girl (*TMP* 5).

BORRIT. Netherlands liaison. Former Intelligence officer at H.Q. on Gold Coast.
Never had woman outside marriage except paying. Peacetime fruit trade.
Canadian wife, dead. Children, Canada. Spanish speaker (*TMP* 1). Returns
fruit trade on demob. (*TMP* 5). Dies when about to marry widow with money.

BRACEY. Soldier-servant of Nicholas's father (*TKO* 1). Unmarried. Melancholic.
Very smart. Large family. France with Jenkins's father, Expeditionary Force.
Killed in retreat from Mons.

BRADDOCK (alias Thorne). Wanted for fraud (*AQOU* 1). Le Bas arrested as him
as result of Stringham's practical joke (see also *TAW* 5).

BRAGADIN, Jacky. Small, nervous. Owner palazzo, Venice (*TK* 1). Mother a
Macwatters of Philadelphia, rich: funded Bragadin Foundation. Unmarried. In
fifties (*TK* 2). Friend of father of Rosie Stevens (Manasch) (*TK* 3). Bad heart,
chest. Fears scandal. Dead (*HSH* 2).

BRANDRETH. Member Le Bas's house ahead of Nicholas (*TAW* 5). Doctor. Looks
after Le Bas during seizure. Father baronet, ear specialist. Looks after Matilda
in pregnancy (*CCR* 2). Overbearingly medical. Interested music. Moreland
breaks from (*BDFAR* 3).

BRAYBROOK, Dolly. Umfraville's first wife. Daughter of Bloody Braybrook, commander of regiment (*TVOB* 3). Marriage lasted year or two. Fell for Foxe.
Wanted divorce to marry him. Umfraville agreed. Foxe dodges. Dolly commits
suicide.

BREEN, Jo. Jockey. Suspended for pulling horses. Joy Grant, Umfraville's second wife, goes to him, having first left Umfraville for Marquess of Castlemallock (*TVOB* 3). Keeps pub, Thames valley, with Joy.

BREEZE, Evan or Yanto, Lt. Platoon Commander under Gwatkin. Married. Age twenty-five (*TVOB* 1). Former accountant. Gwatkin liked sister, but rejected. Exonerated from blame for Pendry's death (*TVOB* 2). Captain Traffic Control Company (*TVOB* 4).

BRENT, Jimmy. Big, fat, with spectacles. Friend Templer, older. Works City (*AQOU* 4). Car crash with Nicholas and others. Affair Jean (revealed *TKO* 3). In army (*TVOB* 3). Oil man, South American office, previously. After Jean, took up with cigarette girl. To marry widow with two grown-up sons (*BDFAR* 3). Gets oil job for Duport. Very fat.

BRIDGNORTH, Mary, Lady. See below. Daughter Scottish duke (*ABM* 4). Distant relative Sir Gavin Walpole-Wilson's mother. Hospital committees, competing with Mrs Foxe.

BRIDGNORTH, Lord. Lives Cavendish Square (*ABM* 1). Father Peggy and Anne Stepney. Owned Derby winner. Also interested in politics. Eddie (*TAW* 4). Eldest son, Lord Mountfichet. Seat Mountfichet (*TAW* 5).

BRIGHTMAN, Dr Emily. A don (*TK* 1). Has written on The Triads. Working on Boethius. Worldly. Cousin of Harold. On Donners-Brebner award panel (*HSH* 2). D.B.E.

BRIGHTMAN, Harold. Acrid colleague Sillery (*AQOU* 4). Reconciled (*BDFAR* 1).

BRUYLANT. With Belgian forces. Replaces Kucherman (*TMP* 5).

BUDD, Colonel. Father of Margaret. Minor Court appointment (*ABM* 2).

BUDD, Lady Frederica. Handsome. Eldest Tolland sister, next Erridge in age. Widow with children. Friend of Mrs Conyers. Lady-in-Waiting, or similar. Thirties. Dresses formidably (*ALM* 1). Husband Robin, Rob, brother or cousin of Margaret. He killed in hunting accident. Self-disciplined (*ALM* 2). Goes to live in country near Thrubworth because of war (*TKO* 4). Isobel joins her while awaiting birth. Udney proposed to her at Ascot(?) (*TVOB* 3). Two sons, Edward, ten, Christopher, twelve, she now about forty. 'Dreadful correctness.' Engaged to Umfraville. They marry. Executor Erridge's will (*BDFAR* 2).

BUDD, Margaret. Eternal socialiser, like female Archie Gilbert. Lives Sussex Square (*ABM* 1). Beauty, like huge doll. Cousin of Budd, Captain of XI, who hit Widmerpool with thrown banana. Marries Scotch landowner; two children at least (*TAW* 2). Still lovely. Husband ill-tempered. Marriage over, cause unknown (*TMP* 5). Marries Horaczko, Polish cavalry officer, register office.

BURKEL. See Strydonck.

CADWALLADER, C.S.M. Ex-miner, Coronation medal and long-service medals (*TVOB* 1). Leaving (*TVOB* 4).

CALTHORPE(s). Boys at school with Nicholas (*AQOU* 1). Calthorpe Major writes home about arrest of Les Bas. Son of nephew of one of the boys involved, as schoolboy, with Pamela (*BDFAR* 5).

CAROLO. Musician. Older than Nicholas. Not real name – could be Wilson, Wilkinson, Parker? Child prodigy. Womaniser. Romantic-looking but mercenary (*CCR* 1). Lodging with Maclinticks (*CCR* 2). Was briefly married to Matilda (*CCR* 3). Goes away to North Midlands with Audrey (*CCR* 4). Leaves her at beginning of war for actress (*TSA* 2). Second violin in *Seraglio* (*TK* 5). White-haired, looks like Liszt.

CASTLEMALLOCK, Marquess of. Takes Joy Grant from Umfraville in Kenya (*TVOB* 3). Twice her age, ugly. Impotent. Family lost money. Joy leaves him. School Chemical Warfare in house, Castlemallock. Predecessor Lord Chief Justice for supporting Irish Union (*TVOB* 4). Caroline Lamb supposedly visited Castlemallock.

CATTLE. School porter (*AQOU* 1).

CHANDLER, Norman. Actor, dancer, director, saxaphonist. Puppet-like face, very thin (*CCR* 1). Bosola in *Duchess of Malfi*. Effeminate. Pursued by Mrs Foxe. She has 'taken him up' (*CCR* 3). Handy and managing. Army (*TVOB* 3). Mrs Foxe follows to Essex. Commissioned (*TSA* 2). 'London's most eminent Teddy Boy' (*TK* 5). Directing Polly Duport play (*HSH* 2).

CHEESMAN. Replacement for Bithel i/c Mobile Laundry. Age thirty-nine, grey-haired, wire spectacles (*TSA* 3). Unmilitary. Peacetime accountant. Singapore. Japanese p.o.w. with Stringham (*TK* 4). At reunion, nearly sixty. Recounts Stringham's death. Picked up from sunk p.o.w. ship.

CHU, Colonel. Chinese military attaché (*TMP* 1). Sandhurst attachment. Wants to go to Eton, aged thirty-eight. Returns China, promoted major-general (*TMP* 4). Killed Mukden.

CHUCK. Boy-friend Henderson, worked same firm as Clare Akworth (*HSH* 6). Involved in gallery (*HSH* 7).

CLANWAERT. Belgian officer, Congo specialist (*TMP* 2). Was Elephant officer, Congo Army. Lives same flat block as Nicholas.

CLAPHAM. Director of firm which publishes St John Clarke's books (*TAW* 4). Admires them. Firm takes over Quiggin & Craggs (*BDFAR* 5). Takes Quiggin and Widmerpool on to board. Dead (*TK* 2).

CLAPHAM, Evadne. Novelist (*BDFAR* 3). Niece of above. Lesbian. Success with

Ada? Book, *Golden Grime* (*BDFAR* 5). Changes to Ada's style. Thirty-fifth novel, *Cain's Jawbone* does well, in her previous style (*HSH* 3).

CLARKE, E. St John. Middle-aged or more novelist, poor in Nicholas's view: windy, empty, weak characterisation (*ABM* 4). Members becomes his secretary. Engages in public controversy (*TAW* 1). Little younger than Wells, Barrie generation. Nicholas liked his books as schoolboy. Reputation made early in life. Tall, cadaverous. Rich bachelor. Likes *beau monde*. To write introduction to *The Art of Horace Isbister*. Turning to modernism? Turns Marxist (*TAW* 2). Quiggin succeeds Members as secretary. In protest march, wheelchair (*TAW* 4). Turns Trotskyist (*TAW* 5). Guggenbühl his secretary. Drifts from Left (*CCR* 2). Guggenbühl sacked. Writing memoirs. Fat and flabby. Has praised novel by Nicholas. Looking after Erridge's business affairs. Dead (*CCR* 4). Poor obituaries. Money left to Erridge, more than £16,000 or £17,000. Royalties eventually to Quiggin & Craggs under Warminster Trust (*TK* 3). Novel *Match Me Such Marvel* to be filmed (*TK* 3)? Books still sell (*HSH* 2). TV programme about him. Homosexual connection Isbister?

COBB, Colonel. U.S. assistant military attaché, known as Courthouse Cobb (*TMP* 2). General (*TMP* 4).

COBBERTON. Housemaster, Eton, parson (*AQOU* 1). Disliked Le Bas (*BDFAR* 5).

COCKSIDGE. Sycophantic captain at Div. H.Q. (*TSA* 1).

COLLINS. See George Tolland and Jeremy Warminster.

CONYERS, General Aylmer. Long-time friend of Nicholas's parents, distant cousin Nicholas's mother (*ALM* 1). Wide interests. Served Afghanistan, Burma, Zululand, Soudan, South Africa. Saved life of native ruler? Praised by Lord Roberts? Womaniser? Bachelor until almost fifty. Married woman nearly twenty years junior. Retired from army as brigadier-general eighteen months later. 'Cello player. Tries training poodles as gun-dogs. Returns to army during First War. Courtier. About eighty, 1935–6. Living Sloane Square area (*ALM* 2). Amateur psychologist. Resolute: deals with naked Billson. Picks up Miss Weedon at concert after first wife's death (*TKO* 4). Has retired as courtier. Marries Miss Weedon (*TMP* 2). Air raid warden in his nineties. Drops dead pursuing looters.

CONYERS, (The Hon.) Mrs Bertha. Wife of above. Eldest of six daughters of Lord Vowchurch (*ALM* 1). Over thirty when married. Sister of Mildred Blaides. Took care of Sybil, Lady Amesbury. Dead (*TKO* 4).

CONYERS, Charlotte. Daughter of above. Married lieutenant-commander, baby at Malta (*ALM* 1).

CORDEREY. Housemaster preceding La Bas (*TAW* 5).

CRADDOCK, Lyn. Subaltern, Messing Officer (*TVOB* 2). Brother of girl to whom Kedward engaged. Killed Caen (*TMP* 4).

CRAGGS, Howard. Managing director Leftist Vox Populi Press (*ABM* 4). Gypsy Jones sleeping with? Early middle-age. Many committees. Rich, oily voice. Involved with Erridge and Quiggin in politico-literary projects (*ALM* 3). Firm now Boggis & Stone. High post Min. of Information. Involved with Pamela Flitten (*TMP* 2) who tipped wine over him. Knighted (*TMP* 3). Runs branch Donners-Brebner. Joins Quiggin in publishing: Quiggin & Craggs (*BDFAR* 1). Married to Gypsy Jones. Fellow-traveller. Randy, says Pamela (*BDFAR* 2). Afraid Gypsy (*BDFAR* 4). Not asked to Quiggin's wedding (*BDFAR* 5). Dies (*TK* 3).

CREECH, Albert. Cook, handyman with Nicholas's parents Stonehurst. In his thirties just before First War (*TKO* 1). Previously hall-boy, footman Nicholas's mother's house. Dislikes women. Loved by Billson. Loves himself. Marries Bristol woman. Bad feet keep him out of army in First War. Cooks in canteen. Two children, boy, girl (*TKO* 3). Works hotels, then manager Bellevue, seaside private hotel. Has not aged much. Has forgotten much about Stonehurst. Dead (*TMP* 3). Wife marries Pole invalided from army. They keep boarding-house, Weston-super-Mare.

CROWDING, Malcolm. English literature don new provincial university (Widmerpool Chancellor). *Fission* group poet (*BDFAR* 3). Little imagination. Puritanical critic. Homosexual? With Trapnel when he died (*TK* 1). Says Trapnel lacked social conscience.

CROXTON. On course with Nicholas (*TVOB* 3). Joker.

CURTIS. Learned corporal (*TMP* 1).

CUTTS, Fiona. Daughter Roddy, Susan. Pretty. About twenty-one (*HSH* 1). Lugubrious. Troublesome. Ran away from schools. Typhoid. Affair with married electrician. Living with Murtlock? Friend of Etienne Delavacquerie previously. Sex rites (*HSH* 5). Tiring of cult life? Living in Delavacquerie's flat. Working in research. To help Gwinnett? Marries him (*HSH* 6).

CUTTS, Jonathan. Son Roddy, Susan, older than Fiona. Married, children (*HSH* 1). Rising in fine art auctioneers.

CUTTS, Roddy. Tall, sandy-haired, smiler. Son Lady Augusta Cutts. Sister, Mercy. Engaged then married Susan Tolland. Conservative Central Office (*ALM* 3). Family, banking, business. M.P. (*CCR* 2). Flat Westminster. Supports Churchill, Eden, on Munich (*TKO* 2). Yeomanry (*TVOB* 3). Major, now Reconnaissance Corps (*TMP* 2). Falls for decoder, Mid-East, wants divorce. Romance over (*BDFAR* 2). Girl left with rich Persian. Holds seat 1945. Susan dominant. Susan has daughter (*BDFAR* 4). Minor Government office (*TK* 1). Likes Widmerpool. Political career over (*HSH* 1). Tolerant parent.

CUTTS, Sebastian. Son Roddy, Susan, older than Fiona. Unmarried (*HSH* 1). Womaniser. Ambitious. Computers. Marries Clare Akworth (*HSH* 6).

DANIELS. Bithel's army servant (*TVOB* 2).

DE GRAEF, Gauthier. Captain. Belgian assistant military attaché (*TMP* 2 and 4).

DEACON, Edgar Bosworth. Artist. Some independent means, low ability, according to Nicholas. Sister married to clergyman. Friend Nicholas's parents and later of Nicholas. Classical subjects. Studio Brighton pre-First War. In Paris just after First War following unspecified incident – presumably sexual – in Battersea Park. Involved in pacifist protest; runs antique shop near Charlotte Street (*ABM* 1). Deals in male erotica. Dubious reputation. Homosexual? Likes Soviet films. Dies after fall at Bronze Monkey club (*ABM* 4). C. of E. cremation, though agnostic. Had been R.C. convert? Work becoming fashionable (*HSH* 7). Exhibition.

DEANERY, Ivo. M.C., pre-war Palestine. Gets command Recce Unit (*TSA* 3) Major-General (*TK* 4).

DELAVACQUERIE, Etienne. Gibson's son. University student where Widmerpool Chancellor (*HSH* 2). Friend Fiona. Scholarship to U.S. New girl-friend.

DELAVACQUERIE, Gibson. Lives Islington. French descent, family settled Caribbean. Lover of Matilda Wilson(?) *HSH* 2). P.r. side Donners-Brebner. In mid-forties – much younger than Matilda. Originally on Donners-Brebner fellowship. Served war Mid-East, India, Royal Signals. Shipping firm. Poet. Critic. Published in *Fission*. On literary award panel. Wife dead ten or fifteen years. Son Etienne, see above. Likes to be thought good manipulator of people. Affair Polly Duport (*HSH* 4). Interested Jacobean and Elizabethan drama (*HSH* 5). Helps Gwinnett. To marry Polly? Not yet. Gives away Gwinnett's address to 'free' Fiona. She living in his flat .In love with her? (*HSH* 6). To marry Polly (*HSH* 7). Book of poems.

DEMPSTER. Looks after Norwegian forces in Britain (*TMP* 1). Timber trade peacetime. Knows Scandinavia. Aunt remotely related to Ibsen. Two M.C.s First War. Pianist. Leaves army (*TMP* 5). Retired from timber, lives Norway (*TK* 4).

DERWENTWATER. See Wentworth.

DIPLOCK. Warrant Officer, Class 1 (*TSA* 1). M.M. Hogbourne-Johnson's chief clerk. Rascal but good at job – Widmerpool disputes latter. Regular army reservist. Red-tape genius. Embezzler? Deserts (*TSA* 3).

DONNERS, Sir Magnus. Rich industrialist. Warned as young man he had fatal illness and spent time reading; doctors wrong. Former member Government, not Cabinet; mid-fifties, looks less, (*ABM* 2). Affair with Baby Wentworth. Parsonic appearance. Lives Stourwater castle (*ABM* 3). Was at 'some quite decent school'? Father knighted? Family Scandinavian or North German? Cliché-king. Pervert? Affair with Baby ends (*TAW* 1). Affair with Matilda Wilson (Betty Updike). Also involved Bijou Ardglass (*CCR* 3). Patron of Moreland and Barnby (*TKO* 2). Was at Sorbonne. Anne Stepney his mistress. Voyeur(?) (*TKO* 3). Matilda returns to him (*TKO* 4). Minister (*TVOB* 4).

Married to Matilda (*TMP* 5). Looks like tailor's dummy. Ill? Dead (*BDFAR* 1). Literary prize in name (*HSH* 2). Bulk of fortune to relations and institutions.

DOOLEY, Ambrose. R.C. chaplain (*TVOB* 1).

DUNCH, Ernie. Farmer neighbour, Nicholas (*HSH* 5), Ill after mysterious experience.

DUPORT, Bob. Friend Templer. Aggressive. Sent down from university first term. Interested Jean Templer (*AQOU* 4). Marries her (*ABM* 2). Mrs Andriadis rents their house, Hill Street. Inherited money. Businessman – metals, Balkans. Womaniser (*TAW* 2). Marriage shaky. Has lost money. Unofficial separation. Abroad. Child, Polly, aged three. Affairs with Bijou Ardglass. Hill Street house sold (*TAW* 4). Marriage patched up? (*TAW* 5). Affair Bijou over. Returns Jean (*ALM* 2). Has been fixed up with job by Widmerpool. South America? Unfaithful (*ALM* 4). Jean leaves him. Divorce (*TKO* 2). Goes Turkey for Donners – chromite. Capacity for money-making. Widmerpool ditches him (*TKO* 3). Man of action. Banters. Melancholic. Board of Trade (*TVOB* 3). Captain, Civil Affairs, Belgium (*TMP* 4). Quieter. Has worked Egypt. Has been in censorship. Stomach trouble. Ageing. Had Pamela Flitton, Cairo. Likes music. Brent finds him oil job. (*BDFAR* 3). Importing oil into Canada (*TK* 5). Ill, crotchety. Wheelchair (*HSH* 7). Collected Victorian seascapes, selling at profit. Seeing lot of Jean. Looks very ill.

DUPORT, Polly. Daughter Jean, Bob. Like father. About seventeen, eighteen (*TMP* 5). Successful actress (*TK* 1). Beauty. Married actor, separated. Not promiscuous. Lead part in filmed Hardy story. In thirties (*TK* 5). To be in Glober film? Possible affair with him. Good part, not lead, Clarini film (*TK* 6). In play directed by Chandler (*HSH* 2). Lead in Ibsen play (*HSH* 4). Affair with Gibson Delavacquerie. Looking after father (*HSH* 5). Playing Celia in *The Humorous Lieutenant*, ascribed Fletcher. To marry Delavacquerie? In Strindberg play (*HSH* 7). Forties looking younger. Will marry Delavacquerie.

EMMOT. Mess waiter with whom Bithel dances (*TVOB* 4).

ERDLEIGH, Mrs Myra. Friend Uncle Giles. Blurred features, large hazel eyes. Fortune-teller. Aged between forty and fifty (*TAW* 1). Widow: husband Chinese Customs? Burma Police? Involved with Stripling (*TAW* 3 and 5). Dominates him. Involved with Trelawney and Giles at Bellevue (*TKO* 3). Like 'blue rinse marquise'. Inherits £7300 from Giles. Living Chelsea, same block as Nicholas (*TMP* 3). Still with Stripling (*TK* 5). Looking very old. Restrains Pamela Flitton and warns her. Dead (*HSH* 2).

ERRIDGE, Lord. Known as this, but first title Earl of Warminster. Head of family in late teens. Eldest brother Nicholas's wife, Isobel. Alford on mother's side. Leftist, with aristo lapses. Seat, Thrubworth Park. Intellectual arrogance. Butler, Smith, sometimes borrowed by Molly Jeavons. Living as tramp, Midlands? (*ALM* 1). Year or two older than Nicholas. Was worried-looking schoolboy. On committee to examine Sedition Bill (*ALM* 3). Beard. Early thirties. Scruffy. Quiggin living in his cottage. Understands causes, not people. Survey of social conditions, not living as tramp, says Quiggin. Keen on Gypsy Jones?

Popular Front supporter. Mona, Templer's first wife, attracted to him. Much of Thrubworth closed; building seventeenth-century. Founding magazine? Family's first appearance in fourteenth century. Money made during Black Death? Kulaks. A Tolland knighted by Edward IV? Another, courtier to Henry VIII, displaced under Bloody Mary, Cavaliers. Peerage under Queen Anne. Wants joint-editorship of magazine, not just to finance. Gives money to good causes, otherwise stingy. China with Mona (*ALM* 5). Mona returns alone (*CCR* 2). Goes to Spanish Civil War. Pacifist. Mad? Thrubworth menaced by death duties after mismanagement. St John Clarke to look after his business affairs while Erridge in Spain. Returns from Spain (*CCR* 4). Ill in nursing home. Typical aristo-idealist, says Quiggin, and politically inept. Inherits St John Clarke money, enough to save Thrubworth. Disillusioned by Communism; against Nazis, but pacifist still, supporting League (*TKO* 3). Blanche Tolland keeps house for him. Smith dead. Troops stationed Thrubworth (*TKO* 4). Antagonistic to this. Ill, Less interested politics, more in history (*TVOB* 3). Dead in mid-forties (*BDFAR* 1). Was to have backed *Fission*. Never Communist. Affair Gypsy? Dead by coronary – result of emotional disturbance over George Tolland's death(?) (*BDFAR* 2). Reverted to aristo values over memorial window in last weeks? Will asks for republication of books which influenced him (*BDFAR* 4).

FAREBROTHER, Sunderland (Sunny). Probably A. S. Farebrother. Friend Templer's father, City. Also distant relative Templer's mother. D.S.O., O.B.E., First War. About thirty, thirty-five (*AQOU* 2). Looks hard up. Saintly appearance, recalling Colonel Newcome. Drawn to Jean Templer. Was at Paris Peace Conference. Mean. Inaccessible, lonely. Something of a butt. Templer says acts poor. Making money? (*TAW* 3). Romantic about war comradeship (*TKO* 1). Brigade-Major (*TKO* 4). Major at Command (*TVOB* 4). Disliked by Widmerpool (*TSA* 1). Conflict between them diminishes (*TSA* 3). Early fifties. Smooth. Shrewdness cannot be disguised. London Territorial Yeoman Cavalry. Knows secret material on Templer? Wrote obituary material on Templer senior in *The Times* and (or?) *Morning Post*. Cloak-and-dagger work. With Poles (*TMP* 1). Parachutist. Lt.-col. Hates Widmerpool. Sycophant? Involved Syzmanski affair (*TMP* 2). In trouble. Disciplined, demoted (*TMP* 3). Civil Affairs, old rank. To marry Conyers's widow, née Weedon (*TMP* 4). At reunion (*TK* 4). Around seventy. Retired from merchant bank. Delighted at Widmerpool's trouble. Flat and country cottage. Around eighty (*HSH* 2). Had Widmerpool removed from bank board (*HSH* 6).

FEINGOLD. Screenplay writer (*ALM* 1).

FENNEAU, Canon Paul. Was at Sillery tea party 1924, met Nicholas (*AQOU* 4). Now at R.A. dinner (*HSH* 4). Father chaplain, Riviera. Interested in scholarly magic. Engages in learned disputes. Suggests Murtlock reincarnates Trelawney. Knew Murtlock as child.

FERRAND-SÉNÉSCHAL, Léon-Joseph. Literary-political figure, minor celebrity (*TK* 1). U.S. during war. Fellow-traveller. Communist propagandist, says Bagshaw. Odd sex tastes. Friendly with Widmerpool. Paris night out. Dead from stroke, Kensington hotel, aged fifty-nine. Wrote novels, plays, philosophic and economic studies, political tracts and possibly verse. Poor writer, says Dr Brightman. Was in bed with Pamela Flitton when died, she says (*TK* 5). Widmerpool watching?

FETTIPLACE-JONES. Member of Le Bas's house who becomes Conservative M.P. (*TAW* 5, *TKO* 2).

FINES. See Sleaford.

FINN, Major Lysander, V.C., Légion d'Honneur, Croix de Guerre *avec palmes* and other foreign decorations. In City pre-1914 War. Then cosmetics, Paris. Returned with Free French Second War (*TSA* 1). Mid-fifties (*TSA* 2). Small. Liked by de Gaulle. Wife, daughter. Like enormous bird. Secretive side. Lt.-col. with General Staff section dealing with Allies and Neutrals (*TMP* 1). Refused promotion for a time. Deaf – simulated? Inherited cosmetics business? Daughter married to Frenchman in British army. Grotesque. Disposition mixes agitation and calm. Stayed army after 1918, returned 1938. Slack on security? Suffers over Szymanski (*TMP* 2). Son-in-law dropped in France and killed (*TMP* 5). Pennistone joining him in Paris cosmetics firm. Retires, then dies Perpignan (*TK* 4).

FLANNIGAN-FITZGERALD. Undergraduate with Nicholas. Connections useful to Sillery (*AQOU* 4).

FLITTON, Captain Cosmo. Married Stringham's sister Flavia. Father of Pamela (but see Umfraville). Lost arm First War (*TMP* 1). Kenya. Heavy drinker. Professional gambler? Unscrupulous in business? Involved Baby Wentworth's divorce. Refused marry her. Left Flavia when Pamela still small. Married American; dude ranch, Montana (*TK* 3). Highly regarded locally. Pamela met Glober at his ranch.

FLITTON, Pamela. Stringham's niece. Daughter of sister Flavia and Cosmo Flitton. Aged six or seven at Stringham's wedding (*ABM* 4). Bridesmaid. Sick in font. In A.T.S., driver (*TMP* 1). Aged at least twenty. Sulky. Abnormal? Claims exceptionally close relationship – possibly sexual – with Stringham. Striking looks. Sexually notorious (*TMP* 2). Lung trouble? Leaves A.T.S. Prefers older men? Secret work. Involved Szymanski somehow? Has given Templer bad time. Knows Lady McReith. Friend Norah Tolland, and dominates her. Widmerpool interested? Affair Theodoric? Cairo (*TMP* 3). Affair Odo. Loves disaster and death, says Mrs Erdleigh. Indicts Odo for poor love-making. Responsible for Templer's fatal risk-taking? (*TMP* 4). Had by Duport, Cairo. Widmerpool took her out. Engaged to Widmerpool (*TMP* 5). Stringham's heir, sizeable amount. Accuses Widmerpool of Templer's murder. Marries Widmerpool (*BDFAR* 1). Unfaithful? To have married John Mountfichet, Widmerpool on rebound? (*BDFAR* 2). Is harsh to him. Deathwish. Meets Trapnel, not friendly (*BDFAR* 3). Likes him (*BDFAR* 4). Leaves Widmerpool for Trapnel. Dislikes *Profiles In String*. Sexually unbalanced, says Trapnel: frigidity mixed with insatiable desire (*BDFAR* 5). Like a child. Throws away *Profiles In String*. Affair schoolboy? Gwinnett calls her the 'castrating girl' (*TK* 1). Marriage continues, though they live in separate Widmerpool houses. Still energetically promiscuous. In bed with Ferrand-Sénéschal on night of his death. In Venice, now late thirties, grey, still beautiful *(TK 2)*. Very frank. Friend of Ada. Affair Glober and to act in Glober film of Trapnel book? *(TK 3)*. Glober to marry? Likes Gwinnett. Widmerpool fears her. Mystic side. Despises Odo. French papers hint she killed Ferrand-Sénéschal. Destroyed *Profiles* because not worthy of Trapnel. Hits Gwinnett. No chance of Glober marriage. Has found Gwinnett's address *(TK 5)*. Looks frightening. Jealousy of Polly Duport – terrible frankness. Accuses Widmerpool of voyeurism in Ferrand-Sénéschal's room. Dead from overdose in hotel where Gwinnett staying *(TK 6)*. C.I.A. involved in death(?) *(HSH 2)*.

FLORES, Colonel Carlos. South American. At Ritz with family party(?) *(TAW 2)*. Jean's second husband *(TMP 5)*. C.B.E. Politics(?) *(BDFAR 3)*. Promoted. Great man. Good speech maker. Head of Government *(TK 5)*. Assassinated *(HSH 5)*. General?

FOPPA. Italian club proprietor, Soho *(TAW 4)*. Long time in London. Cook with British Army during First War. Sceptical about Mussolini. Short, well-dressed. Not naturalised. Gambler. Daughter Fascist, looks after food; beautiful. Competes in trotting events. Disappeared? *(TSA 2)*.

FOXE, Mrs Amy. Stringham's mother. South African beauty and heiress. First married to Lord Warrington, brigadier-general. Divorced from Stringham's father. Political intriguer. Married 'Buster' Foxe. House near Berkeley Square; have footman *(AQOU 2)*. Also Glimber, Warrington home left for her life. Tiring of Buster, another divorce possible(?) *(ABM 1)*. Living at Sunningdale: Glimber let to an Armenian *(ABM 2)*. Has Warrington money, but only for life; extravagant *(ALM 3)*. Fallen for Chandler *(CCR 1)*. Early middle age – beautiful still. Relationship continues *(CCR 2)*. Party for Moreland *(CCR 3)*. She still dazzles. Glimber taken for evacuated Government office *(TKO 4)*. Less well-off. Wants to divorce Buster and live near Chandler; both houses shut *(TVOB 3)*. Left Buster. In Essex cottage near Chandler, who will go to O.C.T.U. *(TSA 1)*. Did not treat Flavia well(?) *(TMP 1)*. Dead *(TMP 5)*.

FOXE, Lieutenant-Commander 'Buster', D.S.C. Polo player. Admiralty. Husband Stringham's mother *(AQOU 2)*. Icy, Well-dressed. Very well preserved. Affair Mildred Haycock(?) *(ALM 4)*. Fatter. Worried about it. Pinched Matilda's leg(?) *(CCR 3)*. Chastened. Likes Chandler. His affair(s) going? Crows over Stringham. Returned to Navy *(TKO 4)*. Extravagant. With secret inter-services organisation at requisitioned Thrubworth *(TVOB 3)*. Umfraville claims Foxe stole wife from him and drove her to suicide. He and Umfraville hate each other. Killed in accident near Lingfield race course *(TK 1)*. Had been made Captain.

GAUNTLETT. Retired farmer, neighbour of Nicholas *(HSH 1)*.

GILBERT, Archie. Devotee of dances *(ABM 1)*. In City – non-ferrous metals? 'Unthinkable in everyday clothes.' Sees it all as sham? North London anti-aircraft battery; married girl from nearby *(TMP 5)*.

GITTENS, Lance-Corporal. Storeman (*TVOB* 2). Cadwallader's brother-in-law.

GLOBER, Louis. American film maker, publisher, art-enthusiast, playboy, tycoon, motor-racing devotee, socialite (*TK* 2). Makes and loses fortunes? Intelligent. Saved famous film actress from fire? Boxer? Self-publicist. In sixties? Nicholas knew him in publishing when young. Short-lived marriages, one to film-star. Last wife Fleurdelys died of leukemia(?). Fascinated by death. About thirty when Nicholas first met him. Very good-looking then; wanted John drawing; had Mopsy Pontner; took pubic hair memento. Russian-Jewish family. Bronx. Father rich builder. To make film of Trapnel book? Wants marry Pamela (Flitton) (*TK* 3). Tough. Gun fight over woman, Montana? Secret contributions to charity. Drops Trapnel novel as film prospect in favour St John Clarke's *Match Me Such Marvel* (*TK* 4). Fallen for Polly Duport. Hits Widmerpool (*TK* 5). Dead in car crash Moyenne Corniche (*TK* 6). Film already abandoned.

GOLDNEY. Secretary archeological society (*HSH* 5).

GOLLOP. Quarry director (*HSH* 5).

GORING, Barbara. Nicholas infatuated by (*ABM* 1). Daughter of Lord and Lady Goring; they took house Upper Berkeley Street for part summer. Lady Goring, Lady Walpole-Wilson sisters, daughters Lord Aberavon. Lord Goring hates London, has experimental fruit farm. Barbara's brother, Tom, contemporary of Nicholas at school; younger brother, David. She, noisy. Good works in Bermondsey. Widmerpool admires. Tips sugar over him. Goring house, Pembringham Woodhouse. Gwatkin (Aberavon) money keeps it up? Engaged to Pardoe (*ABM* 3). Marries and loses baby (*ALM* 2). Pardoe melancholic, Barbara has to run house. Granddaughter marries pop star (*HSH* 2).

GORING, Lord and Lady. See Barbara above.

GORING, Tom. See Barbara above. Commanded brigade (*BDFAR* 2).

GORING, David. See Barbara above.

GOSSAGE. Music critic, friend of Moreland (*CCR* 1).

GRANT, Joy. Professional name. Married Umfraville (*TVOB* 3). Met her at Cavendish. Promiscuous. Split up soon. Leaves with Castlemallock. Leaves him for Breen. They keep pub Thames Valley.

GREENING, Robin. ADC to Liddament (*TSA* 1). Believed dead at Anzio but only wounded (*HSH* 5). Limp.

GUGGENBÜHL, Werner. German. Involved with Mrs Andriadis (*TAW* 4). Trotskyist. Interested socially relevant plays. Writing one. Disturbing presence. Secretary to St John Clarke (*TAW* 5). Leaves for 'something more paying'. (*ALM* 3). University Fellow, now called Vernon Gainsborough (*BDFAR* 1). Affair with Gypsy Jones(?) (*BDFAR* 3). No longer Trotskyist? Publishes *Bronstein: Marxist or Mystagogue?* showing conversion from Trotskyism (*BDFAR* 5). Well reviewed by *TLS* with seven similar books. Dr Gainsborough – academic post political theory (*HSH* 2).

GULLICK, Mrs. Helps at Stonehurst (*TKO* 1).

GWATKIN, Roland. Captain. Company commander (*TVOB* 1). About Nicholas's age. Peacetime in bank. Wants to be good soldier. Married Blodwen Davies, having been rejected by Gwenllian Breeze. No children. Cannot delegate (*TVOB* 2). Little time off. Reads Kipling. Failures during exercise. Farming stock, Shropshire border; distant relation Lord Aberavon(?) (*TMP* 4). Father in insurance. Idealisation of Maureen, daughter local publican. Growing forgetful. Dislikes Bithel. Botches code words because of preoccupation with Maureen. Relieved of command. To await posting. Sees Maureen with Corporal Gwylt. Laughs. Has style. Invalid (*TMP* 4). Acting bank manager. Dead (*HSH* 4).

GWINNETT, Russell. American. Teacher, American women's university. Early thirties (*TK* 1). Ex-alcoholic? To be biographer Trapnel. Homosexual? Likes death? Girl-friend committed suicide? Descended from a 'signer' of Declaration of Independence, Button Gwinnett? Surname from Gwynedd (North Wales)? Buttons, South Wales *advenae*? Grandfather successful lawyer; father bad lot, left Russell's mother. Family moved to New England after Civil War (*TK* 3). Lonely. Connection with Pamela (Flitton). Affair to simulate Trapnel's(?) (*TK* 4). Lives at Bagshaw's. Moves out. Part Trapnel book drafted. Hiding from Pamela. In South Spain (*TK* 6). Broken from academic life. Exonerated over Pamela's death. Water-skiing instructor Mediterranean resort. Liked by Nicholas. Back in academic life? (*HSH* 2). In mid-forties. Book on Trapnel up for prize, *Death's-Head Swordsman*. At obscure college. Much changed (*HSH* 3). Seems old. Very bald. Engaged on *The Gothic Symbolism of Mortality in the Texture of Jacobean Stagecraft*. Staying hotel where Pamela died. Studying Murtlock's group (*HSH* 5). Took notable part in sex rites? Marries Fiona Cutts (*HSH* 6). Great transcendental powers? (*HSH* 7).

GWITHER. Cook with Stringham (*TSA* 1).

GWYLT, Corporal. Small, womaniser (*TVOB* 2).

HAWKINS, Brigadier. Commander Divisional Artillery (*TSA* 1).

HEGARTY. Film scriptwriter (*ALM* 1).

HENDERSON, Barnabas. Late twenties, drop-out. (*HSH* 1). Gave up art-dealer career. With Murtlock. Father killed in war leaving enough to buy art firm partnership. Boy-friend, Chuck (*HSH* 6). Leaves community for him. Art gallery (*HSH* 7). Much smartened up. Was in love with Murtlock.

HEWETSON. Liaison with Belgians and Czechs (*TMP* 2). Sexual adventures? Solicitor. Judge-Advocate-General's Dept., N. Africa. Returns to being solicitor (*TK* 4).

c

HLAVA, Colonel. Czech. Flying ace (*TMP* 2). Major-general (*TMP* 5). House arrest. Dies heart failure.

HODGES, Mrs Baldwyn, Hugo Tolland joins her antique business (*CCR* 4).

HOGBOURNE-JOHNSON, Colonel Derrick, M.C. Regular i/c operational duties, Division (*TSA* 1). Sword of Honour, Sandhurst. Error, Palestine pre-1939 War? Tall, fat, owlish. Rivalry Widmerpool. Clerk, Diplock. Wit? Training Branch (*TMP* 2).

HOPKINS, Heather. Friend, neighbour of Norah Tolland and Eleanor Walpole-Wilson (*ALM* 2). Middle-aged. Butch. Dumpy. Professional pianist at Merry Thought. Broken with Eleanor and Norah (*ALM* 4). Has turned Catholic (*TKO* 2).

HORACZKO 2nd Lt. Assistant to Bobrowski (*TMP* 1). Cavalry. Marries Margaret (née) Budd (*TMP* 5).

HUNTERCOMBE, Lord and Lady. Rich? Neibhbours Walpole-Wilsons in country (*ABM* 1). London house, Belgrave Square. He Lord-Lt. (*ABM* 3). She dresses like Mrs Siddons (*ABM* 4). Daughter Venetia Penistone (*CCR* 2). Lord and Lady interested arts (*CCR* 3). He trustee of galleries. Shrewd.

ISBISTER, Horace, R.A. Artist. Painted Lord Aberavon, Templer senior, Cardinal Whelan and wife of Solicitor-General. St John Clarke to write introduction to *The Art of Horace Isbister?* (*TAW* 1). Ill. At school with St John Clarke? Homosexual relationship with? Has done portrait of him. Dies (*TAW* 2). Memorial exhibition (*TAW* 4). Some satirical comment in later work? St John Clarke to do introduction from Marxist point of view? Married model Morwenna (*HSH* 2).

JAMIESON. Maiden name Clare Akworth's mother – Ardglass branch (*HSH* 5). Husband dead.

JEAVONS, Molly, Lady. Née Ardglass; aunt of Isobel; was sister-in-law to Bijou. Many relations. Lives South Kensington. Married Marquess of Sleaford (John) (*ALM* 1). Seat, Dogdene. She married him at eighteen. He died 1919. Married Ted Jeavons after meeting at Motor Show, though had first seen him as wounded soldier when Dogdene military hospital. Sister Katherine, childless widow, married Lord Warminster as second wife. Keeps monkey in bedroom. Saw lot of Umfraville formerly (*ALM* 4). Nobody ever turned away. Miss Weedon and Stringham have moved into house (*CCR* 2). Hard up. Is left marquetry cabinet by sister (*TKO* 3). Bit tumbledown but could be grand in manner; house a mess. Returning Dogdene with evacuated girls' school (*TKO* 4). Looks like barmaid and Charles II beauty. About fifty. Priscilla staying with her, also Eleanor Walpole-Wilson and others (*TSA* 2). Killed in air raid.

JEAVONS, Ted. See above. 'Adventure'. He and wife not well-off (*ALM* 1). Ill from war wound, unemployable. Tries to sell inventions. Seems relic of First War. Kicks over traces now and then (*ALM* 4). Tart at home? Dominated by wife. Has M.C. Was subaltern. Serving in Machine Gun Corps when hit at La Bassée, after Green Howards and Duke of Wellington's. Spent a leave with Mildred. Too tired for much sex now. Dislikes Umfraville. Reminds Mildred of the leave. Has her again? Selling petrol-saving device (*ALM* 5. Ill, but improves (*CCR* 2). Air raid warden (*TKO* 4). Brother, Stanley, accountant, now Staff Captain, War Office. Ted's sister-in-law, Lil, to live with Mrs Widmerpool. Survives raid (*TSA* 2). Templer moves in (*TMP* 2. About fifty. Tough. Wife had secured home for him. A.R.P. centre of life. At George Tolland's and Erridge's funeral (*BDFAR* 2). Dead (*HSH* 2).

JENKINS, Captain. Nicholas's father. Stationed Brighton before First War, friend of Deacon. Regular. Wounded Mesopotamia. Duty Cairo. At Paris Peace Conference, concerned with disarmament (*ABM* 1). Older brothers include Martin and Giles. Was invalided out of army (*TKO* 1). Dislikes outdoor occupations and socialising. Hunts. Wears eye-glass. Interested in Law and Stock Market. Collects prints and books. Dislikes thinking. Dislikes authority, but also those who criticise authority. Likes power. Sent to France, First War. Survives. Tries to get back in army for Second War (*TKO* 4). Health poor. Ill-tempered. Friend of Tokenhouse, but they drifted apart (*TK* 1). Dead (*TK* 3); 'unphilosophic. mind'.

JENKINS, Giles Delahay, 'Captain'. Nicholas's uncle – father's brother. About fifty (*AQOU* 1). Regarded as joke. Duodenal ulcer. Likes Germans. Was in South Africa. Commissioned. Retired before Transvaal War. Pro-Boer. Supported partially by Trust created by great-aunt – about £185–200 a year. Cause of friction between Nicholas's father and him. 'Bit of a radical.' In Isle of Man; to marry? (*AQOU* 2). Indiscriminate in dealings with women. Unfortunate love affair in Egypt when young. Army Service Corps after line regiment. Affair(s) involving someone else's wife, someone else's money. Debts. Court martial possibilities. Forced to resign. Diamond trade. Tried to get back into army 1914. Refused medically. Work, Ministry of Munitions, Ministry of Food. Worked with 'comforts' for U.S. troops. Opposed to all established institutions. Three nephews (*AQOU* 4). Concerned with paper business (*ABM* 2). At Ufford Hotel, introduces Mrs Erdleigh (*TAW* 1). Just in sixties. Close relationship with Mrs Erdleigh? Working for a charity. Denies knowledge Mrs Erdleigh (*TAW* 5). Let him down? Working 'bucket-shop' – office for advising speculators (*TKO* 1). He and Conyers dislike each other. Uses Bellevue (*TKO* 3). Likes Hitler. Dies Bellevue late August 1939, stroke. Leaves £7300 to Mrs Erdleigh.

JENKINS, Martin. Bachelor brother to Giles and Nicholas's father, on poor terms with both. Killed second battle Marne (*AQOU* 1). Left difficult will.

JENKINS, Mrs. Nicholas's mother. From home with hall-boy and footman. Likes occult (*TKO* 1). Likes simple food. Not social.

JENKINS, Nicholas. Welsh origins. Royal ancient Celtic ancestors? Born about 1907. Public school (*AQOU* 1). Interested in Jean Templer (*AQOU* 2). France, learning language; wants to write (*AQOU* 3). 'In love' with Jean and Suzette. University (*AQOU* 4). Living London about 1928–9, aged twenty-one or two

(*ABM* 1). In love Barbara Goring. Jean, Suzette memories only. Not keen on marriage. Perhaps not still in love. Publishing. Firm specialises art books. Still attracted by Barbara. Rooms Shepherd Market. Incapable understanding Widmerpool. Admits to snobbishness over Deacon and Gypsy Jones (*ABM* 2). Hopes to forget Barbara (*ABM* 3). Still finds Jean absorbing. To write novel(?) (*ABM* 4). Embrace for Gypsy. Consummation with Gypsy, she unimpressed. Not of this world, says Widmerpool. Makeshift love life (*TAW* 1). Has written book. Cold-seeming but with deep affections? Between dissipation and diffidence? Still publishing (*TAW* 2). Working on another book. Consummation with Jean. Political detachment – guys Leftist (*TAW* 4). Would Jean marry him? Apalled by her disclosure of affair with Stripling. Duport's return to bring difficulties with Jean (*TAW* 5). Working in films (*ALM* 1). Has written two novels. Over with Jean. Now about twenty-eight, nine. Interested Isobel Tolland. Worried about marriage. A grey hair (*ALM* 2). Knows at first sight he will marry Isobel (ALM 3). No longer interested in Jean (*AM* 4). Marriage approaches. Engaged (*ALM* 5). Introvert? Cold blooded pleasure in writing (*CCR* 1). Married. Two or three books (*CCR* 2). Has lost film job; reviewing. Isobel has miscarriage. Very interested in Sir Magnus Donner's sex life (*CCR* 3). Feelings for Stringham. Wanted soldiering (*TKO* 2). Affinities with Moreland. Poor financial state; difficulties writing at approach of war. On reserve. Highbrow, says Templer. Isobel pregnant (*TKO* 3). Writing, editing, reviewing. Still moved by news of Jean. Idling at beginning of war (*TKO* 4). In thirties. Journalism. Army, 2nd Lt (*TVOB* 1). Ireland (*TVOB* 2). Aldershot, course (*TVOB* 2 and 3). Mid-thirties (*TVOB* 3). Jean can still cause pain. Son (*TVOB* 4). Castlemallock. Sex deprivation. Posted Div. H.Q. Glad see Widmerpool, but changes: in his power. Temporarily i/c Defence Platoon (*TSA* 1). Sexual longings. Fails language test with Finn (*TSA* 2). War Office (*TSA* 3). Cpt. in Finn's Section, Intelligence Corps (*TMP* 1). Assistant to Pennistone, Polish liaison. Chelsea flat (*TMP* 2). Reading Proust and seventeenth century. Takes over Belgians and Czechs. Major i/c French, Belgians, Czechs and Luxembourg (*TMP* 3). Second i/c to Finn (*TMP* 5). Demobilised. Classical tastes, anti-Blake, regards as cranky. Returns university, aged forty (*BDFAR* 1). Doing book on Burton. Reviewing, spending gratuity. His books well known, though out of print (*BDFAR* 2). Lit. editor for *Fission?* Another son (*BDFAR* 4). A son going to school (*BDFAR* 5). Publication *Borge And Hellebore: A Study*. Likes Tiepolo and Poussin (*TK* 1), though Breugel's *Hunters In The Snow* almost favourite picture. Worked under Tokenhouse. Unshockable (*TK* 2). Gwinnett trust him (*TK* 3). Not working (*TK* 4). Son near military service. In fifties (*TK* 5). Liked Gwinnett and Glober. Wants to avoid Widmerpool. In sixties (*HSH* 1). On Magnus Donners's literary award panel (*HSH* 2). Many books. Suffers from *accidie* – feeling fed-up with life. Reviewing.

JONES, Gypsy. Eton-cropped gamine Leftist agitator, friend of Deacon (*ABM* 1). Stays with him sometimes (*ABM* 2). Pregnant. Father schoolmaster, Hendon: now living there (*ABM* 3). Interested world revolution? Widmerpool attracted and pays for abortion (*ABM* 4). Typical educated middle-class daughter, says Barnby. Working Vox Populi Press. Sleeping with Craggs? On Craggs's knee at party. Has Nicholas, but apathetic about it. Anti-war protest (*TKO* 4).

Marries Craggs – Lady Craggs (*BDFAR* 1). Had affair Erridge? (*BDFAR* 2). In forties. Affair Guggenbühl? (*BDFAR* 3). Custodian of Communist line – ruthless; Craggs fears her (*BDFAR* 4). Attempts destroy Stevens's book (*BDFAR* 5). Widowed (*TK* 3). Living with Pugsley, retains Craggs's name and title. Dead, Czechoslovakia (*HSH* 3).

KEDWARD, Idwal. Subaltern, aged twenty-two. Engaged (*TVOB* 1). Sensible, no dreamer. Peacetime in bank. Castlemallock (*TVOB* 2). Takes over company (*TVOB* 4). To be married. Cpt. in Netherlands advance (*TMP* 4). Married, two daughters.

KERNÉVEL, Captain. Breton (*TMP* 3). Military attaché's office. M.B.E. (*TMP* 5).

KIELKIEWICZ, General. Polish chief of staff (*TMP* 1).

KLEIN, Jimmy. Cousin Rosie Manasch, passion for Peggy Stepney (*ABM* 1). Marries her as third husband (*TMP* 3). Was at Donners-Brebner (*BDFAR* 3).

KUCHERMAN, Major. Belgian military attaché (*TMP* 2). Minister (*TMP* 5).

KYDD, Alaric. Author (*BDFAR* 3). Odd (sex?) tastes. Novel, *Sweetskin*. Much expected of him. Legal case against book. *Sweetskin* disappointing (*BDFAR* 4). Prosecuted. Not guilty (*BDFAR* 5). Poor sales, but picks up? Abroad (HSH 2).

LANNOO. Kucherman's predecessor.

LE BAS, Lawrence, Langton. School housemaster (*AQOU* 1). Footling. Once oarsman, poet? Was good at everything. Arrest following Stringham joke. At Cowes (*ABM* 2). Teutonic-looking (*TAW* 5). Collapse. School librarian (*BDFAR* 5). Eighty-plus, looks well.

LEBEDEV, General. Soviet military attaché (*TMP* 1). Dour.

LEINTWARDINE, Ada. Secretary to Sillery (*BDFAR* 1). Going into publishing. In twenties. Doctor's daughter. Writing novel. Not C.P. Important figure, *Fission* (*BDFAR* 3). Lesbian? Affair with Evadne Clapham? Advances to Sheldon? Friend Pamela (Flitton) (*BDFAR* 4). Marries Quiggin (*BDFAR* 5). Novel published, *I Stopped at a Chemist*, upsets some, but promising. Addresses Venice conference (*TK* 2). Still Lesbian? Twins. Novel filmed as *Sally Goes Shopping*. Has done well. Two dull novels, then *Bedsores* and *The Bitch Meets On Wednesday* – successful. Good at Left talk (*TK* 3). Speech to Men of Letters/Men of Science session. Tries to get Glober to film St John Clarke novel. Does TV programme on St John Clarke (*HSH* 2). Still trying for film. Marriage good. Not writing, busy publishing. Near fifty (*HSH* 3).

LEROY, Commandant and Madam. Live La Grenadière, Touraine, France (*AQOU* 3). Nicholas stays with them.

LIDDAMENT, Major-General H. de C., D.S.O., M.C. In command of Division (*TVOB* 2). Youngish, air of scholar. Dogs; hunting horn in battledress blouse:

affectation? Sees through Widmerpool (*TSA* 1). Observant. Batchelor. Wounded early in war. Likes Trollope. Given Corps (*TSA* 3). Army Council (*TK* 4).

LILIENTHAL. Xenia's husband, see below (*TK* 2). Bookseller. Marries Mopsy Pontner.

LILIENTHAL, Xenia. Redhead. Bookshop (*TK* 2). Uses The Mortimer. Trying sell John drawings for Pontners (flash-back). Went off with Indian doctor.

LOVELL, Chips. Script-writer, journalist; nephew Lady Molly – his mother Lord Sleaford's sister (*ALM* 1). Likes talking about relations. Good-looking. Cheek. Parents eloped. Aged about twenty-three. Father painter. Poor script-writer. Interested Priscilla Tolland. Pushing (*ALM* 4). Lady Molly good to him as child. On gossip column (*CCR* 4). Engaged Priscilla. Married (*TKO* 2). Worried about job. Baby. Officer Marines (*TVOB* 3). Separated by war (*TSA* 1). Priscilla unfaithful? Stationed London after East Coast (*TSA* 2). Romanitc; good journalist. Trying write play. Captain H.Q. Combined Op. Priscilla with Odo Stevens. Child, Caroline, with his parents. Killed at Ardglass party.

LUNDQUIST. Swede. Guest La Grenadière (*AQOU* 3). Thinking of journalism. Row with Örn. Crafty tennis player.

MACFADDEAN. Very keen soldier, ex-schoolmaster (*TVOB* 3).

MACFIE. RAMC Major (*TSA* 1).

MACLINTICK. Music critic. Married to Audrey. Educated Bonn? Devoted to Moreland (*CCR* 1). Rough surface (*CCR* 2). Writing book on musical theory for eight or nine years. Does not get on with wife. Likes whores, not women? Passionate. Squalid home. Anti-Left. Wife leaves him (*CCR* 4). Has lost job. Divorce? Suicide. Tore up book (*TSA* 2).

MACLINTICK, Audrey. Above's wife. Abrasive. Dislikes children (*CCR* 2). Takes Carolo's side. Marriage tottering? Leaves husband for Carolo (*CCR* 4). Living with Moreland (*TSA* 2). Carolo left her after three years, beginning of war. Worked in canteen. Untidy. They do not go out much. Treats Moreland like a child – because she has none? Relationship with him revenge against husband for friendship with Moreland? About forty. Upset on seeing Carolo (*TK* 5).

M'CRACKEN. See Blaides.

MCREITH, Lady Gwen. Friend Barbara and Stripling (*AQOU* 2). Indeterminate age. Theatrical background? Tall, slight, fair skin. Was married to Templer senior's partner, who died. More friendly with Barbara than with Stripling. Lives in world of 'physical action'. Liked by Peter Templer, not by Farebrother. Giggler. Affair Templer? Officer women's services (*TKO* 4). Lesbian(?) (*TVOB* 3). Organised drivers for Belgians and Poles (*TSA* 2). Norah Tolland was with her (*TMP* 2).

MAELGWYN-JONES. Adjutant (*TVOB* 1).

MALIPHANT, Mrs. Aged actress. Slept with Irving and Tree(?) (*TK* 2).

MANASCH, Rosie. Jewess. Parents patrons of arts. At finishing school with Anne Stepney (*ABM* 1). Uncle sold Stourwater to Sir Magnus Donners (*ABM* 3). Likes Pardoe. Marries Jock Udall (*CCR* 3). Billson works for? (*TKO* 1). Uneven marriage? (*TMP* 5). No children. Udall shot. Marries Andrzejewski, Pole, who dies shortly after (*BDFAR* 3). Resumes maiden name. Backing *Fission*. Aged about forty. Pays for party for *Fission* first number. (*BDFAR* 3). Likes Odo? (*BDFAR* 4). Not political, mildly progressive. Affair Odo (*BDFAR* 5). Withdraws backing for magazine over lost MS. Marries Odo (*TK* 3). House Regent's Park, lavishly furnished (*TK* 5). Musical party for charity.

MANTLE, Corporal. In line for commission (*TSA* 1 and 3).

MARINKO. Jugoslave liaison (*TMP* 5). Supported Mihailovich, not Tito, and loses job.

MASHAM, Liaison Free French (*TMP* 2).

MAUREEN. Casual Irish girl idealised by Gwatkin (*TVOB* 4).

MEMBERS, Mark. Writer, critic. Second cousin Quiggin, perhaps from same street. Nicholas's contemporary at university (*AQOU* 4). Early poem in *Public School Verse* – 'Iron Aspidistra' – praised by Gosse. Does not get First? Gains reputation. Less Byronic (*ABM* 4). With Mona, friend of Gypsy. Work for a weekly. Coming man? Secretary to St John Clarke. Three or four books in project, poems, novels, critical study. Responsible for turning St John Clarke to modernism? (*TAW* 1). Verse takes up psychoanalysis (*TAW* 2). Quiggin displaces as secretary. Nicholas thinks him goodish poet. Working Boggis & Stone (*TAW* 4). Verse volume praised by critics. Has arrived? Holding several literary jobs (*ALM* 5). Moving up socially. Been to U.S. Interested German literature, has dropped psychoanalysis. Assistant literary editor (*CCR* 2). Travel book, *Baroque Interlude*. To marry rich girl? Has been at Ministry of Information (*BDFAR* 1). University talk on philosophers. Arranging conferences (*BDFAR* 3 and *TK* 1). Married American journalist and author, slightly older than he; is her fourth. Interested in another woman; novelist? Looking Romantic again (*HSH* 2). Wife, Lenore, in U.S. much. On Donners-Brebner award panel. Poetry prize (*HSH* 3). Poems collected from *Iron Aspidistra* (1923) to *H-Bomb Eclogue* (1966). Writing few recently.

MICHALSKI, 2nd Lt. Pole, ADC to Kielkiewicz (*TMP* 1).

MONA. Model; beauty, nearly six feet tall. With Members (*ABM* 4). Friend Gypsy. Hates men? Wife Templer (*TAW* 2). In toothpaste advertisement. Part Swiss? Father engineer, drunkard. Parents now dead. Aunt, Worthing. Templer obsessively fond of. Untamed quality. Unhappy with Templer (*TAW* 3). Capricious, hysterical. Leaves Templer; is living with Quiggin (*TAW* 4). Likes only herself, says Jean, not men or women. Legacy, £1000 (*TAW* 5). She and Quiggin in cottage (*ALM* 3). Was Lesbian? Unhappy? Thinking of film career. Attracted to Erridge. Flirts with. Accompanies him to China (*ALM* 5). Returns alone (*CCR* 2). At Erridge's funeral, about forty (*BDFAR* 2). Married(?) to Air-Vice-Marshall, Jeff.

MONTSALDY. French Captain (*TMP* 5).

MORELAND, Hugh. Composer. Early twenties, about Nicholas's age (*CCR* 1). Father music teacher. Brought up by aunt. Flat off Oxford Street. Hopeless love affairs. To marry? Music for film of *Lysistrata*, money raised by Donners. Interested in waitress. Interested in Matilda Wilson. To marry her? Writing opera. Marries Matilda. Conducting at resort (*CCR* 2). Matilda expecting. Has given up resort job. Marriage not smooth. Can it continue? Child dies (*CCR* 3). Symphony completed. Lung trouble. Interested Priscilla Tolland? Symphony mild success. Innocent(?) affair with Priscilla. Depressed; breaks with Priscilla following Maclintick suicide (*CCR* 4). Donners had been patron (*TKO* 2). He and Matilda living near Stourwater, Donners having found cottage. Working on ballet. Block because of Hitler. Likes rich life. Matilda leaves him (*TKO* 4). Staying with Jeavonses. Says never had Priscilla. Not sure wants Matilda. Working Edinburgh (*TSA* 1). Temporarily broken up – drinking – when Matilda left but working again (*TSA* 2). Poor health. Living with Audrey. Fire-watcher. Audrey Maclintick manages him. Hates Brahms. Likes Odo. Musical tour with Audrey, Government sponsored (*TMP* 1). Ill (*BDFAR* 3). Baffled by life. Nostalgic (*TK* 2). Worse health (*TK* 3). Quiet life with Audrey. Not married. Cat, Hardicanute. Better off. Still loves Matilda(?) (*TK* 5). Collapses. Dying. Last meeting with Nicholas (*TK* 6).

MOUNTFICHET, Lord. Bridgnorth's eldest son, John. University (*TAW* 4). Married Venetia Penistone, a Huntercombe. Affair Pamela Flitton(?) (*BDFAR* 2). To have left wife for her? Killed.

MURTLOCK, Leslie (Scorpio, or Scorp). Drop-out, cultist, mystic – Simple Life, Harmony. Twenties (*HSH* 1). Homosexual? Named after his Zodiac sign. Was in antiques. Spooky? Began to take over business. Ominous. Sexually aloof. Second sight? Represents revival of Trelawnyism? (*HSH* 2). Was picked up by Shuckerly and installed in flat. Reincarnation of Trelawny(?) (*HSH* 4). TV programme mooted – in *After Strange Gods* series. Sang in choir. Parents in fanatical sect. Scholarship to choir school. Trouble with choirmaster. Uninterested in sex? Interested in moral authority? Choirmaster killed himself? Wants to meet Widmerpool. Struggle with Widmerpool for power? (*HSH* 5). Night rites. Knife's Widmerpool. Finally has Widmerpool under control (*HSH* 7).

ÖRN. Norwegian guest at La Grenadière (*AQOU* 3).

PARDOE, Johnnie. Grenadier ensign, very short. House Welsh border (*ABM* 1). Rich. Big black moustache. Interested music. Staying same Scottish house as Barbara Goring (*ABM* 3). Engaged Barbara (*ABM* 4). Married to her (*ALM* 2). Have lost baby. Melancholic after leaving Grenadiers. Reads religion and philosophy. Does well in Burma, war (*TMP* 5).

PEDLAR, Colonel Eric, M.C. 'A and Q' over Widmerpool (*TSA* 1). Slow, stiff, unambitious.

PENDRY, Sgt. Nicholas's platoon sergeant (*TVOB* 1). Unstable? Wife, Cath (*TVOB* 2). Trouble with her at home. Goes home but remains gloomy. Dead. Suicide? Murder? Accident?

PENISTONE, Venetia. Huntercombes' daughter. Married Mountfichet (*BDFAR* 2).

PENNISTONE, David. 2nd Lt. (*TVOB* 3). Thin, hook nose, fairish hair. Lives Venice with contessa beautiful but not very young. Writing on Descartes. Studies de Vigny. Was at Mrs Andriadis's 'a thousand years before'. In Finn's office, Captain (*TSA* 2). Looks after Poles. Knew Finn, Paris pre-war. Was in textiles. Secretive. Major (*TMP* 1). Nicholas assists in Polish liaison. Book about Descartes – or Gassendi? Fluent several languages. Good soldier. Joining Finn's Paris firm on demobilisation, (*TMP* 5). *Descartes, Gassendi and the Atomic Theory of Epicurus* published (*BDFAR* 5). Marries French girl who had been in Resistance; takes over from Finn (*TK* 4). Rarely in Britain. Writing on philosophical ideas of Cyrano. Cyrano book out (*HSH* 2).

PHILIDOR, Général de brigade. French military attaché (*TMP* 3). From N. Africa to take post. Killed car accident(?) (*HSH* 1).

PHILLPOTS. Nicholas's unit, wounded Crete? (*TMP* 4).

PILGRIM, Max. Young man, professional singer, voice like old lady's (*ABM* 2). Dubious songs. Homosexual? Scene with Deacon. Appearing with Hopkins at the Madrid (*ALM* 2). At Umfraville's club (*ALM* 4). Antique business(?) (*TKO* 3). Sharing flat with Hugo Tolland. Revival at the Madrid (*TSA* 2). Lodging with Moreland. Been with ENSA. To enter decorating business with Hugo. Songs were dating, but fashion for nostalgia during war. Survives Madrid raid.

PILSUDSKI. Leader *coup d'état* Poland 1926 and leads brigade (*TMP* 1).

PINKUS. Adjutant-Quarter master (*TVOB* 4).

PONTNER, Mopsy and husband. Husband older, translator and speculator in paintings (*TK* 2). Beauty. Moreland found her attractive. Sexual encounter with Glober recalled. Refused Barnby. Married Lilienthal when wife left, Pontner having died. Helps in bookshop. Dead.

POPKISS, Iltyd. Padre, C. of E. (*TVOB* 1).

PRASAD, Major. Represents independent State, Indian sub-continent, among foreign officers (*TMP* 4). Religion requires bathroom.

PROTHERO. Commanded Defence Platoon, broke leg (*TSA* 1).

PUGSLEY, Len. Publisher's reader and Leftist writer – *Integral Foundations of a Fresh Approach to Art for the Masses* (BDFAR 5 and TK 3). Affair with Gypsy, who lives with him later.

PUMPHREY. Officer awaiting transfer to RAF. (TVOB 2).

QUIGGIN, Amanda and Belinda. Twin daughters of J. G. Trouble-making undergraduates (HSH 1). Daub Widmerpool in university demo. He brings them to literary party (HSH 3). Associated with underground publication, *Toilet Paper* (HSH 6).

QUIGGIN, J. G. Marxist writer and critic. Gruff. At university with Nicholas (AQOU 4). Modest home. Small college. Second cousin Members. Home near Members? Going bald. Scholarships. Reading history, like Nicholas. Represents 'submerged element' of university? North Country accent. Wants to work. Hard up? Brightman says not (AQOU 4). Father dead. Was railway worker? Or shady builder and politician? Mother, councillor? Keen on Gypsy(?) (ABM 4). Working with Deacon. Magazine contributions. Lost college scholarship, sent down? Smoother. More friendly with Members. Fragments of autobiography to come out? Keen on Mona? Has made a name (TAW 2). Professional reviewer, tough. Literary adviser to publisher. Book coming out? Destroys manuscripts as not good enough. Has displaced Members as St John Clarke's secretary. Renewed interest in Mona (TAW 3). Has turned St John Clarke to active Leftism (TAW 4). Obsessed by wealth. Still preparing book, *Unburnt Boats*. Mona leaves Templer for him. Book finished (TAW 5). Living with Mona in Sussex. Has left St John Clarke. Looking well-fed and spruce (ALM 2). North Country accent discarded. Nicholas's relations with him uneven. *Unburnt Boats* postponed (ALM 3). Communist? Man of will. Supports Anti-Fascist movements. Starting magazine with Erridge(?) (ALM 3). Animosity between him and Mona. Mona leaves him (ALM 5). Did not marry her. Not well situated (CCR 2). Reconciled with Erridge, despite his taking Mona. He criticises Erridge, Nicholas criticises him (CCR 4). Wanted war over Czechoslovakia (TKO 2). With Anne Umfraville (Stepney) (TKO 4). Living with her (TVOB 3). Has given up writing(?) (BDFAR 1). *Unburnt Boats* published. In publishing: Quiggin & Craggs. Looked after firm of Boggis & Stone. Dresses like partisan. Never in Communist Party? Magazine coming out? Enthusiastic publisher (BDFAR 3). *Unburnt Boats*, 'documentary' well received, just before war. Dislikes propaganda in magazine (BDFAR). Quiggin & Craggs taken over (BDFAR 5). Marries Ada. On Clapham board. Twins, Amanda, Belinda (TK 1). Chairman after Clapham's death (TK 2). Less politically committed? (TK 3). Overshadowed by Ada (TK 4 and HSH 2). Stuffy about his children's behaviour.

RAMOS, Colonel. Brazilian (TMP 4).

ROBBINS. Waiter Stringham replaced, ruptured (TSA 1).

RUSBY, Sir Horrocks. Lawyer in Derwentwater case involving Baby Wentworth (ABM 3).

RUSTY. Girl drop-out with Murtlock, about nineteen (*HSH* 1). Tarty. In love Murtlock? Leaves group for Soho (*HSH* 6).

RUYS. Belgian artillery officer, friendly with Pamela Flitton(?) (*TMP* 3).

SALTER, Mrs. Nature Trust. Involved against quarry scheme (*HSH* 5).

SALVIDGE, L. O. Writer (*BDFAR* 3). Praised Trapnel. Essays: *Paper Wine* (*BDFAR* 4). *Secretions*, more essays, published same year (*BDFAR* 5). Devilled for St John Clarke (*HSH* 2). In TV programme about him. Glass eye. Good notice for Trapnel biography (*HSH* 3). Newly married, girl younger than previous wives.

SAYCE. Bad soldier (*TVOB* 2).

SHELDON, Nathaniel. Ageing reviewer and all-purpose journalist, successful (*BDFAR* 3). Sexually encouraged by Ada Leintwardine? Reported Nuremberg trials.

SHERNMAKER, Bernard. Critic of stature (*BDFAR* 3). Writes for *Fission*. Holds critic more important than author? *Miscellaneous Equities* published (*BDFAR* 5). Rejected by Ada? (*TK* 2). Malice towards her. Wrote about Ferrand-Sénéschal. Has not written on Trapnel biography (*HSH* 3).

SHORT, Leonard. Undergrad. a year senior to Nicholas (*AQOU* 4). Comfortable allowance. Sillery's college. Gives lunches. Interested Liberals. Civil Servant (*BDFAR* 1). Cabinet Office during war. Knows Widmerpool. Highly placed. Obstructive? Switched from Liberals to Labour. Unmarried. Knighted (*TK* 5). Prim. Dislikes Pamela (Flitton).

SHUCKERLY, Quentin. Writer. Homosexual? High-quality 'queer' novel, *Athlete's Footman* (*TK* 1). Pillar of cultural conferences (*TK* 2). Poet. Friend of Ada Leintwardine. 'The air hostess of English letters.' Masochist? Picked up Murtlock, no joy (*HSH* 2). Poems delayed. Black boy-friend. Battered to death Greenwich Village (*HSH* 6).

SIEGFRIED. German prisoner Thrubworth working on land and in house (*BDFAR* 2). Establishing himself locally (*BDFAR* 4).

SIKORSKI, General. Pole. Eclipsed after 1926 coup but later takes over (*TMP* 1).

SILLERY. University don, in his mid-fifties (*AQOU* 4). Seeks power. Affects senility. Walrus moustache. Wrote *City State and State of City* at beginning of century. Snob. Knew Asquith. Politician manqué? Admires Russian revolution. Worldly influence? Intriguer. Obliquely involved Derwentwater divorce case. Can assume female characteristics. Non-drinker. To manage Theodoric-Donners-Brebner Fellowships? Funny voices. Portrait for college (*TAW* 4). On Means Test march. Pro-Stalin letter, *Times* (*TMP* 1). Retired, but retains college rooms (*BDFAR* 1). Under eighty. Birth-date never disclosed. Wrote verse in youth, style Patmore. Peer, Sublimated homosexuality? Certainly no interest in women. Working on diaries. C.P. member? Diaries to be published (*BDFAR* 3). Good advance. *Garnered At Sunset: Leaves From An Edwardian Journal* (*BDFAR* 5) – dull but well reviewed. Over ninety (*TK* 1). Dead – almost one hundred (*HSH* 2).

SLADE. Assistant to Pennistone (*TMP* 2). Headmaster (*TK* 4).

SLEAFORD, Marquess of. Geoffrey. Family name Fines. Succeeds John, two brothers between killed. Wife, Alice, mean? Lovell's 'second Sleaford uncle'. No heir (*ALM* 1). Was in South Africa, A.D.C. to Div. Commander.

SLEAFORD, Marquess of. John. Lady Molly's first husband. Lovell's 'first Slea- ford uncle'. Dead, 1919 Spanish flu. Office under Campbell-Bannerman and Asquith (*ALM* 1). Resigned during Marconi scandal. Garter. Chill, serious minded, honourable. Abominated by Edward VII (*TKO* 4).

SMETHYCK, Michael. Museum official. Contemparory of Nicholas at University (*TAW* 4). Vain. Was favourite of Sillery. Retired (*HSH* 4).

SMITH. Butler. Drinks. Erridge's but sometimes lent to Jeavons (*ALM* 1). Irrit- able. Trouble over postal order (*ALM* 5). Dead – septicaemia after bite from Maisky, Molly Jeavons's monkey (*TMP* 2).

SOPER. Div. Catering Officer (*TSA* 1).

STEBBINGS. Liaison, Spain, Portugal (*TMP* 1). Gassed himself (*TMP* 5).

STEPNEY, Lady Anne. Untidy. Reddish hair. Younger daughter of Bridgnorths. Sister Peggy, who marries Stringham. Wants to be different from her. Same finishing school as Rosie Manasch (*ABM* 1). Rebellious: 'on side of the people', re French Revolution. Bridesmaid at Peggy's wedding (*ABM* 4). Involved with Barnby (*TAW* 3 and 4). Over with Barnby (*TAW* 5). Marries Umfraville. Does not last month over year (*ALM* 4). In Paris. Painting. Mistress of Sir Magnus? (*TKO* 2). Attracted by Templer? Affair Templer (*TKO* 3). Broken with Sir Magnus (*TKO* 4). With Quiggin and Members. Living with Quiggin? (*TVOB* 3). Went off with Free Frenchman? (*BDFAR* 2). Married negro painted younger than herself (*HSH* 2).

STEPNEY, Lady. Peggy. Sister, Anne. Bridgnorths' elder daughter. Stringham interested (*AQOU* 4). Coolness between them (*ABM* 1). Klein has passion for her. Engaged Stringham (*ABM* 3). Married to him (*ABM* 4). Divorced and married to older cousin (*TAW* 2). Marriage dead from inanition. Living York- shire. Husband dead (*TMP* 3). Marries Klein.

STEVENS, (Herbert) Odo. Aldershot course with Nicholas (*TVOB* 3). From Birmingham. Peacetime, costume jewellery, also father. Some journalism. Keen on girls. Self-aware. Tough. Too big for boots? Returned to unit (*TVOB* 4). Interested in Priscilla Tolland. With her, Scotland (*TSA* 2). Hero. Did well at Lofoten? Priscilla wants to marry. At Café Royal with her. Lt. M.C. Embarka- tion leave, Mid-East? Musical interests. Jumpy about air raids. Row with

Priscilla. Writes verse and song lyrics. Melancholic. Wounded Mid-East(?) (*TMP* 2). Involved Szymanski escape? Affair with Pamela Flitton (*TMP* 3). Major, bar to M.C. False emotion over Priscilla. Poor lover? Overseas? 'Odo the stoat' (*TMP* 4). In literary world (*BDFAR* 3). Articles. Preparing book, army experiences. Pamela snubs. Operated with Communists in Balkans. Working with Members arranging conferences. Had local decoration, missed DSO. Involved in murders? Book, *Sad Majors*. Liked by Rosie Manasch (*BDFAR* 4). Book too anti-Left. Affair Rosie (*BDFAR* 5). *Sad Majors* serialised and published as book. Married Rosie (*TK* 3). Early forties, not much changed. Two or three children. Matilda Wilson wanted him. Went Ischia with her? Gave Rosie black eye? Quieter. Little work after marriage. No book after *Sad Majors* – a success. Verse collection, never published. Part-time secret service? Shit, says Pamela, despite war record. House, Regent's Park (*TK* 5). Knows something about Widmerpool?

STRINGHAM, 'Boffles'. Charles Stringham's father. See below.

STRINGHAM, Charles. Friend of Nicholas from school, variously described as few months older and about year older. Mimic. Melancholic. Father 'Boffles'. Mother divorced from him, becomes Mrs Foxe. Father remarried to French woman, Kenya (*AQOU* 1). Lives with mother. Family well-off, live at rapid pace? House near Berkeley Square (*AQOU* 2). Like Hamlet. Goes to Kenya. Intensity of Miss Weedon's feelings for him. Late at university (*AQOU* 4). Was injured fall from horse, Kenya. Slept with divorcée. Atmosphere of wealth. Dislikes university. Distancing between him and Templer, then final break. Leaving university? To be personal secretary Donners, with Truscott. Not returning to university. Interested Lady Peggy Stepney. Marriage? More or less engaged, but off (*ABM* 1). Fast? Linked with Mrs Andriadis. Aged twenty-three, four, looks older (*ABM* 2). Been Deauville. Affair Mrs Andriadis ending(?) (*ABM* 3). Engaged Peggy and marries her (*ABM* 4). Leaving Donners-Brebner. Marriage over (*TAW* 2). He and Peggy seldom lived together. Seen with other women. Drinking (*TAW* 4). Living West Halkin Street (*TAW* 5). Alcoholic, Miss Weedon looking after him (*ALM* 4). Hard up? He and Miss Weedon living at Jeavonses' (*CCR* 2). Living at Glimber (inherited by Mrs Foxe from first husband) with Miss Weedon; off drink (*TKO* 2). In London looking for job; trying for army (*TKO* 4). Money problems. Father dead, money left to French wife. Speculation about relationship with Miss Weedon. Has 'dash'. In army (*TVOB* 3). Private RAOC. Not drinking. Mess waiter (*TSA* 1). Transferred by Widmerpool to Mobile Laundry (*TSA* 3). Motives for joining up: rescue self-respect, restlessness, patriotism? Laundry (*TSA* 3). Far East? Will go. At Singapore (*TMP* 1). Missing. Captured (*TMP* 5). Dead. Did well (*TK* 4).

STRIPLING, Barbara. Née Templer, Peter's elder sister. (*AQOU* 2). Left dragoon – a poor husband – to marry Stripling near end First War, while husband at Front. Divorce (*TAW* 3). Marries Lord Perkins, Labour peer and industrial relations expert (*TAW* 3 and *TMP* 5).

STRIPLING, Jimmy. Racing driver. Married to Templer's sister, Barbara (*AQOU* 2). Not in First War and angry if people speak about war. Ran away with

Barbara while husband in France. Rich. Divorce (*TAW* 3). Accident at Brooklands. Underwriter. Taken up mysticism? Going down hill. Affair Mrs Erdleigh. Under forty. Jean confesses to affair with him (*TAW* 4). Affair Mrs Erdleigh continues (*TAW* 5). She 'skinning him'? Would not help Duport (*TKO* 3). Lecturing troops (*TMP* 5). Interested vintage cars. Dead (*HSH* 2). Took up with boy?

STRYDONCK DE BURKEL, General van. Inspector-General, Belgian army and air force (*TMP* 1).

SZYMANSKI Polish(?) trouble-maker. Moved from Free French to Poles (*TSA* 2). Parliamentary question about him (*TMP* 2). Aliases. In detention, escapes with British aid. Job with Stevens? (*TMP* 3).

TEMPLER, Barbara. See Stripling.

TEMPLER, Betty. Becomes this: begins as Mrs Taylor or Porter (*ALM* 4). Pretty. Escorted by Templer. Husband busy money-making. Has married Templer (*TKO* 2). Nervous. Near breakdown. Not 'all there'. Driven mad? (*TKO* 3). Committed (*TMP* 1). Marries F.O. man after Peter's death (*HSH* 2). Happy. Ambassadress.

TEMPLER, Jean. Peter's younger sister, about sixteen, seventeen, couple years younger than Nicholas (*AQOU* 2). Not strikingly pretty. Nicholas interested. In love with 'married man twice her age' (*AQOU* 4). Duport pursuing. Marries him (*ABM* 2). Still interests Nicholas, at Stourwater (*ABM* 3). Reserved. Harsh voice. Pregnant (*ABM* 4). Mrs Erdleigh foresees someone like her for Nicholas (*TAW* 1). Separated from Duport; daughter, Polly, aged three (*TAW* 2). Embrace with Nicholas, then bed. Living near Rutland Gate (*TAW* 4). Confesses affair with Stripling. Over with Nicholas (*ALM* 1). Back with Duport (*ALM* 2). South America. Has left Duport; is staying Rome with Baby Wentworth, now Clarini (*ALM* 4). Divorce; Marries S. American army officer (*TKO* 2). Had affair Brent at time of move to S. America (*TKO* 3). Was running at same time as affair with Nicholas? Poor in bed? She approached Brent (*TVOB* 3). Polly now thirteen, fourteen. She (Polly) revealed affair to Duport. Is Madam Flores; in London (*TMP* 5). Relations with Nicholas formal (*BDFAR* 3). Keen on being rich? Back to S. America. Husband head of Government (*TK* 5). Like grand foreign lady (*HSH* 7). Distant. Seeing Duport now husband dead.

TEMPLER, Peter. School friend, Nicholas, becomes stockbroker. Brother of Barbara, Jean. Mother dead, uncle baronetcy under Lloyd George. Womaniser. Not intellectual or bookish. Sexually precocious. (*AQOU* 1). Family not colossally rich nor poor (*AQOU* 2). Made to leave school early. Amsterdam for father on business. Going into City. Affair Lady McReith? In business (*AQOU* 4). Close of friendship with Stringham. In City doing well (*ABM* 2). Dislikes respectability. Making money; unmarried (*ABM* 3). Married, Mona (*TAW* 2). House near Maidenhead. Lost some money in slump. Marriage not comfortable? Given up womanising? Changed attitude to Widmerpool. Cannot please wife (*TAW* 3). Mona Leaves him (*TAW* 4). Still paying her allowance (*TAW* 5). Selling home near Maidenhead? Sold (*ALM* 2). Recovered from Mona's desertion? Friendly Widmerpool (*ALM* 4). With woman, Mrs Betty Taylor, Porter? 'Fast sports cars, loud checks, blondes, golf' (*TKO* 2). Remarried: Betty. Has slowed, is more serious, almost horrifying change. Lives Sunningdale. Anne (Stepney) attracted? Betty adoring, being driven mad by his womanising? She is mad (*TKO* 3). Big losses in slump, but recovers. Government advisory job, finance? (*TVOB* 3). Adviser to Min. of Economic Warfare (*TSA* 3, *TMP* 1). Wife committed. Deep pain. Flat bombed. Age-conscious. Failure sexually? Room with Jeavons (*TMP* 2). Involved woman? Looking for more active war job. Involved Pamela – unhappily (*TMP* 4). Dead on secret operation. Was abandoned? Widmerpool's fault? (*TMP* 5). Musical comedy death?

TEMPLER, senior. Peter's father. Money made in cement. Widower (*AQOU* 2). Reasonably well-off. Wiry, grim. In sixties. Painted by Isbister. Likes keeping fit. Dead (*TAW* 2).

THEODORIC, Prince. Royal family of unspecified (Balkan?) state. Donners-Brebner expanding in his country (*ABM* 1). Base metals. Brother, king. Descended from Victoria? (*ABM* 2). Macedonia? Diminishing influence? Aluminium? Interested Donners-Brebner Fellowships. With Baby Wentworth and Bijou Ardglass. Still interested Baby? (*ABM* 3). Middle-of-road man. With Bijou and beautiful Brazilian at Lido (*ABM* 4). Bijou his girl? (*TAW* 5). Escapes from own country in war having shot Gestapo agent (*TMP* 1). Involved Pamela Flitton(?) (*TMP* 2). Married, wife in U.S. Country occupied. Still exiled (*BDFAR* 1). Dies Canada (*HSH* 2).

THWAITES, Alan. Husband Caroline Lovell (*HSH* 6).

TOKENHOUSE, Daniel McN. Major (rtd.) Friend Jenkins senior. Publisher, artist. Nicholas worked for him. Subject of flashbacks (*TK* 1). Sandhurst. Legacy. Expeditionary Force, First War. Typhoid. Art books publishing, good at it. Was going into Church. Inveterate Puritanism. Hatred for religion. No sex life. Rift with Jenkins sen. over Munich. Given up publishing for painting, 1938. Mental breakdown over Russo–German pact, 1939. Clinic till German invasion of Russia. Moves to Venice. Leftist letters to Press. Mid, late seventies during Nicholas's Venice visit. Living Arsenal district (*TK* 3). Neo-primitivism art style. *Four Priests Rigging a Miracle*. 'Picture an act of Socialism.' Ideological content required. Wants no religious service at funeral. Painting, *Any Complaints?* Glober buys a painting. Involved in political plot?

TOLLAND, Alfred. Uncle of Erridge (*TAW* 5). Brother of previous Earl. Rambling. Umfraville his fag? Was at Corderey's house – who preceded Le Bas. Guards' Club and Arthur's. Nervous, defensive (*ALM* 1). Likes family gossip. Lonely. Melancholic. Likes good works. Keen on memorial window for Erridge's grandfather. Not educated? (*ALM* 3). Bore? At Erridge's funeral (*BDFAR* 2). Chesty. Can't finish sentences. Umfraville not his fag.

TOLLAND, Blanche, Lady. Sister of Erridge. Good works. 'Dotty': not mad but something 'a little wrong' (*CCR* 2). Gets residue of Lady Warminster estate

(*TKO* 3). To keep house for Erridge, Thrubworth. Remains at Thrubworth with Mrs George Tolland (*BDFAR* 3). Job, animal sanctuary (*HSH* 1).

TOLLAND. See Erridge.

TOLLAND, Frederica, Lady. See Budd.

TOLLAND, George. Brother, Erridge, next in age. Contemporary Nicholas. Cold-stream. Then City (*ALM* 1). Does well. Very correct. Snob. Marries Mrs Veronica Collins, who divorced husband; she has two children, Angus, Iris (*CCR* 2). Wife older. Returns to regiment (*TKO* 4). Captain, France, with Guards (*TVOB* 3). Lt.-Col., wounded mid-East (*TMP* 2). Hospital Cairo. Cannot be moved (*TMP* 3). Dying (*TMP* 5). Brought home; dies (*BDFAR* 1). Veronica pregnant. Son, Jeremy (*BDFAR* 3). Succeeds Erridge. Wife lives Thrubworth with Blanche.

TOLLAND, Hugo. Youngest brother of Erridge. Eccentric, odd clothes; aesthete at university (*ALM* 1). About to be sent down? (*CCR* 2). No; gets degree (*CCR* 4). To inherit £300–400 at twenty-one. Pro-Franco – as pose? Job, Baldwyn-Hodges antiques, interior decorating. Tough? Good at job. Breaks leg. Rival sick-bed to Erridge. To share flat with Pilgrim (*TKO* 3). Gunner, in ranks (*TKO* 4). Bombadier S. Coast – does not want commission (*TVOB* 3). Only surviving Tolland male (pre-Jeremy) (*BDFAR* 2). Executor for Erridge. Does not want title. Remained bombadier, ack-ack. Back to antiques: own shop with army friend, Sam. Attracted to Pamela (Flitton) (*BDFAR* 2). Pleased at birth of Jeremy. Sad figure (*HSH* 1). Sam dead. Working hard in antiques.

TOLLAND, Isobel, Lady. Second youngest sister Erridge. Becomes Nicholas's wife. 'Different'. Bit of highbrow(?) (*ALM* 1). Getting engaged to someone else? At first meeting, Nicholas knows will marry her (*ALM* 3). Engaged Nicholas (*ALM* 5). Marries him (*CCR* 1). Ill – miscarriage (*CCR* 2). Starting baby (*TKO* 3). Going live with Frederica in country (*TKO* 4). Near delivery (*TVOB* 3). Son (*TVOB* 4).

TOLLAND, Jeremy. See Warminster, Earl of.

TOLLAND, Norah, Lady. Sister of Erridge. 'Dotty'? Living with Eleanor Walpole-Wilson (*ALM* 1). Swears. Lesbian? Chelsea flat. Masculine. Driver, women's services (*TMP* 2). Friendly Pamela Flitton: relationship with? Was with Lady McReith. Friendship with Pamela broken (*TMP* 3). Reunion, Pamela? (*BDFAR* 2). Affair with Eleanor, does not resume post-war (*HSH* 1). Job car-hire firm. Becomes director. Legacy from Eleanor, money and two pugs.

TOLLAND, Priscilla, Lady. Youngest sister Erridge. Lovell interested (*ALM* 1). About twenty (*CCR* 2). Several beaux. To work in opera. Affair Moreland? (*CCR* 3). Unconsummated. Over (*CCR* 4). Engaged Lovell. Marries him (*TKO* 2). Daughter, Caroline (*TVOB* 3). Interested Stevens? Marriage difficulties – believes Lovell not trying to get house together. Various men mentioned (*TSA* 1). With Stevens, Scotland (*TSA* 2). Caroline with Lovell's parents. Stays at Jeavonses'. At Café Royal with Stevens. Killed by bomb at Jeavonses'.

TOLLAND, Robert. Brother, Erridge: seventh child, third son. Mysterious (*ALM* 1). In business but may not stay. Age about twenty-four (*CCR* 2). Nonpolitical. Correct, yet suggestion of dissipation. Likes ageing night-club hostesses. Musical. Likes making money? Likes Matilda Wilson (*CCR* 3). Takes flat on death of Lady Warminster and becomes hard to trace (*TKO* 3). To join navy (*TKO* 4). Lance-cpl. Field Security (*TVOB* 3). On way to commission? Affair Mrs Wisebite–Stringham's sister. Stationed Mytchett. Intelligence Corps corporal. Embarkation leave. France. Has withdrawn name from applicants for commission. Recalled. Killed Dunkirk period (*TVOB* 4).

TOLLAND, Susan, Lady. Sister of Erridge. High-spirited and occasionally melancholic. About twenty-five or six (*ALM* 3). Engaged Roddy Cutts; marries (*CCR* 2). He wants divorce (*TMP* 2). No divorce; has behaved well; she in ascendant (*BDFAR* 2). Daughter.

TOMPSITT. Young, large, fair. Entering F.O. Protégé Sir Gavin Walpole-Wilson (*ABM* 1). Involved with Barbara Goring. She attracted, he casual. Min. of Defence (*TMP* 2). Ambassador (*TK* 5). Married rich European. Scruffy.

TRAPNEL, Francis Xavier – known as X. Novelist, critic. To be published by Quiggin & Craggs (*BDFAR* 1). *Camel Ride to the Tomb* (how he sees life), best first novel since war? Was clerk, RAF India. Not very political. Worked films. Leftish Social Democrat (*BDFAR* 3). Lapsed Catholic. About thirty. Beard. Thin. Decadent look. Once had eye-glass? Tough. Family spent much time Mid-East. Father secret-service? Only child? Looks suggest family link with Asia Minor. Theories about writing and the writer. Insistent talker. Does imitations. Volume short stories. Working on new novel. Short of money. Doctrine of 'panache' in living. Short story in first *Fission*. Unimpressed by Pamela (Flitton). Has to act a part (*BDFAR* 4). Lives hotels, flats with various girls, who may keep him. Nights on Embankment. Successful with women; long-lasting relationships. Holds court at pub, The Hero Of Acre. Borrower. Cash on nail wanted for writing. Likes drinking clubs, but not great drinker. Regular contributor *Fission*. *Bin Ends*, short story collection, out. Reputation growing. Novel, *Profiles in String*, under way. Seeking advance. Girl, Tessa, leaves him. In love Pamela. Disappears. Parodies Widmerpool and Evadne Chapman. Ill. Living with Pamela, Maida Vale. Dispute with her over *Profiles*. Nervous state (*BDFAR* 5). Not working properly. Afraid she will leave. Novel script in canal. Pamela leaves. Loved her, though sex was no good. Suicide? Father, jockey. Going to pieces, no new novel. Nicholas thinks him very good writer (*TK* 1). Dead. Gwinnett to do biography. Posthumous conte, *Dogs Have No Uncles*. Legal trouble over it. Did radio and TV work. Died in gutter. Uncollected stories. *Commonplace Book*. List of girls: Tessa, Pat, Sally, Jacqueline, Linda, Pauline – now call-girl. Gwinnett has written biography, *Death's-Head Swordsman* – after stick he carried (*HSH* 2).

'TRELAWNEY', 'Dr'. Cult leader, near middle age 1914 (*TKO* 1). Catch phrase – 'The Essence of the All is the Godhead of the true.' Not real name. Grubb or Tibbs suggested facetiously by Moreland. Had Temple, North Wales; girl killed herself there. Educated Bonn. Drugs(?) (*TKO* 3). At Bellevue. Friendly

Mrs Erdleigh. Asthma. Sees future (*TSA* 2). Dies at Bellevue. Murtlock his reincarnation? (*HSH* 4).

TRUSCOTT, Bill. Few years ahead of Nicholas at university. Great potential. Well-off; father Harley St specialist (*AQOU* 4). Also called Bob. Narrowly achieved First. Tall, dark, going grey. Works for Donners, recruits Stringham, perhaps as entrée to Mrs Foxe's social group. Personal secretary to Donners. Great career continues to elude (*ABM* 2). Approaching thirty. Fails to publish. Spare man. Recruiting Widmerpool. Removed from Donners-Brebner through Widmerpool (*TAW* 2). Working with by-products of coal (*ALM* 2). Vehemently against Widmerpool. Still not fully realised (*BDFAR* 1). Wrote verse. Going NCB? Much demoralised by sacking. Bachelor (*TK* 4). Not invited Sillery's ninetieth birthday party. In sixties.

UDALL, Jock. Married Rosie Manasch. Heir to newspapers which opposed Donners. P.o.w. (*TMP* 5). Killed by S.S. after escape attempt, Germany. No children.

UDNEY, Jack Elderly courtier. Proposed to Frederica at Ascot? (*TVOB* 3). She denies.

UMFRAVILLE, R. H. J. (Dicky). Gambler, socialite. Own estimate 'professional cad'. Forties (*TAW* 4). Has been in Kenya. Aura of money. Brigade of Guards tie. Gentleman rider. Le Bas's house, but began in Corderey's. Was asked to leave school. Took two women St Moritz and left them to pay? Anne Stepney interested? Was in Cuba with Mrs Andriadis. Marries Anne (*TAW* 5). Fourth wife. Married in Paris. Marriage over? (*ALM* 4). Managing club. Knew Molly Jeavons well. Was in Cannes with Mildred Haycock (Blaides) about 1923. First War, Captain, Foot Guards (*TVOB* 3). Army again, Staff of London District. Railway Transport Officer. Engaged Frederica. Knew Flavia Wisebite in Kenya. Had her. Mad? Father bred horses, having married rich woman. Remained army after First War. First wife Dolly Braybrook, who fell for Foxe and wanted divorce. Foxe would not have her. She killed herself. Had to leave army when he married Joy Grant. Went Kenya. She left with Marquess of Castlemallock. Takes wife from District Commissioner. 'Rough house' over this. She dies. Hates Foxe. Commands transit camp (*TMP* 2). Major. Civil Affairs (*TMP* 3). Lt.-Col. Military Govt., Germany (*BDFAR* 2). Married to Frederica. Claims to be Pamela Flitton's father; Nicholas sceptical. Retires from job as Thrubworth agent (*TK* 1). Melancholic. Nearly eighty (*HSH* 6). Stick. Deaf.

UPDIKE, Betty. See Matilda Wilson.

VAN DER VOORT, Colonel. Netherlands (*TMP* 2).

VOWCHURCH, Lord. Family name Blaides. Friend Edward VII. Father of Mrs Conyers and Mildred (Haycock). Buffoon (*ALM* 1). Motoring accident; limp. Produced no heir and Baby Wentworth's father succeeded (*ALM* 4). Rode horse upstairs. Practical joker.

WALPOLE-WILSON, Eleanor. Sir Gavin's daughter. Countrified and hates London. Dislikes feminine pursuits (*ABM* 1). Girl Guides. Dislikes house parties (*ABM* 3). No sign of marriage; going on banana-boat to Guatemala with Janet Walpole-Wilson (*ABM* 4). Much in country, breeding dogs (*TAW* 4). Friendly Norah Tolland. Ménage with her, Chelsea (ALM 1). Heather Hopkins a friend. Pork-pie hat, bow tie? Swears. Grows serious. Interested politics (*CCR* 3). Has given up Hopkins. Staying at Jeavonses' (*TSA* 2). Survives bomb. Mid-thirties; in uniform. Urban district councillor (*HSH* 1). Affair Swedish woman doctor. Dies Stockholm. Legacy to Norah, includes two pugs.

WALPOLE-WILSON, Sir Gavin, K.M.G. Retired diplomat. Has flat Paris at end First War; working with refugees after Diplomatic Corps (*ABM* 1). House Eaton Sq. Was Minister to S. American republic. Made error; resigned. Mild eccentricities of dress. Limp. Country house, only recently bought, Hinton Hoo. Moves Left (*TMP* 1). Dead (*TMP* 2).

WALPOLE-WILSON, Janet, Miss. Sir Gavin's sister. Younger. Not well-off. Jobs, secretary, governess (*ABM* 3). Opinionated. Not liked by Lady Walpole-Wilson. Can be malicious. Friendly Mrs Widmerpool (*ABM* 4). Going sea voyage with Eleanor. Living with Mrs Widmerpool, near Stourwater, but WVS work takes her elsewhere.

WALPOLE-WILSON, Lady. Daughter of Lord Aberavon. Nicholas likes (*ABM* 1). Gavin's wife. Daisy. Nervous. Dislikes Janet (*ABM* 3).

WARMINSTER, Countess of. See dead Earl of. An Ardglass. Stepmother Erridge, Isobel etc. Katherine. Invalid. Eccentric (*ALM* 3). Witch-like. Lives Hyde Park Gardens. Hypochondriac? (*ALM* 5). Older than Molly. Good-looking, ordered. Writes unscholarly books on women in history. Bears no children (*CCR* 2). First husband stockbroker, who dies. Centre of family gatherings. Cassandra-like air. Withdrawn from world. Writing on Maria Theresa. Prone to fortune-tellers; Knows Mrs Erdleigh. Dead (*TKO* 3). Leaves little.

WARMINSTER, Earl of. Dead. Brother Alfred Tollard, father of Erridge. Ten children (*TAW* 5). First wife an Alford. Married Katherine, sister Molly Jeavons, childless widow as second wife. Died blood poisoning Kashmir (*CCR* 2). Liked big game shooting.

WARMINSTER, Earl of. See Erridge.

WARMINSTER, Earl of. Succeeds Erridge. Jeremy. Son of George Tolland. Best man at Sebastian Cutts's wedding (*HSH* 6). Junior Research Fellow. Daunting. To make Thrubworth research centre. Stepbrother, stepsister, Angus, Iris, children of mother's first husband, Collins. Angus journalist, Iris wife of architect – husband a Vowchurch. Mother living London.

WARTSTONE, Miss. Manages Chelsea flats where Nicholas lives during war (*TMP* 2). Difficult.

WAUTHIER. Belgian artillery officer (*TMP* 3).

WEEDON, Geraldine. Known as Tuffy. Was Flavia Stringham's governess; then secretary to Mrs Foxe. In love Stringham? About thirty, thirty-five (*AQOU* 2). Has left Mrs Foxe, following legacy (ABM 2). Stringham still sees her. Late forties (*ALM* 4). Friend of Molly Jeavons; some work for her. Chilly. Is looking after Stringham, who drinks. She and Stringham living at Jeavonses' (*CCR* 2). Susan Tolland dislikes her. Firm with Stringham (*CCR* 3). Tough. To marry General Conyers (*TKO* 4). Conyers dead (*TMP* 2). In MI5 supervising girls. Marries Farebrother (*TMP* 4). Dead (*HSH* 2).

WENTWORTH, Baby. Father was brother of Mrs Conyers' and Mildred's father and became Lord Vowchurch. Brother, Jack. Divorced. Cosmo Flitton involved but refused marriage. She involved Flavia's divorce; also mentioned, not culpably, Derwentwater case (*ABM* 2). Pursuing Prince Theodoric? Mistress Sir Magnus Donners and Barnby interested? (*ABM* 3). Barnby has painted her. Barnby going to see her (*ABM* 4). Affair Sir Magnus over (*TAW* 1). Marries Italian, living Rome. In fifties, married to film director, Clarini, but living apart (*TK* 2). Not fond of him? Pursuing Glober. Growing hard, man-like. Atmosphere of 1920s. Wants to marry Glober (*TK* 3). Dead Montego Bay, having recently married rich Greek (*HSH* 3).

WIDMERPOOL, Kenneth G. School contemporary of Nicholas, though two or three years older. Only child. Ugly. High-pitched voice. Spectacles. Low school status (*AQOU* 1). Figure of fun. Odd overcoat? Had boy expelled for homosexual note to Templer? Fish-like appearance. Leaves school before Nicholas. In France (*AQOU* 3). Less of an oddity. Obsessed with self-improvement. No university. Articled to solicitors; father dead. Considering business, politics later. Lives with mother, Victoria, near Roman Catholic cathedral. Distressed that Nicholas lacks career plans. Paternal grandfather Scottish businessman named Geddes; took wife's name for higher social standing. Family Nottinghamshire. Financial crisis on father's death. Ashamed father's occupation? Fixer – the tennis dispute. Smarter (*ABM* 1). To become symbolic figure, linking past and future. 'Embodiment of thankless labour and unsatisfied ambition.' Jaundice. Exercise at Barnes. Solicitors, Turnbull, Welford & Puckering. Political pronouncements. Father used to supply liquid manure; then living on Pembringham estate. 'Frog Footman'. Nicholas does not know his Christian name. People recognise his potential. Regards arts books published as 'not very serious'. Sugared. In love Barbara Goring. No money for marriage. To join Donners-Brebner? (*ABM* 2). Unfortunate manner. Interested Gypsy(?) (*ABM* 3). Working Donners-Brebner. Paid for Gypsy's abortion. Promoted (*ABM* 4). Christian name terms with Nicholas? Leaving Donners-Brebner (*TAW* 2) to become bill-broker. Schemed to have Truscott removed from Donners-Brebner. Then Widmerpool also removed. Templer treats him as normal city acquaintance. Templer wants him to help Duport (*TAW* 5). Fatter. Little over thirty. 'Innate oddness'. Lives by will alone. Territorial officer. Old Boy Dinner speech. Engaged Mildred Haycock (*ALM* 1). Looks older than years, i.e. little over thirty. Smartish club (*ALM* 2). Has secured job for Duport. Sexual worries. Captain, Territorials. Hated by Truscott. No intellectual or aesthetic interests (*ALM* 3). Jaundice (*ALM* 4). Has not slept with Mildred. Sexual failure (*ALM* 5). Recovers morale. Approves Russia (*CCR* 2). Returning Donners-Brebner? Nursing home. Growing more social. Closer to Templer than is Stringham (*TKO* 2). Wrong estimate about war. Cancelled Duport's credit (*TKO* 3). 'Embodied' – joined up (*TKO* 4). Staff College? Regards Duport as insolent. Major at Division (*TVOB* 4). Rivalry, Farebrother (*TSA* 1). Rivalry, Hogbourne-Johnson. Cools towards mother. Has Stringham transferred to Laundry (*TSA* 3). Unfeeling about Bithel's fall and Stringham's posting. Promotion? Moving to Cabinet Office. Sharply appraises Nicholas. Outsmarted by Farebrother. Lt.-Col. Cabinet Office (*TMP* 1) Worker.. Military Assistant Secretary. Interested Pamela Flitton? (*TMP* 2). Goes to tarts. Colonel (*TMP* 3). Involved Pamela (*TMP* 4). Engaged Pamela (*TMP* 5). OBE. Not returning to City? Likes power. Labour M.P. at by-election and PPS to Cabinet Minister (*BDFAR* 1). Married to Pamela. Trouble with her? Moving Left (*BDFAR* 2). But esteems Attlee. Interested *Fission*. Will write for it. Fellow-traveller(?) (*BDFAR* 3). Secures paper supply for *Fission*. Satirised by *Daily Telegraph*. *Fission* article: 'Affirmative Action and Negative Values'. Touched by Trapnel for £1. Trying displace Bagshaw? Crypto-Communist line on Greece. Pamela leaves (*BDFAR* 4). Confronts her at Trapnel's. Going to E. Europe. Had poor sex life with Pamela (*BDFAR* 5). Minor Government office. Pamela back with him. Friendly Ferrand-Sénéschal (*TK* 1). Outing together Paris. Loses seat 1955. Fellow-traveller? Like to be part of Communist apparat though so bourgeois? Conyers's verdict 'typical intuitive extrovert' recalled. He and Pamela only nominally together. Have been married dozen years. Two houses – flat Westminster, cottage Stourwater. Life Peer. Not a Communist? Did lean that way once? Involved Burgess, Maclean? Not homosexual? Active East/West trade. Rich? Furthered Balkan wine trade? Mother dead, missed funeral (*TK* 2). Looking for Belkin. Pornographic picture collection? Excited by Pamela's talk of Donners as voyeur? (*TK* 3). Spy? Denounced as Stalinist or Revisionist at East Europe state trial (*TK* 4). Bluff – to show he is anti-Communist? Denounced as British agent. Relationship with Pauline, call-girl: photographs. Question in House on commercial deals, East Europe; untaxed? Escapes prosecution (*TK* 5). Was subject to blackmail? Voyeur – Pamela and Ferrand-Sénéschal. Struck by Glober. Unhinged? (*TK* 6). Disappears for year (*HSH* 2). Chancellor of newish British university. C.I.A. involved in his fall and Pamela's death? Has had U.S. university and research posts. Changed. Faith in youth stuff. Book in preparation, *Pogrom of Youth*. Nobel recommendation? When returns Britain much on TV. No political life. Daubed and assaulted in university demo. Bald. Broad-minded Chancellor. Trustee of literary fund. Signs as 'Ken'. Close interest in difficult students. Unconcerned about disparaging references in Gwinnett's book (*HSH* 3). Great esteem among students. Scruffy and liberated in dress. Brings Quiggin twins – who daubed him – to literary party. Anti-order speech. Late sixties (*HSH* 4). Interested Murtlock's commune as 'vehicle of dissent'. Obsessed with need to uproot bourgeois values. Is running kind of commune. Resigns as Chancellor (*HSH* 5). Sees Murtlock's group as power base? Struggle between him and Murtlock? In naked dance rites. Knifed by Murtlock. Out running with the group (*HSH* 6). Looks bad. Hardly recalls Bithel. Was removed from board of bank by Akworth and Farebrother. Abases himself before Akworth.

Cravenly subordinate to Murtlock. Wants to leave, but continues sexual rites (*HSH* 7). Was finally under Murtlock's dominance. Bequeaths house to cult? Cannot get Murtlock out. Dead, sprinting for lead in group run.

WIDMERPOOL, Mrs Widow (see above for husband). Kenneth's mother. Flat, Victoria. Friend Janet Walpole-Wilson. looks late forties, but is more (*ABM* 4). Cottage near Stourwater. Janet staying with her (*TKO* 4). Dominating. Lil Jeavons to live with. Opposes son's marriage (*TMP* 5). He sending her to live Scotland, an old lady. Admires Stalin (*BDFAR* 4). Dies, cottage Kirkcudbrightshire (*TK* 2).

WILSON, Matilda (Betty Updike). *Jolie laide.* Father chemist. Brought up near Stourwater. Actress. Mistress Donners after Baby Wentworth (*TAW* 1). Moreland interested (*CCR* 1). They marry. Baby daughter dies (*CCR* 3). Attracts women but likes men. Gone off social life. Knows about Moreland and Priscilla. Discloses she was married to Carolo. Spending more time with theatrical people (*CCR* 4). Cottage near Stourwater (*TKO* 2). Wants social life again. Ambitious. Envies Anne Umfraville's (Stepney's) hold on Donners. Has returned to him (*TKO* 4). Donners wants to marry her. Behaved well over Priscilla. Marries Donners (*TSA* 2). Seems settled with him (*TMP* 5). Wanted Stevens (*TK* 3). During widowhood went Ischia with him? To tease Rosie Manasch only? Is calm — superior — on seeing Carolo again (*TK* 5). Interested in reviving Donners's memory when widow (*HSH* 2). Organises literary prize. Comfortably off under will. Well-preserved. Living Eaton Sq. flat. Remained in love Moreland till death. Dead (*HSH* 6).

WISE, Rupert. Dancer. Friend Chandler. Strict morals; little small talk. Engaged member corps de ballet (*CCR* 3).

WISEBITE, Flavia. Stringham's sister; older. Persecuted by mother. Pamela Flitton's mother. Liveliness weighed down by melancholy, like brother. Married first Cosmo Flitton. Divorce. Then Harrison F. Wisebite, American. He died of drink, Miami. Living with Robert Tolland (*TVOB* 3). Older than he. Had affair Umfraville, Kenya. He Pamela's father — claims so, but discounted by Nicholas (*BDFAR* 2). Clare Akworth's godmother (*HSH* 6). Has suffered from nerves. Mad?

WISEBITE, Harrison F. Second husband Flavia, Stringham's sister. From Minneapolis (*TVOB* 3). Dies of drink, Miami. Invented cocktail, 'Death Comes to the Archbishop' (*BDFAR* 2).

WISEBITE, Milton. Nephew of Harrison F. Works *Time-Life* (*TMP* 2). Was in Europe with army. Affair Pamela Flitton?

Theme

Near the start of *AQOU* we get an explicit account of what Powell means by his overall title *A Dance to the Music of Time*.

> The image of Time brought thoughts of mortality: of human beings, facing outwards like the Seasons, moving hand in hand in intricate measure: stepping slowly, methodically, sometimes a trifle awkwardly, in evolutions that take recognisable shape: or breaking into seemingly meaningless gyrations, while partners disappear only to reappear again, once more giving pattern to the spectacle: unable to control the melody, unable, perhaps, to control the steps of the dance.

Life, then, has shape, method, pattern: it would be hard to imagine music or dance without. There is order. What sort? Not only are the dancers unable to control the melody but they may lack power over the steps they perform. (That late 'perhaps' is sizeable.) In Powell's title 'dance' does not evoke primarily rhythm, harmony, gaiety. Instead the word is at least ironic and possibly derisive, echoing the use in a phrase like 'led a dance'. The intricacy of the measure is sad and demeaning, not elaborately beautiful, since those engaged have no choice but to take part, and their responses are like those of a complicated machine. Their lives have some kind of meaning – are only 'seemingly meaningless' – but they do not know what and do not consciously express it. We hear of life as a 'ritual dance' in *ABM*. Ritual is metaphor so this, too, suggests underlying meaning. Yet it is the other, less heartening aspects of ritual which sound most strongly here, and once more the intent is ironic: people behave as if they can play fresh, original parts in life, whereas really the lines have been laid down from far back, and all the moves are inflexibly formalised, limited and repetitive. Life has some system but it is hard to find comfort in the fact. Patterns exist but they may be utterly destructive of those which people would wish for themselves.

The human will can look very feeble. The contrast between how people might want to behave – or might have been expected to in view of upbringing and background – and the actual performance imposed as time calls the tune is a main theme.

We had better not overstate Powell's view, nor confuse it with other philosophies on the imperiousness of time. We are not in Hardy country. And Hotspur's dark, dying glimpse of life as 'time's fool' goes further than anything we find in these books. What we do find is the insistent suggestion that people's lives may be linked in strange, unpredictable, often perverse fashion. Time will secure these couplings, and break them. ('Partners disappear, only to reappear again.') Sometimes the results will be intriguing, sometimes droll, sometimes devastatingly harsh. This provides the 'meaning' of the dance: we shape and condition each other's lives in ways which may seem at the same time spectacularly random and ferociously intense.

This thesis acquires exceptional impact because we are, for the most part, among a small section of upper-class and upper-middle-class English society, the level being generally higher than in *AM*. Close interrelationships are basic. But presumably the reader is to take it that we are all in the dance, regardless of class, all subject to the music, all liable to exercise strange influences over those near us: Powell has chosen this segment of the world because he knows it best and because it most effectively demonstrates the theme.

Presumably, too, we are all as unreliable as Powell's narrator, Nicholas Jenkins, at reading the signs of how people will develop and how they will impinge on each other. This is an extension of Powell's view, and an important one: at least some indications of the future are available to us. Although the music moves irresistibly on and governs the dance regardless of the dancers, we may be given a glimpse of what is coming up on the score. But we are often too blind, prejudiced, insensitive or ignorant to take it in; only hindsight makes things clear. Or clearer: as Nicholas puts it in *HSH* old age provides as one of its compensations

> a vantage point for acquiring embellishments to narratives that have been unfolding for years besides one's own, trimmings that can even appear to supply the conclusion of a given story, though finality is never certain, a dimension always possible to add.

True, this dependence on hindsight is not a much more cheerful philosophy than one which sees Mankind skipping out into the un-knowable, like rats behind the Pied Piper. It is the difference between being lost without a map and lost with a map we do not or cannot read; the difference, possibly, between pessimism and irony. But we have to ask here, who made the map? Or, to go further, who, or Who, made the ground it charts? Do the books suggest that time alone holds all the power? Or does Powell give any sign that time itself might be subject to control; might not be the ultimate force; might be the music but not the conductor? Apparently not. There are few hints of a supreme being in even the vaguest, least religious sense. In *AQOU* we do hear of the 'transcendental manipulation' of 'certain people who seem inextricably linked in life', but no details of this other worldly force are given, no delineation. Signs of second-sight attend Mrs Erdleigh, Trelawney and Murtlock: yet, although we have to take it that there is something beyond the rational and workaday, it remains mysterious, vague, touched by hocus-pocus, and only rarely involved in the narrative. Of course, here and there time will take on for a brief while characteristics of fate or chance or destiny: god-like qualities. That is probably as much as we can say. The degrees of contrariness, inevitabity, coincidence and determinism with which time works out its designs in *ADTTMOT* are so enormously and fascinatingly varied that it becomes dangerous to speculate beyond what we are directly told. Time rules.

We may see how in one of the books' chief relationships; the one between three characters we meet first as schoolboys in *AQOU*, four if we include Nicholas. They are Kenneth Widmerpool, Peter Templer and Charles Stringham. Widmerpool, a little older than the others, is an oddity. It may, or may not, have something to do with an overcoat he wore as a new boy, which was marginally out of line with school regulations. Nicholas has forgotten the details, but they are not important; for whatever reasons, Widmerpool became fixed in the minds of his contemporaries as a freak, to be treated with amusement or contempt. Against Stringham and Templer he seems particularly blighted. Although these two are graphically differentiated they have in common an aura of unquestioned superiority over Widmerpool, a superiority which arises in part from class (Stringham's mother was once married to Lord Warrington); in part from money (Stringham's family have the reputation of great wealth, and Templer's is 'not poor'); in part from appearance and general *savoir faire* (Widmerpool is ugly and ungainly and wears squeaky boots). The first words we hear attributed to Stringham concern Widmerpool's 'good, sensible shoes'. And Templer's opening remark is, 'I'm afraid I'm wearing rather Widmerpool socks today.' For them he is a standard of both the dull and the crassly *outré* and Jenkins shares their attitude. He sees Widmerpool at school as an automaton with defective machinery; a fish-like creature; someone doomed to struggle for distinctions he would never achieve. The reader who takes the narrator's impressions for truth would foresee Stringham and Templer moving easily towards success in later life, while Widmerpool flounders in hard-working mediocrity, at best.

Fiction tends to avoid the predictable and the reversal of these expectations is total. Widmerpool eventually achieves such power that he may certainly be accused of causing Stringham's death; and is possibly also implicated – a far more sombre matter – in the death of Templer. Long before this Jenkins has been forced to see that his school verdict on Widmerpool was faulty. Early in *TAW* it shocks Nicholas to hear Templer speak of Widmerpool as a normal business acquaintance, not now a natural subject for laughter and condescension. Towards the end of this book, Jenkins and Widmerpool put a drunken Stringham to bed after an Old Boy Dinner at the Ritz for members of their house at school. Jenkins reflects on the strangeness of this new situation in which Widmerpool is now able to dictate behaviour to Stringham. 'That suggested a whole social upheaval: a positively cosmic change in life's system. Widmerpool, once so derided by all of us, had become in some mysterious manner a person of authority.'

Time has begun its changes. So far, though, there is not really very much to shock the reasonably alert reader. These processes might even be seen as natural, inevitable. Simply, Jenkins, Templer and Stringham read the early signs badly. The point is made during a description of the Old Boy Dinner: Jenkins tells us that no matter how important Widmerpool had become it was the school rating of people which operated at the Ritz reunion and by this Widmerpool remained a nonentity. That view is arrantly and wilfully wrong, if career advancement and power are the criteria; and in adult life such criteria sometimes matter. Snooty disdain for Widmerpool's industry is shown to be misplaced. Once he is out in the world it pushes him on so far and so fast that deeper matters than career success are involved: in *TKO* Jenkins wonderingly records that Widmerpool has gone 'miles ahead' of Stringham in friendship with Templer

To suggest that character appraisal in a public school (we assume Eton) may be naïve is a modest enough thesis requiring a view of time as nothing more than an agency which exposes and corrects errors founded on inexperience, prejudice and cabalism. There is no lurid contrariness here, no upsetting of expectations for the titillating sake of it. If the reversals went no further than this we would be witnessing a very elementary exercise of irony. Such changes are part of the routine of things; and particularly at the period concerned, from the 1920s to the present. Jenkins speaks of 'a whole social upheaval' being apparent in Widmerpool's ascendancy over the drunken Stringham. Although in those early parts of the dance at school Widmerpool might seem hopelessly awkward, while Stringham, Templer and Jenkins himself follow the steps with inborn ease, the music is to change. There will be political shifts to the Left and the 1939 war. The assumptions of Stringham and Templer, and of the school in 1921, will no longer have much bearing on reality. Widmerpool, who knows how to intrigue, work and flatter for what he wants, and is a Labour man, will do much better. The school may not have endorsed his final report, 'Should go far'. But what time makes of British society after he has left will ensure that someone of his qualities does. The music of time here encompasses the idea of political change, of revolution, though a muted one. This, again, is a concept unlikely to startle the reader: hindsight makes such moves look inescapable. The music of time, playing through the thirties, was bound to reflect political upheaval, and the dancers' positions were sure to be affected.

We must now move on from what are virtually routine processes of change. During army service in the war Widmerpool begins to advance at a more spectacular rate. Near the end of *TVOB*, Jenkins, now a junior officer in a Welsh regiment, reports after a posting to Divisional Headquarters and finds he is to work under Major Widmerpool. Momentarily Jenkins is pleased to see someone who reminds him of a life that is lost. Only a few pages later, though, he grows uneasy at the realisation that he is under Widmerpool's control. Time – plus luck – continues to readjust the balance of power. It is still not an outrageous exercise of luck, either, since coincidences which brought old acquaintances together in the Services were commonplace. Another is on its way. In the next novel, *TSA*, Jenkins realises that an officers' mess waiter with unusually refined voice is, in fact, Stringham. This is time working out a programme of reversal with especial neatness and savagery. The formerly rather dandified Stringham (at school he reminded Jenkins of those sad young men in ruffs who appear in Elizabethan miniatures) once bearing with him the aura of family wealth and distinction, is forced to put up with the complaints and abuse of Biggs, Staff Officer Physical Training, and Soper, Divisional Catering Officer. More to the point, Stringham, like Jenkins, is now in Widmerpool's power. And Widmerpool, uneasy at Stringham's presence in the Mess, uses this power ruthlessly. Under his orders, Stringham is posted to the Mobile Laundry, Widmerpool knowing that the Laundry may soon leave for the Far East. Eventually, Stringham is captured by the Japanese and does not survive. Widmerpool's victory goes further yet. He will marry Stringham's niece, Pamela Flitton, for whom Stringham had special, possibly sexual, affection. He has left her a respectable fortune from which Widmerpool may expect some benefit. He has the girl and the money.

With apparent ferocity and obvious thoroughness time has turned inside out the comparative status of these two men. This is something a good way beyond the routine processes of change. Coincidence has now begun to ride tirelessly and brings further elements of retribution into the corral. Templer, unhappily married (his second wife has lost her reason, allegedly because of his womanising) likewise seeks an affair with Pamela. Although avidly promiscuous she will not gratify him. He feels he must be ageing and volunteers for a dangerous war mission to prove otherwise. He, too, is killed. And, in *TMP*, Pamela accuses Widmerpool of complicity in his death: she says he 'put up a paper' recommending withdrawal of support for such ventures and that, as a result, Templer was abandoned. Widmerpool's denials do not convince.

It will be obvious that we are not talking here about the kind of incidental piece, or pieces, of luck that a novelist may find handy to push his plot along: say the sudden recognition of Henry Wilcox by Jacky Bast in *Howards End*, or the elaborate structure of chance required for the accident in *The Great Gatsby*. These are instances where the novelist decides to take a risk and hopes that the reader will not notice a sudden straining of likelihood; or will, out of affection and approval for the rest of the work, swallow it. Powell, on the contrary, is telling us that in the affairs of Widmerpool, Stringham and Templer – and to a much smaller degree Jenkins – time has applied coincidence according to a flagrant and exact scheme. We are invited not to close one and a half eyes to unlikelihood but to watch, wonder at and learn from the ways in which life – the dance – will arrange almost unbelievably interlocked connections and events in order to ensure dizzy and often chilling alterations in fortune.

A qualification is needed. There is one sense in which time changes nothing. Careers and power are important but they are not every-thing, certainly not in novels. Regardless of what progress Widmer-pool may make in business, the army or politics his basic rating as a character remains constant. He begins grotesque and is never any-thing other to Jenkins or – I think it is fair to say – to the reader: the more eminent the more ludicrous. Powell's books may offer some satire on the outmoded, cloistered, disintegrating values of Eton in the twenties. Yet at the same time they will assert the basic right-ness of those values. Time will play tricks with superficials – com-parative power, wealth, rank – but cannot touch the essentials. The dance will force participants to change position, but it cannot change their worth: throughout Widmerpool will be fool or villain; String-ham, Templer and Jenkins variously flawed heroes. I look at the pro-cess in notes on some of the books where it is most obvious. Enough to say now that we may feel some sentimentalising here. An eleva-tion of school-based insights into inflexible truths suggests a high estimate for juvenile wisdom and for the perceptiveness of cliques. One may think of the Romantic yearning for time to be fixed at its most happy and full moments; Lamartine at the lake calling for the hours to stop. It could be argued that *ADTTMOT* asserts that Eton-ian relationships get things right and that it would be nicer if there were no need for change. Nor is it simply a matter of declaring that early judgements on character will be correct. Widmerpool not only remains personally objectionable throughout the books (with his repellent appearance duly complemented later by shaky sexual resources), but at the end his career, and his very personality and physique, break up. This makes Jenkins's youthful estimates for-midably immune to the processes of time, even if we make allow-ance for the fact that he is a narrator looking back who might pick out only those early opinions which the future will endorse.

To return, though, to the pattern of reversals and coincidences: some would argue that these are so mathematically worked out that credibility has no hope; the technique, they would say, falls be-tween the disciplines of realism and fantasy and is outside the scope of serious fiction, operating only to amuse the reader with its ex-haustively neat ironies, and to hold the volumes together with com-plex, intriguing but factitious links.

Concentrated in one volume, even a very large volume, they would certainly be preposterous. Over a long series, though, a gradualism in development is possible which effectively prepares the way for these otherwise strange events. For example, there is room and time to explain convincingly the otherwise monstrous improbability of Pamela's marriage to Widmerpool: it remains bizarre, but these are bizarre people.

Essentially, though, the question is whether we can take certain cornerstone assumptions – often honestly and directly spelled out – on which *ADTTMOT* is built. The main one is that characters pass very closely related lives and that this will be true not merely in the limited geography of well-to-do London – what Bernard Bergonzi in *Writers and their Work 144* (London, 1962) calls the 'extreme cohesiveness of English upper-class or upper-middle-class society' – but also in the worldwide setting of the 1939–45 war: to take only one instance, Nicholas's meeting with the South American husband of Jean at the Victory Day Service.

On the one hand these nicely fashioned surprises are the entertaining tricks of fiction, and let us be grateful for entertainment. They also represent, of course, elements in the dance thesis: further affirmations of another basic assumption of the books that links between people, once established, may well find ways of reasserting themselves, and that not even vast international disruptions will prevent this; rather, the rearrangements caused by war produce even more startling contacts, especially when someone like Pamela is shuttling tirelessly – sexually unsatisfied and unsatisfiable – between the men.

Powell has made an entirely believable whole of this. He (or at least Jenkins) holds as a further premise that in all our lives there is someone like Widmerpool who will reappear at crucial stages and around whom key events will form. I am not sure that many of us could think of such a person in real life. That is not the whole question, though. We demand that a fiction writer should by technique or art, and maybe both together, convince us that this is how the world as he sees it might behave. Through a number of skilfully employed devices Powell is able to make us accept the existence of a tight-knit, limited and very tangible world. He establishes, for example, a remarkably dense texture of resemblances and connections between characters by continually comparing their appearances, careers and dispositions. In *ABM* we will find Mrs Andriadis described as being like both Stringham's mother and Miss Weedon, her secretary; and Mr Deacon and Sillery, a scheming university don, are elaborately compared and contrasted. At these points it is as if the fiction had only itself to draw on for allusion and this sets up an immensely powerful impression of inter-dependence between characters. It can be overdone and there are times when one fears that every male character in the novel resembles Uncle Giles.

Again, footloose, errant or privateering figures, as well as one or two with supposed supernatural powers, act as unifying agents, bringing far-flung characters and items in the narrative into sometimes surprising juxtaposition: as chief of these purposeful wanderers we may note Uncle Giles; Odo Stevens, soldier and author; Dicky Umfraville, five times married and possibly – only just – father of Pamela; and, of course, the female sexual nomads like Pamela, Anne Stepney and Jean. Then there are Mrs Erdleigh and Dr Trelawney, able to establish special connections through time.

Also, we have the repeated, explicit, persuasive statements from the narrator that pattern is to be found in the movements of time by those able to see. In *TAW* Umfraville invites Jenkins and others to visit Mrs Andriadis with him. Jenkins has been there before with Stringham and ruminates: 'I could not inwardly disregard the pattern of life which caused Dicky Umfraville not only to resemble Stringham, but also by this vicarious invitation, to re-enact Stringham's past behaviour.'

All these techniques lead the reader towards what we might call acceptance of Powell's world. They would not work, though, if time were shown to operate always with the startling exactitude apparent in the reversals of the Stringham–Templer–Widmerpool relationship, because credibility would give way. Although the dance will almost always lead to irony, it will not necessarily be in that sharply retributive style. It may simply assert what Powell sees as the norm. For example, time makes its impact on Lord Erridge, Earl of Warminster, Jenkins's brother-in-law. When we first hear of him Erridge is deeply Left in outlook and behaviour. Like Orwell he apparently dresses as a tramp (denied by Quiggin) to discover conditions for the down-and-out; he attends Popular Front meetings; stocks his room at Thrubworth, the family seat, with volumes of what sound like the Left Book Club; and eventually goes to Spain to support the Republic – though in a pacifist role – having already given a good deal of money to the cause. He returns disillusioned, again like Orwell. And now time begins to nudge him irresistibly back to the interests of those with title, money and lineage. Erridge inherits £16,000 from St John Clarke, a once popular novelist, who himself turned Left politically in later life. First assumption among Erridge's family is that he will give the money to his 'Spanish friends'. This begins to look unlikely. At the end of *CCR* we are led to believe – not more than this – that the legacy may well be used to pay off an overdraft on the estate account. This means that the sale of some Thrubworth woods, proposed to raise the wind, might not be necessary. Erridge seems to have been brought back – literally – to his roots. And the fact that the timely funds come from another well-heeled and inconstant convert to the Left emphasises the irony. There is more. In *BDFAR* Erridge dies. We learn that his last week was spent in making arrangements for a memorial window to be installed at Thrubworth in tribute to his grandfather. Previously he would never display more than a grudging and guilty interest in ancestors. As Norah, his sister, says, Erridge appears to have turned his values upside down. What happens to Erridge may be seen as something like the affirmation in *FAVTAD* that the inner strength of established families is formidable; formidable enough to see off the aberrant whims of their own renegades.

Time cuts through other characters' poses, too. Powell, as we shall see throughout *ADTTMOT*, is hard on Leftists. Quiggin, a scholarship boy of great ability and drive, is a fierce Marxist when we first meet him, and remains more or less so for much of the sequence. In *BDFAR*, though, the rot – if we view it like that – has set in. Quiggin abandons his revolutionary-style dress for something better suited to one who now aims to make his name as a publisher. His marriage is presented as a career step, and he soon reaches the boardroom. By *TK* he has sunk so many of his principles that he can bring out, very successfully, the memoirs of a retired Tory politician; in *HSH* the anti-authoritarian behaviour of his daughters has begun to irk him deeply. The irony is heightened by the fact that Quiggin berated Erridge after his backsliding for the naïveté of 'a typical aristocratic idealist'.

Given time then truth will out, taking truth here to mean what people were bred up to, or what are their ruling passions: in Quiggin's case self-advancement. A far more striking instance of this latter – obsessive career progress – is seen in Widmerpool, the novel's major character development. He begins as an exemplar of vehemently willed ambition and ends, or at first appears to, deep in self-abnegation, seemingly contemptuous of everything that previously governed his life. Is this, then, one of time's swingeing ironies? Not quite. In fact, Widmerpool, naked, ill and in his sixties, dies while urging a group of cultists to greater speed while out on a ritual run in the early hours of one morning. Widmerpool draws ahead. 'I'm leading, I'm leading', he shouts. Even in self-abasement he had to be the top: time finally asserts what was always there.

We may object – and I do at some length elsewhere – that the theme of a return to the inner 'truths' should be so regularly slanted against the Left: St John Clarke, Quiggin and Erridge are all instances. Mode Leftists were such a feature of the period that one can understand to some degree why Powell comes down on them so hard. In any case, the theme goes beyond politics. We are watching beautifully paced and documented examples of Bacon's 'inseparable propriety of time, which is ever more and more to disclose truth.'

But time and the dance will also activate in Powell's books occasional patterns of breathtaking coincidence which seem to prove nothing except that funny things do happen. Some of these are sexual and I examine their impact on Powell's treatment of love, marriage and women in a self-contained chapter. To take one example now, though: in *AQOU* Stringham and Jenkins are at university and receive a visit from Templer with two friends, Bob Duport and Jimmy Brent. After dinner the five go for a drive in an ageing Vauxhall which Templer has recently bought. They pick up two girls, crash the car and have to return by bus. It is a small, amusing adventure, apparently of no great significance, though it does signal a rift between Templer and Stringham. However, before the end of the sequence Jean Templer will have had sexual connections with three of the men in the car: affairs with Jenkins and Brent, marriage with Duport. This is a remarkable percentage if we exclude her brother from the possibles. Of course, it could be argued that this is natural rather than otherwise, Jean having a ready link with all three through her brother; and it is true that we are given an early hint of Jean's sexual restlessness, 'in love with a married man twice her age', Peter reports. All the same, Powell does seem deliberately concerned here with the symmetry of fluke; and we have to take into account with it that other roaring coincidence of Jean's love life, when her second husband is chaperoned by Jenkins at the Victory Day Service.

The Vauxhall episode and what follows seems on expression of Powell's (or Jenkins's) thesis that life has moments which, although apparently of no great moment at the time – say a spin in a car for five young men and two local girls – will vividly colour later life. It is a fiction writer's grateful assertion that now and then, and here and there, time will formulate arbitrary links across the years and, for no reason beyond a tendency to pattern, will carry out the sort of shaping described at the beginning of *AQOU*. But it is only now

D

and then and here and there. Intriguing examples of such links occur between *AQOU* and *BDFAR* (that is, between Book 1 and Book 10). In *AQOU* a boy called Akworth is expelled from school for passing what we take to be a homosexual note to Templer. Widmerpool intercepts it and shows it to Le Bas. Making arrangements in *BDFAR* many years later for a son to go to school, Nicholas meets Le Bas working as a librarian. A boy comes, ostensibly seeking a book, but probably to perpetrate some sort of rag on Le Bas. The boy's name is Akworth. Revenge across the generations? That idea receives added impact in *HSH* when Widmerpool meets the original Akworth – now Sir Bertram – and, in an overwrought state, kneels to him for forgiveness. Again: in *AQOU* a boy called Calthorpe Major is first to write home with news of Le Bas's arrest following a practical joke. A page or two after his meeting with Akworth in *BDFAR* Nicholas meets Widmerpool who tells him that Pamela is closeted with a schoolboy, a schoolboy who is almost a man. His name is Calthorpe, 'son or nephew of one of the Calthorpes'. No matter of retribution seems involved, only simple coincidence and pattern; the two incidents, so close together, make for a remarkable sense of interconnection.

The view of life contained in the title and notion *A Dance to the Music of Time* has a remarkable flexibility and range and comes over as generally credible and satisfying. It avoids the temptations to flippancy, off-handedness and formula which can occasionally turn irony into something less. Time, the reader agrees, could work like this, or this, or could even fail to work at all on the important things. And we accept, too, that time may put characters (and, by implication, us) through the hoop or the dance in a way which, when seen in retrospect, may give evidence of a scheme, even of a meaning.

Style

What strikes one first about the prose of *ADTTMOT* is its elaborate texture and seemingly cast-iron poise, qualities suiting the narrator's wisdom, favoured status, knowledge and assurance. Nicholas senior sets the past's uncertainties against the comparative – and only comparative – clarity of hindsight. Above all, the style is a generalising instrument, designed to bring apparently fragmented material into unity. By continually opening its focus wide the writing places incident and feeling of the moment in their background.

We may look at the first two paragraphs of *AQOU* for early evidence of Powell's method. The prose is smooth, belligerently sure of itself, measured and parenthetical. Simile abounds and especially simile not meant so much to make accurate parallels as to satirise through fanciful, even outrageous, allusion: 'as if ', which appears twice in the first paragraph, is a favourite Powell device, often raised aloft when one of these jokes is on the march. It is a technique bringing great pictorial richness, along with a sense of amused, knowledgeable detachment: the writing sees beyond the obvious and actual and can appraise situations by wide-ranging – free-ranging – standards. Only a little later than these opening paragraphs Jenkins describes his housemaster Le Bas standing 'as if he were about to leap high into the air like an athlete or ballet dancer; and in this taut attitude he seemed to be considering best how to carry out his threat, while he breathed heavily inward as if to inbibe the full savour of sausages.'

Colons do heavy duty in *ADTTMOT*. In these opening two paragraphs, and throughout, the prose is largely appositional: to borrow the mode, plain statement followed by commentary or modification or conjecture, so that the reader feels himself presented with a very wide choice of possible responses; the uncertainties of real life are caught. Colons give Powell the ferry between immediacy and perspective, between events and their interpretations, and – as at the start of the second paragraph here – between statement and generous extension.

The book opens with the narrator watching men engaged on road works during a snow shower. The scene invokes images from history, from art, then from Jenkins's own schooldays, and the novel is under way. Polished, mandarin syntax catches a party of workmen in attitudes which are all near absurdity; comic faces made to look more so when reflected in the fine curve of a silver spoon. To the narrator they have the quaintness of a different and distant class and are beguiling show-pieces, 'making pantomimic gestures', behaving 'like comedians'. One resembles a Shakespearean clown. Their activities are mock-heroically likened to a rite and to observances. They work in an 'abyss' among 'subterranean drain pipes', neither of these being quite the terms such men would pick themselves to describe their work. For the narrator they are almost another species, performing unthinkable duties in frightful conditions. Such phrasing represents a deliberate posture, of course – the narrator exaggerating both his own sheltered timorousness and the horrors of low-class life, a familiar upper-class mannerism: 'I am glad to say that I have never seen a spade', Gwendolen says in *The Importance of Being Earnest*.

Combined with this suavity and impression of social aplomb, though, is a strong element of self-mockery. It is, after all, the comic workmen's brazier, brightened momentarily by the remains of what look like two kippers wrapped in newspaper, which sets Jenkins off on his big-time flights about legionaries, centaurs, legend and Poussin. Often in the series one meets this balance. Jenkins's oracular stance will be given a shove by the drolly, sometimes even sleazily, matter of fact. In *A Quintet, Sextet And War* (Indiana, 1970) John Russell is interesting on what he calls 'relapse diction' in Powell's prose; the technique in which a dignified paragraph may be abruptly shaken by the use of low-status idiom.

In other words, the style of *ADTTMOT* helps establish the novel's basic duality: the poise of hindsight against the intransigence of fact and actuality. There is, of course, detachment and assurance, but they are not absolute; the prose can be high-flown but it will often be reeled in again pretty sharply. Although the opening of *AQOU* certainly laughs at the workmen – perhaps at workmen, as *AM* laughs at flunkeys and Powell's play *The Rest I'll Whistle* (London, 1971) laughs at domestic helps – it is also making sure that Jenkins and his tone of voice remain down-to-earth, if not subterranean. This modulated dignity, mandarin with the skids under it, gives Powell's style its distinction. We may see it at work again in the discussion over Haig's statue in *ABM*. The conversation, begun by Widmerpool, is of supreme comic banality. In the course of it, Barbara Goring, by whom Nicholas is besotted at this time, asks him why, to help with realism, the statue of the horse should not be made from the model of a real horse. 'Couldn't they do it in plaster of Paris or something. Don't you think?'

For Nicholas, 'This last question, propitiatory in tone, and addressed in a fairly low voice to myself, could still make me feel, for reasons quite subjective in origin, that there might be something to be said for this unconventional method of solving what had become almost the chief enigma of contemporary aesthetic.' Elegantly shaped, resonantly Latinate, the prose is calculatedly knocked sideways by the stupidity of the basic subject, and the special idiocy of Barbara's contribution.

We will often meet this comic method in *ADTTMOT*: the presentation of fatuously trivial or even degraded subject matter in elevated language. It is, of course, a standard issue for humorists, with Wodehouse as possibly its greatest modern exponent. Perhaps the mode has lost, or is losing, some of its effectiveness now, since straight mandarin writing is so out of fashion that to parody it might seem self-indulgent; or even meaningless to younger readers. Dangers have always stood very close to this comic technique. If it fails – if the joke misses – we are left with what looks like wilfully ponderous prose and a strong smell of at best facetiousness and at worst pomposity. I will return to this.

For the most part, Powell uses the mock-ponderous, or mock-matter-of-fact, admirably, as we have already seen in the discussion over what tip to give the man who recovers Pringle's clothes in *AM*. There is a fine example in *AQOU* where Stripling as a joke is about to substitute a chamber pot for the top-hat in Farebrother's hat-box. Jenkins records:

> My immediate thought was that the relative size might prevent this plan from being put successfully into execution; though I had not examined the inside of the hat-box, obviously itself larger than normal (no doubt built to house more commodious hats of an earlier generation), the cardboard interior of which might have been removed to make room for odds and ends.

Busy, ponderous writing, devoted to the logistics of this operation, rather than to pointing up its farcical nature heightens the humour (though use of 'commodious' without apparent awareness of its potential double sense in the context seems to indicate an untypical insensitivity). This is the narrative technique of 'brutal thoroughness' with ludicrous material which V. S. Pritchett referred to in his *NS&N* review of *ABM* (28 June 1952). That lavishly documented kitchen argument in *TKO* over whether or not Billson did right to give one of Dr Trelawney's young followers a slice of stale seed cake pleasantly loads a negligible incident with all the pernickety shifts and queries of intense moral debate. Similar very thorough and inappropriate solemnity attends General Liddament's reflections on porridge for the troops in *TVOB*; and Widmerpool's account of how he reconciled the two embittered tennis players, Örn and Lundquist, in *AQOU*. In the same volume, a lavatory drawing of Widmerpool is used as grounds for a delightful skit on the hard-working machinery of detective fiction and of art criticism as Jenkins tries to identify the perpetrator.

This contradiction of style by subject matter is one way towards deflation, perhaps the simplest. There are others. Throughout *ADTTMOT* we come across instances of highly-fashioned and, or, potentially dramatic and earnest prose tugged sharply back on the short leash. Jenkins first takes Jean Duport (Templer) in his arms during a drive along the Great West Road, in *TAW*. The writing is intermittently sonorous and passionate; but both qualities are kept in check – at least that – by a description of the locale: an 'electrically illuminated young lady in a bathing dress dives eternally through the petrol-tainted air' as part of an advertising display. And there is an unglamorous doubt: were Nicholas and Jean thrown together by complicated psychological and emotional causes or by pot-holes in the road?

In *TMP* Nicholas goes to Normandy near the end of the war with a party of allied officers, virtually on a sightseeing tour. To be back in France in such circumstances he finds powerfully moving. Yet, although the prose catches those feelings, it also applies repeated correctives. The landscape is a mixture of untouched loveliness and equipment smashed in battle: Corot-like colours and vistas have to accommodate a camouflaged, rusted staff-car, wheels in the air. Nicholas is overwhelmed. 'A gigantic release seemed to have taken place . . . I was briefly in tears.' What provokes this is the sight of an old, bearded Frenchman who stops and delightedly waves to the convoy. The incident is as much comic as dramatic and touching.

The Frenchman may look 'like a peasant in a fairy story who has found the treasure', but he is wearing that most inelegant and unromantic of garments, an olive-green British anti-gas cape. The whole sophisticated apparatus of understatement is here; and is carried, too, in the slight ponderousness and step from immediacy of 'I was briefly in tears', rather than 'I wept'. To use some of Powell's own words from a little later in *TMP*, the prose seems designed as 'a reminder of the eternal failure of life to respond a hundred per cent; to rise to the greatest heights without allowing at the same time some suggestion, however slight, to take shape in indication that things could have been even better.'

Nowhere, I think, is the self-deflating purpose of Powell's style better seen than in a sequence I refer to in the chapter on Narrative: the air raid at the beginning of *TSA*. This book's ironic tone is set early on when an assistant in an outfitters' assumes that Nicholas is being fitted with a military greatcoat for some stage role; and the theme of war as a show, a performance, is smartly pursued. A little later the air raid is treated as a spectacle, the landscape caught in a light, a 'refulgence' to be precise, 'theatrical yet sinister'. Cloud masses change colour 'as if' phased in some way with the searchlights. The view is 'resplendent' and 'transcendentally speaking' seems to promise some sort of revelation from above. The flares are 'like Japanese lanterns at a fête'. They are 'apparently' on long wires from an invisible ceiling. 'As if' at a signal the flares meet smoke from the ground. It is 'the penumbra of Pluto's frontiers'.

Literally, then, high-flown. As a matter of fact, I find it gives as vivid and realistic impression of a raid as more seemingly business-like pieces of reportage. But one cannot dispute, of course, that it is a deliberately gorgeous and ostentatiously fanciful account of something that would also have its painful and infinitely grim aspects. The prose could be regarded as not so much theatrical as up-stage.

At least, it is until near the end of this paragraph of description. Then we hear suddenly that 'The reek of scorched rubber grew more than ever sickly.' Exciting pictorial features have been summarily dispelled and the passage moves on to its real let-down. Nicholas has been watching the display with Bithel, officer i/c the Mobile Laundry and, overall, a figure designed to counter any suggestion of nobility or grandeur in the pursuit of arms; this destructive role strengthened, if anything, by his fraudulent claim to be brother of a V.C. At the end of the set-piece on the raid, 'Bithel fidgeted with the belt of his mackintosh. "There's been a spot of bother about a cheque," he said.' The let-down, then, is towards not the dirt and agony of war, which might have their own sad dignity, but towards one of its niggling, bureaucratic ennuies: the Pay Department has been late in transferring field allowances to Bithel's account and a cheque has bounced; even Bithel, scruffy, wearing unbelievably ill-fitting false teeth, and generally disorganised, is bound by the protocol which requires an officer not to shame himself and his commission by passing cheques unbacked by funds. In a sense, the conversation is about soldiers' honour; but on what a drab scale, and what a soldier. The incident continues with Bithel declaring – shouting against the din of ack-ack fire – that he always imagined himself as the hero of serials in *Chum* and *Boy's Own Paper*, and sees his present experience as akin to crises in those yarns. ' "Coming under fire for the first time" – that was always a great moment in the hero's career. You must remember. Where he "showed his mettle", as the story usually put it.'

In the group of books to which *TSA* belongs, Powell is often trying to say something about the nature of war and military values. In this passage – beginning with the imaginative account of the air-raid – there is a careful, subtle and complex demonstration that war can be as much Bithel's tiresome personal problems as it can be 'the penumbra of Pluto's frontiers'. Against the 'refulgence' of the flares and searchlights we may catch sight of Bithel's 'double row of Low Comedy teeth', as he laughs at himself and at notions of heroism. The writing has abruptly debunked itself. It is another controlled nose-dive, and immensely skilled.

Such control is customary, not invariable. Powell will take fearful risks, and seems ready to accept that an intensely literary style may stray occasionally into blatant over-writing, pedantry and word-spinning. In his review of *HSH* in the *Sunday Telegraph* (7 September 1975) John Lehmann spoke of parts of the sequence which came 'very close to a wordy flatness'. There are times in *ADTTMOT* when the prose is caculatedly – arrogantly – distanced from clear, everyday patterns; the writing of what a miner-soldier from *TVOB* might call 'an educated Evans'. The opening of *HSH* is an example.

Duck, flying in from the south, ignored four or five ponderous explosions over at the quarry. The limestone cliff, dominant oblong foreground structure, lateral storeyed platforms, all coral-pink in evening sunlight, projected towards the higher ground on misty mornings a fading mirage of Babylonian terraces suspended in haze above the mere; the palace, with its hanging gardens, distantly outlined behind a group of rather woodenly posed young Medes (possibly young Persians) in Mr Deacon's *Boyhood of Cyrus*, the picture's recession equally nebulous in the shadows of the Walpole-Wilsons' hall.

Without the first chapter of ABM reasonably clear in his mind, a reader might have trouble sorting out the meaning here; might be baffled by the word 'recession' (signifying obscurely hung). A little later the metaphors will grow uncomfortably numerous and competitive: a peak, coagulations of cottonwool, perforations and loopholes. Elsewhere in ADTTMOT humour can shrink to drollery. What starts ironic may end soft. A sequence characterised only by lightness of touch and unfailing precision may be followed by a paragraph or two where one is conscious chiefly of abstract and evasive diction, strained fancy and an apparent belief that if a piece of prose lacks architecture one should compensate by making it arch. Generally, Powell's aim at these points is the same as elsewhere: to diminish through over-dignifying. Restraint and economy are lost, though. Jokes may be stifled by their own fat.

This is not an objection to intricacy or allusiveness: a long conceit comparing the officer group to carved Roman deities in *TSA* is tortuous, yet more or less comes off. But take the comparison drawn in ABM between the Sword of Damocles and the large sugar caster which Barbara Goring holds over Widmerpool's head in joke. The caster does not remain merely poised and threatening, like the Sword, but suddenly pours sugar on to Widmerpool's head. Or, to put it another way, 'unlike the merely minatory quiescence of that normally inactive weapon, a state of dispensation was not in this case maintained.' This is, of course, an attempt at humour by overstatement, but so energetic that one feels bruised by the rib-digging. Similarly, it would be very hard to put up with Nicholas if he addressed us always, instead of only sometimes, in this sort of sentence, again from ABM, where the subject is an acquaintance and sexual rival, Tompsitt: 'The wine had the effect of making him discourse on racing, a subject regarding which I was myself unfortunately too ignorant to dispose of as summarily as I should have wished of the almost certainly erroneous opinions he put forward.' Too often in ADTTMOT one feels that the prose is sweatily on the run from plain statement. What are we to make of a passage like this from BDFAR,

in which Jenkins reflects on autobiographies written by his contemporaries?

However, nearly all revealed, if not explicitly in every case, a
similar reorientation towards the sixth climacteric, their narrative
supporting, on the whole, evidence already noticeably piling up,
that friends, if required at all in the manner of the past, must
largely be reassembled at about this milestone.

It could be argued, I know, that this is Nicholas getting on a bit
and exercising in character a fussiness and solemnity which are quite
credible. To that one must say that here and elsewhere Powell puts
under stress the reader's affection and respect for his narrator, a
dangerous tactic.

The unhappy examples just quoted come from a fairly late book
in the sequence and from the second. It is sometimes said that
Powell's style straightens itself out during the course of *ADTTMOT*,
particularly in and after the war volumes. It is true that the first two
books are the most liable to over-blown complexity; but the novel
is never altogether free of it, *HSH*, the last volume, providing several
examples. Once or twice, as in *TKO*, Powell will lamely concede he
is asking for too much. He will seek what effects he can from slave-
driven whimsy and subsequently dismiss these as foolish. Jenkins
ponders whether Templer's new wife Betty, a nervy, dazed character,
might have been only recently released from one of the dungeons
at Sir Magnus Donners's home, Stourwater. The notion is worked
over and then followed by the abrupt disclaimer: 'Of course, I did
not seriously suppose such a thing.' But seriously, folks. Elsewhere in
TKO we meet a similar creaky flight of fantasy when Jenkins affects
to take literally an exclamation of his mother, 'I thought it was the
end of the world.' Having done some stunts with thoughts on the
Last Trump, the Day of Judgement, Sheep and Goats, figures risen
from the tomb, Jenkins concludes: 'No doubt my mother used only
a figure of speech.' No doubt.

What we are talking about are two different kinds of result from
the literary or mandarin style. For the most part, Powell's prose,
although richly imaginative and atmospheric, will remain convincingly tied to reality. There will be instances, though, where the
writing is literary in the sense that it is not cogently lifelike; the
minimal links with common sense are broken which should be
present even in jokes. Admittedly the distinction between success
and failure is narrow; narrow but deep: what a character in Peter

de Vries's *Forever Panting* calls 'the gulf between the OK and the de trop.' Regrettably, enough facetiousness and middle-grade drollery exist in *ADTTMOT* for some casual readers to take this as the regular Powell tone, and to be seriously discouraged. All humorous writing involves risk: what sparkles for one reader will wrap another in a pall. To say what works and what does not may seem an attempt to promote personal taste into a rule. One can only hope to enlist agreement by giving examples. What the examples I have cited say to me is that here and there Powell, after the style of some essayists who wrote in a more leisurely and less generally educated part of our century, believes that an imperturbable and fluent manner will do a lot to cover slight matter. *The Times* fourth leaders used to get away with it until fairly recently. They had to go, though.

Generally, what one is reaching out for and failing to find in some of these examples is concreteness in the prose; some sharpness of definition and signs of solid contours behind the cloudbank of words. Although occasional uneasiness with Powell's style on these grounds is inescapable, we do need to keep in mind what his intentions are. Perspective on what happens is as important to him as what happens; and he has evolved a prose which will quite calculatedly lower or even kill the impact of some potentially exciting situation for the sake of reflective comment or allusion. It is deflation, but of a different kind from what we have already discussed: a deliberate reduction of vivid, sharp, perhaps even pacey writing to the less lively language of analysis and interpretation. The technique is particularly apparent in Powell's treatment of love and sex, and one can see why. The overall attitude to love – Jenkin's marriage and a couple of others excepted – is anti-romantic and ironic. Nicholas looks at the social and dynastic consequences of liaisons and changed liaisons, usually finding them bizarre. When it comes to his own love affairs, apart from the one with Isobel, we are dealing in relationships which the mature narrator knows to be ultimately unsatisfactory; and therefore the prose will not do very much to capture passion or feeling, but set these passing relationships in their context. Experience, worldliness and truth demand that Jenkins look at love as sometimes bleak, sometimes empty and almost always desperately fragile. The style rightly echoes these reservations. When dealing with love – and sometimes with war and other violent action – it will quite often relinquish its hold on the immediate and actual because these are less significant than they seemed at the time;

allow them to sink from view beneath a surface of generalisation and long-view complexity: as far as war goes, I examine the process in the notes on *TMP*. And as far as sex goes, Nicholas's experience with Gypsy Jones in *ABM* provides a remarkable piece of writing.

This is not simply a question of delicacy, though we had better notice here that these early books are much less frank in language than, say, *TK*, published during more easy-going times. The object of the prose in the Gypsy Jones episode is not to keep things clean but to keep them cool; to keep them flaccid, one might almost say; to depersonalise. Coupling takes place.

> In spite of the apparently irresistible nature of the circumstances, when regarded through the larger perspectives that seemed, on reflection, to prevail – that is to say of a general subordination to an intricate design of cause and effect – I could not help admitting, in due course, the awareness of a sense of inadequacy.

It we look at that sentence we will see a pretty clear statement of Powell's purpose. The sexual impulse of the moment might have seemed 'irresistible' then, not at all a subject for qualifying adverbs and parentheses; but hindsight must modify matters with 'apparently'. Urgencies of desire have to give way in this account to 'larger perspectives' and 'reflection'. Although exciting accident might have seemed to put Nicholas and Gypsy together in circumstances right for love-making, Jenkins the narrator can now look back and see 'an intricate design of cause and effect'. It is this which interests Powell; and so the emptiness of the incident itself – recalling similar unhappy, mechanical sexual encounters in *AM* and *V* – is deliberately captured in words which have nothing to do with love or lust but only with the intellectualising of desire when recollected in tranquillity. So unspecific is the prose in this sequence that Robert K. Morris wrongly assumes in *The Novels Of Anthony Powell* (Pittsburgh, 1968) that Nicholas does not make it but 'cerebrates away the first serious opportunity to lose his virginity.'

Similarly, Nicholas's jealousy of Barbara Goring's interest in Tompsitt, also in *ABM*, is recorded, but cannot be felt in the prose. In *ALM* Nicholas seems much more at ease theorising about love and love affairs than in giving us some idea, through the precision and warmth of the words, what his love life is actually like. Even in *TAW*, which does contain very moving glimpses of the shocks, pain and disgust in Nick's affair with Jean, the prose will turn aside at crucial moments and wander in general reflections about women and love, allowing some of the pain to dissipate. The style is, then, trying to say in its texture what has to be said about love, and saying it on the whole honestly and effectively. Most of us would be prepared to concede that the fictional treatment of sexual love is habitually glamorised. Powell avoids that, while also avoiding cynicism, in a style shaped to suggest amusement, melancholy, pain and heartfelt uncertainty.

Although the writing can lose its balance, for the most part it is a subtly controlled means of setting against each other immediacy and retrospect, surface and substance, incident and theme, impulse and perspective, social poise and the signs of powerful change. Uniquely Powell's, it is a style which for many, including myself, can become addictive. It can certainly be accused both of stopping short and of going much too far. It is, though, never long separated from the novelist's main task: the creation and sustenance of people who live, and whom we come to care about.

Narrative Method

Powell's narrative method in *ADTTMOT* is, of course, crucial to the novel's shape, a uniquely subtle and complicated device. More than a little arbitrarily, I would like to break it into three elements, for the sake of keeping my own mind clear and, I hope, the reader's: the relationship of sheer, basic story-telling requirements to those of commentary and reflection; the personality of Nicholas, Powell's narrator; and the means by which Powell brilliantly widens, varies and extends what can be done within the 'I' formula.

Like most first person narrators, Nicholas Jenkins participates in the action; he observes and comments; and he reminisces, from a position often decades ahead. It is the degree of tilt towards comment and retrospective judgement which makes Jenkins exceptional. For a novelist with a thesis about intricate relationships formed and burnished by time, a method of story-telling which can present complementary views by the central figure from at least three chronological situations (there may be more) is obviously very attractive, and Powell uses it with resourcefulness and flair. He did not invent the technique, but takes it on, employing it with a new thoroughness, continually changing perspectives and making adjustments of focus, sometimes subtle, sometimes huge. An omniscient author might have done as much, it is true; but the first person stance means that ironic comment – and most of it is ironic – strikes one as more humane when expressed through a fallible protagonist, less hatched, pat and superior.

Nicholas moves easily out of actuality into retrospect. One of the most illuminating examples comes at the beginning of Chapter 3 of *ABM*. Jenkins is reflecting on a party he has attended recently at Mrs Andriadis's. It marks a stage in his development from youth to adulthood: life is opening up. He is conscious of 'having travelled a long way' during one evening out. He has learned, among other things, that the demarcations which he was accustomed to make in life (treating love and enmity, work and play as opposites, for instance) lacked flexibility. People do not belong to different worlds but are 'tenaciously inter-related'; these worlds lie closer to each other than he had thought, or at least 'to some pattern common to all'. These notions are, then, very much part of Powell's dance theme: the patterns, configurations and links. He wishes to sound this note for us; but it would be unnatural for Jenkins to understand all this, whole and clear, in his early twenties. What Nicholas does get is the unspecific feeling that changes have taken place, plus partial glimpses of new complexities, new depths: he has learned a lesson, knows it, but has not yet got it formulated. Experience is in three stages: the immediate impact of the party; the groping theories upon it, a short time afterwards; the more distant retrospect, which includes placing of these events in their context. 'I did not of course come to these conclusions immediately,' Jenkins tells us. He suggests, in fact, that to have known in advance all the 'infinite complications' of personal links at Mrs Andriadis's party – those tenacious inter-relationships – might have spoiled his enjoyment of the occasion. Powell has allowed him to speak here the whole narrative strategy of *ADTTMOT:* the reader may take pleasure in direct, immediate presentation of an event; ponder the contemporaneous reflections of it; and then look for evidence, hints, as to how these circumstances and people fit into the overall time scheme. One example will be enough to show how Powell uses this flexibility of narrational position to draw the patterns of coincidence and connection which, stretching across time, make up the dance. (I hope the cataract of names which follow do not swamp the point.) In *TMP* Nicholas runs into an American soldier he has met before, Colonel Cobb, an assistant military attaché. It is January 1943, time of the German surrender at Stalingrad. The narrative appears to hop and meander. Cobb makes a joke. Jenkins recounts that 'years later' in New York he repeated Cobb's words to Milton Wisebite during a publisher's party. Milton is the nephew of Harrison F. Wisebite, second husband of Flavia, Stringham's sister, and mother of Pamela Flitton, Cosmo Flitton having been Flavia's first husband. He ran away with Baby Wentworth, though would not marry her. At the publisher's party, Milton asks about Pamela, and confesses to some sort of relationship with her years before. This would be 'appreciably later' than the German Stalingrad surrender, though during the war. The mesh of connections suddenly revealed – Milton is, after all, a kind of relation of Pamela – is as comprehensive and startling as anything in

ADTTMOT; and the seemingly off-hand, rambling quality of the narrative, the casual switch of period, gives this sequence of fortuitous incident (for Jenkins to encounter Milton; for Milton, with the American forces in Britain, to have met Pamela and had an affair with her) the kind of undramatic tone which Powell wants for his scheme: fluke is normal, coincidence routine.

We often find Jenkins as narrator looking back on Jenkins the protagonist looking back: both *AQOU* and *ABM* open like that, as if Powell wished from the start to give the 'present' of the book fluidity and a time context. Period movements are especially complex at the opening of *ABM*. Jenkins looks back to a sale. Pictures by E. Bosworth Deacon on offer there make him think back a further stage, to his first visit to the house of the Walpole-Wilsons in Eaton Square, because of a Deacon hanging in the hall. But we have already been taken even further back to accounts of the friendship between Jenkins's parents and Mr Deacon.

The effect of such roving narration is, inevitably, to catch in the construction of the books the theme of time's sameness beneath seeming change. It is as if it does not much matter from which chronological point we view the incidents and characters. Mr Deacon will be already dead when we first hear of him in *ABM* and his work (on historical themes, as it happens) so dated that Jenkins fears it will cause laughter at the auction (those vast canvases which are to grow modish again in *HSH*). Yet we will move not simply to days when the adult Nicholas associated with Deacon but to an encounter with him at the Louvre during the First War, when Nicholas was a child.

We must not make too much of the time-shift. As Ford Madox Ford says in *It Was the Nightingale* (London, 1934), 'There is nothing really startling in the method. It is that of every writer of workmanlike detective stories . . . [a] technique . . . identical with that of all modern novelists, or of myself . . . Or Proust.' All the same, it is hard to think of any novelist who makes such subtle, effective and continual use of it to support a theme as Powell. The description of events as they occur tends to be less important than the placing of them in the overall scheme, a scheme we are constantly reminded about. It is only one of Powell's objectives to convey the flavour and freshness of a moment, and possibly not the chief objective. As a result, he needs a specially devised style, which I have commented on more fully in another chapter: here, one may briefly say that it is a style which rarely strives for narrative pace, and which may down-play and blur the impact, edge and immediacy of events as they happen. He needs, also, of course, a carefully devised narrator. It is time to look at the character of Nicholas.

There is more than one Nicholas. Jenkins, the elderly narrator, is a lavishly developed character, opinionated, learned, prosy, philosophical, reflective and copiously articulate. There is also Jenkins a participant in the events recalled; though 'participant' may be putting it rather strongly. Jenkins senior keeps Jenkins junior pretty well battened down except for occasional exercise spells and airings. As I will show in notes on several of the books, very important aspects of feeling and behaviour are left out almost altogether; Nicholas's relations with his wife, both before and after marriage, are treated with glaring economy, for instance. The fact of his marriage is covered in one sentence at the end of a chapter in CCR. If we fail to keep in mind the conventions of this type of narration – the duality, or multiplicity, perhaps, of the recounting figure – we may find ADTTMOT lacking in core, and perhaps in impetus: some readers feel a gap, an emptiness, or even a wetness, at the centre of the novel because of the contemporary Jenkins's passivity and self-effacement.

But is it practical to require readers to allow for the conventions of a narrative method? Novels are not written for critics or other novelists. The public do not consciously read with an eye to technique; though they may sense soon enough when a technique has come unstuck. (On some matters the ordinary reader may have very pronounced technical views and one will often hear people say they do not like 'I' books at all; in their defence we may recall James's words in a letter to Wells about 'that curst autobiographical form'. Powell was no doubt aware of such prejudices when he began, but decided to take the risk.) There is an obvious in-built hazard to the 'I' narration. It is that the reader will confuse the narrator and the author. This may sound an almost unbelievably illiterate and primitive error, but is it? In *The Years with Ross* (New York, 1958) James Thurber relates how Wolcott Gibbs, in a fascinating and rivetingly sensible guide to the craft of fiction-editing for the *New Yorker* magazine, said it had always irritated him when a story was written in the first person but the narrator's name was different from the author's. In ADTTMOT the possibilities for confusion are considerable. For a start, the 'I' of this narration is spread over a long distance and so becomes very insistent. Second, though this might not be known to the general reader, autobiographical facts or approximations from Powell's life are pervasive: army family; public school; publishing career changing to writing. Third and most important, where, as in *ADTTMOT*, the 'I' figure is so industriously reflective, so given to detailed, distanced, retrospective commentary, the narrator's and author's voices are almost bound to merge: this is the kind of moralising we have come to expect from intrusive, omniscient authors.

The danger here is that the reader will then feel that the author should tell us less about 'himself', obtrude 'his' personality and views less, and get on with developing his character, Nicholas Jenkins. This is what I meant in making what may have seemed a pedantic, naïve suggestion that the reader ought to be aware, and remain aware, of the rules of a first-person novel. What happens is that the novelist creates a character to tell the story: he is not that character. This accepted, the reader may see that Jenkins is, in fact, an elaborate and very well defined piece of characterisation. His character is, though, that of an elderly man, the mature novelist and scholar who is looking back over his life. He will, of course, try to recall and recreate what the younger Jenkins did and felt in the past, and these incidents as they occur will have their own interest; but it is a minor interest when isolated: the interest of an episode, or of a step in the dance. Imposition on those events and feelings of the later Jenkins's perspective is what interests Powell most; and is crucial to his presentation of a theme concerned with the patterns of time. If we accept that the personality of the narrator is at least as important in flashback as it is during the actual passage of recollected events, Powell's reasons for choosing this method of presenting his novel will look cogent if not irresistible. Reticence over the younger Jenkins's love life then becomes a positive feature of the older Jenkins's character. Powell is not attempting what Defoe did in *Moll Flanders*: a formal framework of recollection, with incident, as it occurs, given the full treatment of immediacy and suspense. Nor is his model that strange composite which Thackeray used for *The History of Henry Esmond*: supposed recollections written by Esmond himself, 'edited' by the author, and occasionally moving abruptly between a third and first-person narration in order to achieve both immediacy and an appearance of detachment. In the *Music of Time* the recollective, distanced point of view is continuously vital, not something extra.

To those who find Nicholas the protagonist a toweringly non-committed figure this may sound academic and far-fetched. I must say there are situations in this novel, as in *WBOW*, when I long for Nicholas to do – or even say – something that would influence the course of events, rather than simply record them for ironic treatment later. His inactivity can put a strain on our affection for him, and upon credibility: could anyone be so neutral? We see characters caught up in the political battles of the thirties, but not Nicholas. Adultery encompasses almost everyone, but not Nicholas: along with Bagshaw's father, who is white-haired and doddering, he seems to be one of the very few men she knows whom Pamela does not try to seduce. (Templer appears to be another.) Nicholas will privately escort her when she wishes to vomit, but no closer or more bracing intimacy seems conceivable. One feels drably certain that, even though Pamela likes older men, she would never grab Jenkins's testicles in the Basilica of St Mark's, Venice, as she does Russell Gwinnett's, the American scholar, in *TK*. It is as if the characters know that Nicholas must not lose his cool, so that all those polished, ironically slanted memories will come out smooth one day. As the sequence proceeds he becomes less and less personally implicated and in *HSH* has shed almost all personality. Matters of acute social or matrimonial tension may take place near him but he will say next to nothing. We might even question whether a man of such sensitivity and rectitude would put up to the degree he does with someone like Widmerpool. Powell shows himself conscious of this difficulty and makes the narrator explain the relationship, or try. In *TKO* Duport asks Nicholas whether he does not find Widmerpool odious. 'He and I rub along all right', Nicholas replies. Then, in *TVOB* Jenkins says Widmerpool was acceptable because of what he stood for: that is, he recalls pleasurable phases in Nicholas's life. But what one feels sometimes is that the protagonist Nicholas is so bland and amorphous that he can accommodate almost anyone as a friend.

We know what Powell wants. He has certain basic hazards to counter. In the letter to Wells, Henry James went on to make his objections to the first person novel very explicit. It had, he thought,

'no authority, no persuasive or convincing force – its grasp of reality and truth isn't strong and disinterested . . . There is, to my vision, no authentic, and no really interesting and no *beautiful*, report of things on the novelist's . . . part unless a particular detachment has operated . . . and this detachment, this chemical transmutation for the aesthetic, the representational, end is terribly wanting in autobiography brought, as the horrible phrase is, up to date.

What is sometimes called Nicholas's passivity may also be termed, more favourably, his detachment, and often is. To go back to politics, for an example: Nicholas can look at the idealogical flutterings of Erridge, Quiggin, Sillery, St John Clarke with something like the scepticism of ordinary, uncommitted common sense. Possibly that common sense has about it a consistent hint of the Right, but the circumstances almost require such a bias in the cause of independence: Nicholas's attitude does not seem much out of line with, say, Orwell's middle-of-the-road campaign against parlour pinks; a mild corrective at a time of modish Leftness. His treatment of Member's high-flown theorising about politics and psychiatry as they affect St John Clarke in *TAW* comes from a free and perspective intelligence. In a novel of extraordinary and volatile people a narrator lacking emphatic personal traits and of consistently steady disposition will help maintain contact with normal standards. That was one reason for presenting Gatsby's dream through Carraway, and must at least partly explain Powell's motives, also.

Two questions arise. Is Nicholas then only a foil character? Can a twelve-volume novel be sustained by a foil, even if he has a double personality, that of protagonist and narrator? There are those who would answer first Yes and then No to these questions, and for them *ADTTMOT* is incomplete, or worse. What we have to recognise, I think, is that the protagonist Nicholas, as depicted by the older Nicholas, is a character most notable for qualities like temperateness, reticence and equilibrium. These would not suit the first-person hero of a story-telling novel, of course: if Jim Hawkins did not frequently allow boldness and curiosity to rule him there would be no *Treasure Island*. And, even in a work of unconventional narrative structure like Powell's there will be sequences where Nicholas's coolness looks like intolerable or incredible coldness; and where self-effacement makes us suspect a local failure in characterisation. Yet gentleness, balance, resolution are not negative qualities. Throughout the books Jenkins has a very active life under way, though it tends to be dealt with in asides rather than with the directness given to the exploits of others. It is in the nature of this kind of work that the presentation of Nicholas should be so unemphatic. The novel's direction and tone come, after all, from applying an ironic eye to the externals of life and viewing these against deeper factors. Like John Aubrey, whom Powell has written about and edited, Jenkins is a masterly gossip. He is more, though. The narrator knows from the start what lay out of sight in himself – the weakness, uncertainties, fears and excesses – and so there is no call to spend much time on behaviour as a guide to, or denial of, personality. Jenkins senior can go straight to the heart of Jenkins junior. In a style not uncommon to the twentieth-century novel, Nicholas emerges as a tentative, often baffled, sometimes defeated central figure. This kind of character is current not because novelists have lost the ability to depict sterling, successful extroverts, but because they believe he mirrors many of their contemporaries. Nobody could deny that there is a pallor about the character of the younger Nicholas. Some people are by nature pale.

Nor, when seen whole, is he as pale as all that, either. It is primarily, I think, the way in which Powell shows his love affairs which makes Nicholas look wan. Certainly in the famous Gypsy Jones seduction (by or of) in *ABM* we meet a deliberate avoidance of verve and exactness in the prose. Sex is strangled by subordinate clauses. Against this, though, we have touching and intense moments with Jean and the sad yearnings for Barbara Goring: 'That was the last day for many months that I woke up in the morning without immediately thinking of Barbara.' This has about it a genuine, simple directness. On a lighter note, Nicholas's distant affection for Suzette at La Grenadière in *AQOU* and even the comically misdirected avowal have the feel of life. There are, in any case, other emotions besides the sexual, important as these are to novels. The surprise, reverence and delight with which Nicholas finds in *TMP* that he and his party of allied officers have been staying in Cabourg – Proust's Balbec – are marvellously given. Excitement about literature is as valid in a man of sensibility as more carnal responses. To be back in France at all fills him with an exhilaration mirrored in the prose.

Friendship, too, is powerfully felt and conveyed. We can experience Nicholas's horror in *CCR* on discovering how Stringham's family treat him now he has become an alcoholic: 'as if he had been put away from view like a person suffering from a horrible, unmentionable disease.' Nicholas's disgust with Widmerpool, for sending Stringham to the Far East, and the regret as Moreland moves towards death in *TK* are forcefully though tactfully conveyed.

I am not discussing here what we know about Nicholas, what we are told, but what we see and feel in operation. We are, in fact, told an immense amount about his life as it unfolds: the documentation is thorough. Some of it remains at that level: that is, it is never 'embodied', to adapt a Widmerpool term, never really made part of a character, though it is part of the machinery of characterisation. The 'torments of thwarted desire' during military life, which Nicholas claims for himself near the beginning of *TSA* seems a barrack-room generalisation, quite unworked for in the presentation of Jenkins as an individual so far. Likewise his conjecture in *TAW* that he may be transfixed somewhere 'between dissipation and diffidence' could certainly be substantiated as to diffidence, but dissipation?

Where Jenkins is most alive, and then considerably and interestingly alive, is in friendship, in devotion to his work and art (though we should note that even this is muted: he speaks of 'that hard, cold-blooded almost mathematical pleasure I take in writing and painting'), in wit, in the gossip's curiosity about odd sexual habits (Sir Magnus's primarily), and in an occasional sharp animosity towards people he feels have fallen below standard: towards Odo Stevens, in *TMP*, who had 'corroded' Chips Lovell's last year of life by ostentatiously carrying on an affair with Priscilla, his wife: in that one word is something on the way towards hatred.

Nicholas, the participant, is then a character whose actions, thoughts, attitudes and emotions are given to us through the filter of retrospection and which are therefore short of vividness, actuality, suspense. The younger Nicholas will have some of the characteristics of an exhibit. On top of that, he is not by nature a raucous, swashbuckling or aggressive figure. Of a recognisable upper-class English type, he is endowed with considerable self-control and calmness and a notable taste for understatement. I say English. This restraint – so often used in lampoon portraits of, say, the Foreign Office man – does have its counterpart elsewhere. An Italian word – *sprezzatura* – best sums up Nicholas's qualities. And, as Frederic R. Karl points out in 'Sisyphus Descending: Mythical Patterns in the Novels of Anthony Powell (*Mosaic*, University of Manitoba Press, vol. 4, no. 3, 1971) Nicholas is 'a cool cat, a hip operator': a figure, in other words, whose deadpan character has contemporary currency far beyond Britain. Occasionally, Nicholas may look not so much cool as lethargic or null. Occasionally the voice of retrospection may intone the life out of things with its heavy abstract nouns and posturing Latin syntax. We will grow bored with the endlessly deft commentary on this most elegant *Come Dancing*. But, overall, what Powell is trying to do through this difficult narrational method succeeds very well. And what he is trying to do is worth the risks and small failures.

Inevitably there is a certain amount of tolerated duplicity in this kind of narrative stance. A man looks back over his life; many of the uncertainties and imponderables of a particular time are so no longer: he knows the upshot. But where the 'I' of the story is an active central figure we accept that he will recount his adventures as they unfolded for him at the time, with all the unknowns and obscurities of that period kept in. This the technique of, say *David Copperfield*, or *Jane Eyre*. Powell is not quite in this category, though. He is not telling an unfolding story. Although by and large the books advance in time and finish about fifty years later than the sequence began there is no straight, chronological flow from beginning to end as in a more conventionally plotted novel. *TKO*, for example, opens with Jenkins as a very small child before the 1914–18 war although the preceding book, *CCR*, closed with him as a married man in the period of the Spanish Civil War. It is, in fact, crucial to Powell's purpose that the novel should be able to move about in time, so that he may show the complex relationships of one period with another. As Proust puts it in *Time Regained*, reality is a relation between sensations of the moment and 'those memories which simultaneously encircle us'. There will be flashes forward and back.

Another point: as we have seen, Jenkins is not in any simple sense the hero of this novel. He is an observer more than a participant; much more. He does not put before us simply a series of adventures in which he figures, but describes an incident or a relationship and reflects upon it, drawing from many sources, some of them natural to the Jenkins of the period we are seeing, some not. Many first-person narrators do this, it is true, but not on the same scale.

What this means is that we are given continual reminders that Jenkins is at once a participant in the events described, or, at least, a contemporary witness; yet someone, virtually omniscient, looking back from anywhere up to fifty years ahead. The result is a narrative method which is not completely logical – or to use a word more often applied to detective story writers – fair. An example will clarify the matter.

In *TMP* Jenkins tells us that he doubts Odo Stevens's claim to live a highly charged sexual life with Pamela Flitton. We take this as a speculation, perhaps true, perhaps not. Later in *BDFAR*, Trapnel explains that Pamela suffers from a kind of frigidity. It seems apparent from the way in which Trapnel's statement is given that this is the one we should believe. (He speaks with 'absolute simplicity' and his tendency to play a role has disappeared. Further, Jenkins explicitly reflects that Stevens had not told the complete truth.)

Now, at the time of Stevens's boast, Jenkins the narrator – as against Jenkins the contemporary listener – would know of Trapnel's disclosure. It would be absurd, though, to expect Powell to reveal at that stage a very dramatic and intriguing piece of material before its time. What one does feel to be cheating, however, is the narrator's comment on Stevens's words. 'Emphasis expressed as to the high degree of sexual pleasure to be derived from a given person is, for one reason or another, always to be accepted with a certain amount of suspicion.' I have called it the narrator's comment. I think this is reasonable: it is written in the present tense, as a general timeless observation.

The narrator is getting it two ways. He is using Odo's words as the occasion for a display of what one takes to be perception based on acumen and wordly wisdom. We are to find later, though, that he knew the real situation all the time. The uncertainty was wilful and assumed, the speculation bogus.

Does the reader notice? Does it matter? I think the answer in both cases is No, and I give the example only to show the kind of options open to an author who can use this narrative method skilfully; and I include sleight-of-hand as a skill. One quite important constructional point is involved, perhaps. I know from talking to Powell that he regarded each new book in the *ADTTMOT* sequence as something with its own separate, organic life. It had to link properly with the other books, of course; but its own particular vitality is crucial: he had no overall, detailed plan because this would not have allowed each book to develop its own life. If we apply this general principle to the Odo Stevens example just mentioned we can, I think, see what has happened. What *TMP* requires here is a gradual, clouded revelation of sexual incompatibility between Pamela and Odo. If one read that book and not *BDFAR* the situation would remain intriguingly uncertain. In *BDFAR*, though, Powell is after another effect: the sudden, paradoxical disclosure that a woman of such apparent sexual appetite is, in fact, sexually defective. The reader will forget the circumstances in which the doubts about Odo's claims were created in *TMP* and so Powell will get away with two essentially contradictory devices; contradictory, that is, if we take the books together. He is concerned with a basic, mechanical continuity for the two books; but for the sake of a particular effect in each is prepared to break an underlying dictate of his chosen narrational position. Powell is demonstrating his ability to 'bounce' the reader as Forster calls it in *Aspects Of The Novel* (London, 1927) that is, to make us accept a shifting viewpoint in the author, even though it might be against formula and strict logic. In fact, Forster claims that the novelist's right to shrink or extend his knowledge and perception is a great advantage of the form; and not at variance with real life, either, since our ability to perceive varies from day to day. English novelists have always 'played fast and loose' with their characters, and are entitled to, in Forster's view.

In such an example we see a sharp differentiation between Jenkins the narrator and Powell, the author. It would be intolerable if Powell were really telling the story of his life and said, on hearing Odo's boasting, 'I've always found it was wise to take with a pinch of salt a man's claim to be enjoying exceptional sexual pleasure from some particular woman', when it turned out later that he knew the boasting was only that. But, as author, Powell can exercise a prerogative to manipulate us as his immediate purpose needs (though I do not think the lumpily passive and abstract construction of the sentence 'Emphasis expressed as to . . .' indicates a reluctance to fit this thought firmly on Jenkins.)

In Powell's hands the first-person narrative is, in fact, an extremely elastic and varied device. It is a form of story-telling which has, in principle, certain very obvious limitations: we are largely confined to the judgements and experiences of one person. This can be both tiresome and baffling; tiresome because the single tone of voice grows monotonous; baffling because we may not be altogether sure how we should 'take' the narrator, whether as entirely credible and estimable or faulty: thus the *Moll Flanders* debate. Powell very successfully skirts or utilises the limitations. One of his chief methods is explicitly to imagine Jenkins viewing events through the eyes and mind of someone else, and particularly through those of Uncle Giles, who becomes at times a kind of second-string narrator. This is a most remarkable technique. It is not simply a matter of augmenting the chief narrator's information by getting reports from temporarily better placed characters, which goes on all the time in first-person novels. Nicholas will actually surrender his point of view, his judgement, to Giles for a while. That, in itself, brings a notable complexity. It is more than this, though. 'To look at things through Uncle Giles's eyes would never have occurred to me,' Jenkins reflects in *ABM*. The book then, naturally, goes on to do exactly that: look at things as Giles might have assessed them, had he been present at the time; it would be difficult to get more notional. It is the mature – indeed, elderly – Jenkins who gives us what he takes to be Giles's way of judging matters, while pointing out that the younger Jenkins would never have considered such a stratagem. What we are getting here is a narrative viewpoint from fifty or so years on, based on a hypothetical version of what someone other than the story-teller might have felt about people and events he did not even see. ('This concept of regarding one's own affairs through the medium of a friend or relative is not, of course, a specially profound one; but in the case of my uncle, the field of vision surveyed was always likely to be so individual to himself that almost any scene contemplated from this point of vantage required, on the part of another observer, more than ordinarily drastic refocusing.')

This is fiction, so perhaps one should not speak of hypotheses as a departure from the rule. The whole world is make-believe and there is a sense in which the author can just as validly see matters as Uncle Giles as he can see them as Jenkins. Within the limitations which he has set himself, though – those of the 'I' narrative – this is a fascinating means for an author to secure himself more elbow-room. At the opening of Chapter 2 of *ABM* he provides us with a triple view of the events of the moment: Jenkins's contemporary reactions; Jenkins's hindsight; Giles's notional contemporary opinions as imagined by the mature Jenkins in retrospect. (Giles 'would, for example, have dismissed the Huntercombes' dance as one of those formal occasions that he himself . . . found utterly unsympathetic.') It is a technique which takes us even further than Proust's prescription of reality as a relation between present and past, and further than the great narrational subtleties developed by Conrad.

What one gets from Giles, as interpreted for us by Jenkins, is generally a point of view touched by considerable malice, suspicion and disguised envy. There is an aggressiveness, a bloodymindedness, about him which is quite alien to Nicholas's own placid outlook on life; so, Uncle Giles supplies a tone which would not otherwise have been available. We discount most of what he says as springing from prejudice; Powell is telling us as much about Giles as about what Giles is describing. Yet, however partial his views, they do add to what we are shown; do free us from Jenkins's single-tone tolerance and blandness, and from the limitations which comparative youthfulness imposes on Nicholas. The contrasting estimates of Conyers provide an example. There is Giles's, hostile and backed by personal knowledge of Conyers's past; and Nicholas's, affable and dependent largely on hearsay.

This does not dispel the kind of uncertainties natural to a first-person narrative. We have Nicholas's point of view which, by and large, we accept; and Uncle Giles's which, by and large, we reject. 'Uncle Giles disapproved on principle of anyone who could afford to live in Belgrave Square', for instance, is an observation which does not suggest a particularly balanced outlook; he was in favour of Hitler, at least for a time, and felt there would be no Second World War. Nicholas will report much of what he sees with the fairly tolerant irony of a full participant in the life being discussed; to the same people, institutions and events Giles, also an insider, but by no means a full participant, will bring a much franker, much less controlled dislike. The truth about life cannot be set down by a novelist in simple, cut-and-dried terms. Giles represents some of the doubts.

His role is interesting when taken alongside reflections on character portrayal in fiction given to Jenkins in *TAW*. I have mentioned these briefly earlier but would like to go into the question more thoroughly now. Prejudice, he suggests, might be a very useful element in the novelist's equipment, enabling him to 'pin down unequivocally the otherwise elusive nature of what was of interest, discarding by its selective power the empty, unprofitable shell making up that side of Members untranslatable in terms of art.' (No, one cannot always be happy with the handling of metaphor in Powell.) Now, we are not entitled to attribute this view on his craft to Powell. It is Jenkins thinking to himself, and only about the way to deal with one man, Members, if he were to be used as basis for someone in a novel. (Powell could be satirising himself here; or employing a traditional trick for suggesting realism in a novel: referring to fiction as if it were some different species from what this particular fiction writer is engaged on.) And, in any case, the argument in favour of prejudice is put up as only one side of a debate; before this, Jenkins has suggested that prejudice should, in fact, be avoided if a lifelike picture of Members is to be attempted. The ground under us is uncertain. I think it fair to say, though, that some of Giles's judgements, biased, crabby and extreme as they may be, do provide a view which demands attention, and which extends the narrative; ensure a lifelike complexity and ambiguity which might not be possible in a more narrowly conceived first-person narrative.

Standard practice is for a first person narrator to use other voices to recount in conversation or some different form of statement sections of the story which the 'I' figure could not witness or know. *Wuthering Heights* rests on this convention; in *The Great Gatsby*, Michaelis, the coffee shop proprietor, tells the inquest of events leading up to Myrtle Wilson's death. Carraway having been elsewhere. Powell also does such in-filling, sometimes without much subtlety. Isobel Tolland gives an unbelievably thorough recapitulation of a telephone talk with her sister, Priscilla, in *CCR*. Sillery can be used to tell us that Pamela Widmerpool is unfaithful and, incidentally, to take a kind of Chorus role and, from his position as collector and font of information, inform us near the opening of *BDFAR* that Prince Theodoric is in exile and Sir Magnus dead; Mopsy Pontner can describe her sexual adventure with Glober on the table among after-dinner liqueur glasses in *TK*.

These are routine aids to the first person technique. The point is that Powell goes much further. He will frequently stop the 'story' in order to present through flashback a flight of hypothesis by Jenkins which is not so much essential linking material as a judgement or philosophy based on an entirely different life-style from his own. We have seen how it happens through Giles. Again, Jenkins will refer continually to Barnby's opinions on women and art. Since Barnby is an industrious womaniser and a successful painter, the third in family line, we are shown quite a different version of the world from Jenkins's own guarded treatment of love; and from his appreciative, but non-practising, attitude to art. Barnby's attitude to women, says Moreland, is direct, like his approach to work. 'If he sees a girl he likes all he has to do is to ask her to sleep with him.' Whereas Nicholas might dwell on the sentiment and sensuality of a love affair, Barnby, we are told, was more interested in aspects of 'action and power' in a relationship and would rarely admit to being in love. Nicholas may intellectualise about art, but Barnby will point out that few artists had much idea what 'branch of aesthetic' colleagues worked to. With a tough, practical, rather selfish outlook he corrects the central narrational view given by Nicholas.

We have seen that, for the sake of balance and change, Powell will summon up not simply a recollected opinion from Giles on some event or person (though there are plenty of those) but a completely notional view: what he might have thought given these or those circumstances. He will do the same with Mrs Erdleigh; and here, since we are dealing in clairvoyance, the elements of speculation and hypothesis are even more pronounced. 'If Mrs Erdleigh had been able to examine the astrological potentialities of that day she would perhaps have warned groups of lovers that the aspects were ominous,' Jenkins reflects in *TAW*, during a visit to Foppa's restaurant. Mrs Erdleigh is not present, any more than Giles was at the *ABM* scenes; an 'if' is buttressed by the shakiness of a 'perhaps'. All this is a ploy for allowing the mature Jenkins, the retrospective Jenkins, to hint at the separation he knows will come between himself and Jean, and between Barnby and Anne Stepney, who are also at Foppa's, without actually resorting to an equivalent of 'little did we know then that . . .', a crude, tease formula. It is a formula, just the same, and I imagine that some might find the contrived suspense sham and tiresome: Powell has already darkened the affair between Jean and Nicholas, and Barnby and Anne are due to separate before the end of *TAW*. It is a question of which convention we find more acceptable: an intrusively omniscient retrospective author; or an occasional flaggrantly concocted uncertainty. Powell, in fact, employs each method from time to time. Although there are moments when we hear both techniques creaking, the books keep moving pretty well. Forster, at least, would not ask for more.

It is worth spending a little time examining how Powell does make use of uncertainty and imprecision as a narrative aid. The aim, of course, is naturalness, realism: many of our impressions in life are fragmentary, partial, faulty, either at the moment of receiving them or in retrospect. Powell catches this quality. Jenkins will continually express doubts about his own reading of a situation or assessment of a character. This is akin to what Henry James calls in the Preface to *The Ambassadors* Strether's 'more or less groping knowledge' of things; these very uncertainties figuring, in James's opinion, among Strether's 'most interesting motions'. Where Jenkins requires to pass on others' impressions the possibility of mistake is greater still; tentativeness in the narrator's version becomes obligatory.

Powell gives Jenkins explicit, and far-reaching, reflections to make on the problem in *TK*. Pamela Widmerpool, has been discovered naked at night in Bagshaw's house, where Gwinnett was a lodger. Pamela was seen in what was probably the downstairs hall by Bagshaw's father, a short-sighted, elderly, retired insurance employee who had got out of bed to go to the lavatory. The description of this extraordinary event comes to us, then, from an original source of questionable reliability (Bagshaw we know to be older than Nicholas, who is in his fifties; so Bagshaw senior must be well on); via Bagshaw himself to Jenkins. 'To express how things turned out is to lean heavily on hearsay,' Jenkins explains. Or, to put things infinitely less categorically we have the thunderous double negatives of 'What Bagshaw himself later related was not necessarily untrue.' For a moment here Powell raises explicitly the whole question of how a novel is told, quoting Trapnel, as a matter of fact, though it could as easily have been Henry James or Percy Lubbock. Trapnel believes that every novel must come from 'a point of view'. Jenkins takes this thought further and says that the reader of a story, or the listener, must adjust his responses to the known or suspected prejudices of the teller. This is, of course, Powell commenting on his own method in *ADTTMOT*. If anything, Powell actually emphasises the unreliability of his narrator's perceptions; and the continual eruption of comment from Giles, Barnby, Sillery and others is to stress Jenkins's limitations and partialities. Overall, the effect is of a naturally fallible, many-faceted presentation of truth.

In the episode at Bagshaw's house there is, perhaps, another reason for the doubtfulness of the story. It is an incident which puts some strain on credence. Why should Pamela – even Pamela – be naked in one of the house's public thoroughfares? Gwinnett's bedroom would be another matter. How did she get in unobserved by the family? Why did Bagshaw senior do nothing about the apparition? There are answers to all these objections but, even for Bagshaw's house, where eccentricities were numerous, the situation and responses to it may seem far-fetched. By recognising from the outset this possibility of uneasiness in the reader, Powell attempts to forestall criticism. It is another example of an author using his technique – tolerably, I think – to get things two ways. He wants the drama and comedy of the incident; at the same time he knows he is pushing us a little hard and so has Jenkins say that the account is not put forward as what actually happened. The debate about truthfulness or not is conducted in weighty, solemn language ('On the other hand'; 'immediate assumption'; 'whatever he did or did not take in') which, although possessing a facetious undertone, is also intended to distract the reader into wondering whether the incident was mechanically possible, rather than whether it is acceptably likely as a piece of serious writing.

Perhaps this makes the device sound less an element in the craft of fiction than in its craftiness. There is a more reputable side to it, though. The arduous amassing of doubts around the night encounters in Bagshaw's house do, in fact, strengthen credibility. The tale is not over-neat; the rough edges suggest actuality, not contrivance. The seeming inconsistencies in the story are frankly put to us, and because the dramatic events of real life often have about them illogicalities or almost unbelievable chance or aspects that defy comprehension, we may feel that Bagshaw senior's story gives the feel of reality. Powell, in fact, draws attention to the technique, having Nicholas mention it as a reason for believing Bagshaw; and there is a built-in hope that the reader will take the message. It turns out that there are doubts over whether Pamela was actually seen in the downstairs hall or on a landing. 'Here again the narrative lacks absolute positiveness. In a sense, the truth of its essential features is almost strengthened by the comparative unimportance adjudged to exact locality.' The use of 'almost' is fascinating and gives in miniature the whole method. Part of the general atmosphere of manufactured imprecision, it is employed to achieve the opposite of its face meaning: if the claim is muted to 'almost strengthened', the effect will in fact be of considerably strengthening. Jenkins is saying that one does not fret too much about getting the circumstantial matters immaculately correct as long as the central truth is unquestionable.

These devices work, I think. We do accept the episode of the naked visitor as credible; a further strange event in a strange household, and involving in Pamela a central character whose habits have never been conventional and who has shown several signs of mental derangement in *BDFAR* and *TK*.

Elsewhere in *TK* we meet a different kind of displaced or assisted narrative. Pamela is once again near the centre of the incidents concerned. Towards the end of the book we hear of a complicated disturbance in the darkness of a London street involving several principal characters, Jenkins not being present. Finally, Glober hits Widmerpool, breaking his glasses.

Once more Powell works hard to create imprecision. His narrative is full of phrases like 'there is some corroboration,' 'Some doubt existed', 'uncertainty prevails'. Powell's method of bringing basic uncertainty here is not to make Jenkins's informant fallible through physical weakness, like Bagshaw's father, but to use a pair of informants, Moreland and Stevens, neither of whom, we learn, is especially truthful. Although they agree on the fundamentals of what occurred there are divergences. For instance, they differ over Polly Duport's reaction when Pamela, seeking to destroy the relationship between Polly and Glober, announces that Glober has been promiscuous and always takes a cutting of pubic hair from women he has made love to; there is a cushion stuffed with these mementoes. Stevens declares Polly to have been offended by this open statement; Moreland says she was calm.

The overriding purpose is once again credibility and control. By Powell's standards this is an extremely strident and violent scene. (We have already noticed, as a general change, that with the emergence of Pamela in the later books the degree of outspokenness mounts briskly in the novel.) Here, besides seeking to shock Polly, Pamela proclaims disgusting allegations about Widmerpool and utters chilling laughs. Mrs Erdleigh cries transcendental warnings. Widmerpool seizes Pamela (by the throat according to Stevens; perhaps by the arm, according to Moreland.) Stripling possibly grapples with Widmerpool. Then Glober strikes Widmerpool.

Such material is close to melodrama and perhaps to grotesque farce. The debate over whether it is 'true' serves the same purpose as in the incident at Bagshaw's house – to cut the ground from under those readers who might feel Powell has gone too far. On top of that, it enables Powell to bring the temperature of the sequence down from time to time. By introducing legalistic, often ponderous, discussion about what went on, he prevents extremes from running into excess. Take this impossibly arch and contorted sentence: 'Stevens, more down to earth in affecting to regret unachieved refinements of the boxing ring, seems also to have been a little shocked, a condition vacillatingly induced, in this case, by the age of the antagonists.'

It is probably not an accident that two of the most striking examples of what one might call second-hand narrative occur in *TK*, a book dominated by Pamela. She is unique to *ADTTMOT* in that she continually produces moments of lurid dramatic force. She carries her own purple patch with her. To accommodate such a character within the generally subdued tone of his novel Powell will distance her by deflected reports of her behaviour. He will blur her in doubts. It is a notably shrewd recognition of a problem, of a limitation, in fact; and a notably skilful way out. He knows himself to be not well equipped to deal with direct versions of forceful action and, in finding a means to compensate, has usefully extended the capabilities of the 'I' narrative.

Love, Sex and Marriage

Sexual passion is treated mainly from the point of view of an observer, not a participant, in *ADTTMOT*. Of course, the narrative method ensures this: Jenkins can tell us at first hand only about his own love affairs, and on those aspects of his life he tends to close up. It is not simply a matter of narrative method, though; or, to put it another way, Powell chose the method and with it the limitations: these include a distanced, ironic treatment of most characters' sexual behaviour, interest in the social effects of liaisons taking a higher priority with Powell than their emotional content.

Promiscuousness, infidelity and impermanence are at least as prevalent here as in *AM*. As in *AM*, too, the suggestion comes over strongly that adultery and infidelity are less habitual among the lower classes (despite a denial of this by Lovell in *TVOB*). There is an excellent piece of observation – also in *TVOB* – when Nicholas asks Kedward how Gwatkin's marriage – with a second-choice woman – has worked out. ' "Why what do you mean?" he said. "All right. Why should it not?" ' Although a few central established upper-class marriages seem to survive without the remotest menace – notably those of Jenkins and his father – they are small rocks of stability among acres of shifting sand. Such volatile relationships are basic to the music of time theme. Near the end of *TAW* Jenkins ponders the nature of sexual love, its changeability and the strange, interweaving threads it can produce. He is looking at a French picture postcard portrait of a couple.

> I had enacted such scenes with Jean: Templer with Mona: now Mona was enacting them with Quiggin: Barnby and Umfraville with Anne Stepney: Stringham with her sister Peggy: Peggy in the arms of her cousin: Uncle Giles, very probably, with Mrs Erdleigh: Mrs Erdleigh with Jimmy Stripling: Jimmy Stripling, if it came to that, with Jean: and Duport, too.

E

This is something other than the endless cycle in *La Ronde*: here, the possible liaisons are not so much endless as infinite. In *La Ronde* the affairs come full circle; in Powell ramifications go madly in all directions. What one has to ask, I think, is how far sex – love might be putting it high – is utilised in the novel simply as a means of keeping the patterns of the dance in a constant, interesting state of change.

It is not by any stretch a simple question. For one thing, we have learned from the pre-war books that Powell's view of sexual love – the happiness it can bring, its stability, its authenticity – is sceptical. We may accept this as an honest, entirely credible outlook. A superficial treatment of sexual relationships would then become the only one possible. There is a second matter. In fact, Powell does not treat all sexual liaisons in this way. The *Music of Time* contains one very thoroughly and sensitively drawn love affair not involving Nicholas – and love here is the right word – though it does come very late and inevitably raises some questions.

These are important reservations. We may say, though, that one result of Powell's fascination with the externals of fragile sexual relationships is that *ADTTMOT* offers a large number of women who, although of expertly differentiated personality, seem, as to their feelings, all made to similarly tough, shallow or even negative pattern. They move between men without showing what impels them; at least, what beyond mere acquisitiveness or whim. They travel through the narrative like a missile on a pin-ball machine, occasionally lighting up a man for a brief while, but almost immediately bouncing off to another, not quite at random, but only not quite. Lady Anne Stepney, for instance, drifts from Barnby to Umfraville, whom she marries, then turns to Sir Magnus Donners, from him to Templer, from Templer to Quiggin, and from Quiggin to a Free Frenchman. Baby Wentworth and Bijou Ardglass seem present only to shift from man to man, a touch of whorishness being more obvious here than with Lady Anne. Then there is Mildred Blaides who has allegedly worked hard at promiscuity on the French Riviera, and who is 'as hard as nails'. For a time she is engaged to Widmerpool. Gypsy Jones, the virulent Leftist, has an arduous sex life (including what seems to be the taking of Nicholas's virginity) but we see no evidence of love in her.

Powell's intention is clear. Lady Anne provides, through her liaisons, intriguing links for the dance between different classes, age groups and political philosophies. By implicating both Barnby and

Sir Magnus she contributes to one of the novel's primary themes, the relationship between the artist and the materialist, between the man of imagination and the man of will (though Barnby's will is pretty good, too). Mildred Blaides brings widely separated eras into startling contact: she had a short affair with Ted Jeavons during the First War, while Widmerpool was still a child, and seems in Jenkins's view to belong to that epoch 'by some natural right'; and she is sister-in-law of General Conyers, a friend of Jenkins's father, in his eighties at the time of her engagement to Widmerpool. By her association with Murtlock, Fiona Cutts in *HSH* breaks out from upper-class confines in what has become during our time a fairly routine abandonment of family standards.

What we are discovering is that sex produces some of the most bizarre effects in time's dance. Not many of us would dispute the relevance of such a thesis to real life. What we do not see in these women, though, is evidence of love or sexual excitement. Mona, Templer's brassy, tall, peroxide-blonde first wife, who has already had adventures before their marriage and then moves to Quiggin, from him to Erridge and finally to Jeff, an air vice-marshal, is another whose changeability obviously speaks a message about the strange dictates of sex, but who appears notably short of feelings: early on she is 'hard and untamed' and she grows 'firmer, more ruth-less'. Real life can, it is true, produce in all classes women whose emotions are taken up largely with themselves. The proportion in this novel seems high, all the same, and one occasionally suspects that the approach is flippant rather than sharply truthful; convenient as much as accurate.

Happily, there are other women in *ADTTMOT*, with comparable roles as sexual shuttles in preparing the fabric of time, whose feelings Powell is able to portray with remarkable sympathy and precision from Jenkins's external point of view. Few of these come anywhere near happiness or satisfaction; but one senses, and sometimes sees, the force of their yearning for love, and can understand how this need may drive them into apparently irrational or unusually promiscuous behaviour. We feel this, I think, about Jean Templer. Several of her love scenes with Jenkins are touchingly written. Although the dialogue still has something of that clipped, off-hand quality which characterises the love talk of *AM*, Powell is now able to do much more with it. In the exchanges between Jenkins and Jean towards the end of *TAW* we become aware of her vulnerability on the one side and, on the other, that reserve and capriciousness which mean Jenkins will never really possess her. Jean's mixed shame and belligerence when telling him of her affair with Stripling, also in *TAW*, gives a poignant insight of the clash between good taste (as Jenkins would judge it) and emotional susceptibility.

In much the same way, Powell can with astonishing economy suggest an intense, gentle, idiosyncratic emotional life for Matilda Wilson, another sexual rambler. She has an important function in demonstrating further steps in the dance to the music of time, something in the style of Lady Anne. An actress, Matilda moves in her love life between on the one hand the musicians Carolo and Moreland, and, on the other, Sir Magnus Donners, 'the Great Industrialist' as Moreland calls him, prime representative of money and status. She marries all three but ends with Donners, and we are meant to deduce that most women will direct themselves if at all possible towards men of power, wealth and undistinguished intellect. ('The minds of most women are unamusing, unoriginal, determinedly banal,' says Moreland. 'Matilda is not one of the exceptions. Is it surprising one is always cuckolded by middle-brows?') In *CCR* there is a sequence in which she first of all discloses to Jenkins that Moreland is her second husband; then almost shyly displays her admiration of Moreland's greatness; and lastly reveals her anxieties about the marriage because Moreland is engaged in an affair with Jenkins's sister-in-law, Priscilla. This conversation catches exactly the feelings of someone a little out of her depth in a sexual relationship, yet resourcefully trying to hang on. Melancholy and confusion will break through and show that although she refers to herself as 'an old tart' she, too, is searching like Fotheringham in *AM* for 'something beyond all this sex business'. Jenkins has said of the perpetually warring Macklinticks that it cannot be much fun to be married to either. Matilda replies by asking whether it is ever fun to be married to anyone. ' "I mean *married* to someone," said Matilda, speaking quite passionately. "Not to sleep with them, or talk to them, or go about with them. To be *married* to them. I have been married a couple of times and I sometimes begin to doubt it." ' Her establishment of a literary prize to commemorate Donners in *HSH* seems to show that, although she sold out, some sensitivity lingered on.

Despite Jean and Matilda, however, the treatment of women until quite late in *ADTTMOT* is for the most part strikingly external, sketchy. Then comes Pamela Flitton, by far the most ambitious piece of female characterisation attempted by Powell and the only woman projected with the thoroughness of the novel's chief men. So considerable is her impact on several of the later books that the reader is bound to wonder whether Powell consciously attempted to offset male dominance in the earlier volumes (it had been picked up in at least one review) and amend the impression that young women have only a passive or indirect function in furthering the dance proposition, through their influence on men. Another consideration is possible, although I must say at once that Powell himself will allow no weight to it. Pamela could not have been presented in her uninhibited, robust style before the *Lady Chatterley's Lover* 'censorship' case and the relaxation which followed. When I put this to Powell in conversation he said that such liberalising was not very important: the skilled novelist could suggest what he wished, regardless of prohibitions. In a sense, that is true. With someone like Pamela though, whose very outrageousness is basic to her personality, I am not convinced that the argument holds. It is important to our picture of her, for instance, that she should have been had by Duport in the sordid circumstances he describes and that he should use the crude, degrading language he does when recounting the episode to Nicholas. Before the *Lady Chatterley's Lover* case it could not have been put like that, or anything like that.

At any rate, Pamela emerges suddenly in *TMP* as a woman of exceptional sexual éclat and ruthlessness, the impression growing in the books that follow, until she dies in *TK*. As a means of contriving the extraordinary turns of time and the dance she is supreme. I mention elsewhere how she sets up a complicated and painful series of reversals involving Stringham, Widmerpool and Templer. Her affair – possibly too strong a word – with Milton Wisebite contains equally complicated links, though without the sombre elements, Milton being the nephew of Harrison F. Wisebite, who was Pamela's mother's second husband. Pamela has an affair with Odo Stevens who has had a previous relationship with Priscilla Tolland, Jenkins's sister-in-law. Jenkins has a link with Pamela via her Duport encounter, too, of course. Then, it is said that she was to have married Mountfichet, Lord Bridgnorth's eldest son, and Anne Stepney's brother: this would have raised more connections – though at a remove – with Templer again, through his affair with Anne; and with Umfraville, also through Anne, whom he marries for a short while. Further, Umfraville at one point claims to be Pamela's father (this being fairly convincingly disputed by Jenkins) and has certainly been her mother's lover.

Yet although her function as creator and tangler of relationships is so patent – even blatant – and although she shares with some of the other roving women a surface personality of startling toughness and consistent aggression, Pamela receives a degree of character development unequalled among other women. This is not to say that she is entirely convincing. The portrait is perhaps tinged with sentimentality and its psychology over-simple. But it has some very accomplished features. As a result, Pamela can hold some of our sympathy, and a good deal of our curiosity, even when she appears at her most pugnacious or sullen. She has enabled Powell to break away from what had become almost a female stereotype and create someone who is a complicated living woman with elaborate emotions. One feels blistering energy whenever she is present, combined with a sense that she is looking, hopelessly, for a fulfilling response somewhere in life, and chiefly through love. Her promiscuity is a symptom of despair, as is her marriage to Widmerpool. Her disgruntled restlessness recalls Prosper Bland in Powell's play *The Garden God* (London, 1971), who momentarily breaks down and bemoans the tedium of lechery.

Pamela's sexual mobility and general toughness of shell are well documented not long after our first meeting with her as an adult in *TMP*. (She has been fleetingly seen as a child bridesmaid at Stringham's wedding in *ABM*.) Now an A.T.S. driver, she has caused sexual complications among the Polish army contingent in Britain, probably ending with a major's appearance before a Court of Honour; has occasioned a fight between two R.A.F. officers, also resulting in court proceedings; has brought about a severe reprimand for a Naval paymaster lieutenant-commander; possibly provoked an unofficial strike at the docks; caused the transfer of a Treasury official – a married man with several children – who fell into indiscretions because of her. She may have tipped wine on the floor during a dinner with Howard Craggs, may even have poured it over his head, though he continues to pursue her. She seems to flirt with Prince Theodoric and Roddy Cutts, the Conservative M.P. Her reputation for unfaithfulness continues after her marriage to Widmerpool and gives Sillery great amusement in *BDFAR*. She is involved, seemingly or evidently, with a schoolboy; with Louis Glober, who possibly wanted to marry her; and with Gwinnett. She grabs Gwinnett by the testicles in the Basilica of St Mark's, is continually rude to Widmerpool, abuses Odo Stevens in public and seeks to disrupt the relationship of Polly Duport and Glober by proclaiming his allegedly odd sexual habits.

On the face of it then she is not merely of a pattern, but the most startling model produced from it. We are required to look deeper in her case, though. Her sexuality is part of the essence of her personality, not an incidental, and it is accounted for in both physiological and psychological terms. Lady Anne's and Gypsy Jones's promiscuity may be a credible feature of their liberated, militant character outlines. For Pamela it is integral.

Her culminating love affair with the novelist X. Trapnel is the most fully and sensitively documented in Powell's novels. She leaves Widmerpool for him. In fact, Nicholas visiting the two of them in Trapnel's ground-floor flat north of the canal at Maida Vale, lights suddenly on the idea that she had married Widmerpool only in order to run away with Trapnel. What he means by this, apparently, is not that she had in mind a move between two specific people; Trapnel had not come into her own or Widmerpool's life when they married. But she sought, according to Jenkins, 'anarchic extremities of feeling'. Widmerpool's way of life – high-level politics, reasonable prosperity and influence, social eminence – represented one sphere which she could move into; as she did, though, she intended, perhaps consciously, perhaps not, to seek its antithesis, and Trapnel's existence in seedy accommodation on very little money and with cachet only from literary accomplishment drew her to him. It would seem to be a taste for violent, possibly painful, change for its own sake. Nicholas explains it with St John Clarke's rather lurid phrase to 'try conclusions with the maelstrom'.

Now, obviously, a woman who moves between men and who represents 'extremes' has a part in proving the odd consequences of time; but Pamela's personality outstrips the role. Her love for Trapnel is not shallow. It begins, in *BDFAR*, with a disaster. Pamela behaves with resonant dislike and he aggravates her hostility by mistaking who she is. 'Girls like that are not in my line,' says Trapnel, bruised by the encounter. 'I don't care how smashing they look. I need a decent standard of manners.' That is asking a lot of Pamela.

And a little later on in the same book it is her very rudeness which seems to have helped win Trapnel over. By now he is 'mad about her'. He has listened to her berate on the telephone a man who had sent her a jar of pickled peaches as a present, which she had disliked. Whether that in itself captured him he is not sure, but captured he is. What is more, he has the idea that she likes him, but is afraid to show it. This is no conventional opening to a love affair, but in its uncertainties, hesitances and seeming contradictions, is entirely right for these characters. (It owes a little to Benedick and Beatrice, perhaps, but not over-much.) Pamela's aggressiveness does not disappear during her affair with Trapnel but becomes part of her love: in other words the standard female hardness of earlier books has been embodied as one part of a developed character; it no longer constitutes the bulk of the portrayal. As an accompaniment to leaving him, Pamela throws the manuscript of Trapnel's uncompleted novel, *Profiles in String*, into the canal, hoping he will find it on his way home from the pub and suffer. In Bagshaw's words, the novel was Trapnel's 'life work'. Yet Pamela claims in *TK* to have had a good motive: she says the book was unworthy of Trapnel and that he himself knew it should be destroyed. So convinced is she of her rightness that she threatens to destroy another of Trapnel's works, *A Commonplace Book*, if she considers that also poor. The belligerence, the apparent bitchiness – to use a term she moots herself – are, then, according to her claim, based on esteem. Whether or not we take this as wholly true, there is certainly more to her than shell. Throughout this affair one feels that these are people drawn together against likelihood who have made something genuine together; not permanent, obviously, but substantial. This relationship has its bearing on the message about artists and others, certainly: Pamela has moved from the supreme careerist, Widmerpool, to Trapnel, the most fully and convincingly drawn man of imagination and creative talent in *ADTTMOT*. But it is also a relationship which is admirably and complicatedly alive. Some lines Pamela speaks to Jenkins at the close of Chapter 4 of *BDFAR* catch the limitations of Powell's method when dealing with love affairs, yet also show its possibilities. Jenkins has gone to see Pamela and Trapnel in their flat in Maida Vale. At the end of the visit, Pamela makes him a formal, even ladylike, goodbye. Then, before he can reply, she says:

'Bugger off – I want to be alone with X.' The intensity of her emotions cannot be given from outside, and we cannot be present at what happens when Nicholas leaves; but her strength of feeling is marvellously, economically, captured in that abrupt break from a style of speech unnatural to her (i.e. polite) to the urgent, crude frank plea of those final words. It is an apparent deflation used, in fact, to give the moment stature.

Powell offers physiological explanation for Pamela's behaviour. She suffers from a form of nymphomania. Trapnel's description of her love-making in *BDFAR* is to be taken as authentic and is full of sadness and pain. 'It's when you have her. She wants it all the time, yet doesn't want it. She goes rigid like a corpse. Every grind's a nightmare. It's all the time and always the same.' Widmerpool, who has his own troubles, apparently gives up any attempt at sexual relations with her.

I am not sure that everything in Pamela's dossier sounds completely right. Perhaps the characterisation owes something to that of the tart with a heart of gold; perhaps, too, the resounding paradox of the woman who endlessly wants sex but does not really want it is better known to novelists than to doctors. It does not greatly matter. Intimidating, poignant, honest, Pamela is a fine creation, particularly in *BDFAR* (matters grow a little strained in *TK*). The relationship with Trapnel is treated like a real love affair, not as a symbolic, intriguing, passionless, jokey coupling. And yet it is symbolic and intriguing all the same.

Most other love affairs or marriages in *ADTTMOT* also bring pain and disruption, sometimes to a shattering, even fatal, degree: the Maclinticks, the Morelands, the Lovells, the Widmerpools, the Peter Templers. Against them, the Jeavonses, the Conyerses, Nicholas's parents, Jean Templer and Carlos Flores, provide rare moments of concord (and one has to note that a good number of these are past their physical best: stability is what you decline into). What is more, not all even of these have impeccable sexual records: Lovell says Ted Jeavons brought a tart home, though Nicholas is sceptical; Jean has been around; Conyers was a womaniser.

Where views on marriage and love are explicitly given – quite often – the tone is generally brittle or disillusioned. Conyers thinks marriage resembles war, 'a terrible and passionate drama'. Moreland has a theory about 'the attraction exercised over women by men to whom they can safely feel complete superiority'. Umfraville holds, in a deeply wry assessment, that 'The nearest some women get to being faithful to their husband is making it unpleasant for their lover.'

Settled marriages are not the stuff of which novels are easily made. One feels at times that Powell's dance thesis – the duty to work changes – limits what he can say. The chaste are virtually disenfranchised. And one comes back at the conclusion of this look at sex and marriage to a point of view which is bound to recur in any examination of Powell's work. It might be easier to accept the sombre opinion of sexual relationships if it were consistently followed. In fact it is quite startlingly discarded where Nicholas's own romance – not an extravagant term – with Isobel is concerned. 'Would it be too explicit, too exaggerated, to say that when I set eyes on Isobel Tolland, I knew at once that I should marry her?' Nicholas asks this in *ALM*. Although disarmingly phrased this is still a statement of love at first sight; magical *rapport* where, for almost everyone else, calculation, chance, curiosity and lust are the cause of union. Thereafter we hear so little of her, let alone actually encounter her, that the discretion takes on a kind of flamboyance. A reader sees so many love affairs on the rocks that he craves information about this nominally central one which so effortlessly keeps afloat.

Perhaps one should recognise that sexual passion in *ADTTMOT* is treated with something other than absolute realism. In Powell's view, desire – for someone, for status, for the quiet domestic life, for change – transforms people; so sharpens and emphasises this one impulse that they become for that time single-dimensional characters, swift-moving counters on a board. These movements themselves may then be fascinating and exciting to watch; the causes, though, are secondary, banal, scarcely worth talking about: simply what the dice dictate.

There will be effective departures from this method, as with Pamela above all. And the method itself is generally all it needs to be in a work of irony, more concerned with social patterns than with feelings. When, though, as in Nicholas's and Isobel's case, a love affair is ostentatiously exempted that irony; and when this particular pair of counters do not speed separately around the board but settle together snugly in their square, we are bound to ask why this should be.

The Volumes in Sequence:

A Question of Upbringing

AQOU circles, seeming to leave Nicholas pretty well where he started and this helps bring an almost emphatic shapeliness to the book. In the first chapter, Nicholas's Uncle Giles, nosy, aggressive, a little shady, calls on him at school to discuss family business, centred on the Trust from which Giles draws an income. Nicholas is embarrassed and inconvenienced by the visit. Then, as an undergraduate, near the end of the volume, he meets Giles again, this time in a London restaurant: once more the atmosphere lacks conviviality, once more the conversation is the Trust. Giles still treats Nicholas as something of a child, expecting him to drop everything and dash to London when called.

Between these two cheerless meetings, Nicholas has observed vivid changes in others and believes that 'a new epoch' is starting for himself. In those closing moments, though, as he eats with Giles, *faute de mieux*, at the Trouville, we are most conscious of a similarity between the young man and the senior schoolboy, as we are meant to be. Like Salinger in *The Catcher in the Rye*, Powell has posted his hero to a transit camp: that painful, confusing, absurd, anxious and, for some, protracted waiting time between late youth and full adulthood. But whereas Holden Caulfield is precocious, Nicholas is in several senses, and above all the sexual, one of life's late developers. His two school friends, Templer and Stringham – both slightly older, it is true – have left him behind. Whatever one may make of Nicholas during later stages of the dance, for most of *AQOU* he remains very much a wallflower. Templer's adventures with women began while he was still at school, making both Nicholas and Stringham feel backward. On a visit to Templer's family home Nicholas spots signs of an advanced relationship between Peter and Lady McReith. Then, at almost the end of *AQOU*, it is Stringham's behaviour over a woman which makes Nicholas aware that time has turned a corner. Stringham is thinking about marriage to Lady Peggy Stepney and cuts an appointment with Nicholas on the chance of seeing her at a party, a discourtesy marking for Nicholas 'the final remnant of life at school'. As if to contradict these signs of change he turns to Giles again; but we are to take it that, while things may look the same, essentials have begun to alter: the surface seems as ever but in fact a great deal of water has gone under the bridge. Gradualism, tentativeness and occasional reversals attend Nicholas's development in a fashion which seems exactly right.

Although he does not get too far in this volume Nicholas reveals a fair amount of his character. Innocence sets him apart. Apartness – or detachment, non-involvement, distance – attend him throughout the series, of course. Innocence fades. Or perhaps it changes nature: the mystification, shock, even awe at worldliness will gradually evaporate in the books which follow *AQOU*: naïveté is no good to an ironic narrator. The *TLS* review (16 February 1951) saw the process already at work in *AQOU* and found the theme of the volume to be 'the passing of youthful preoccupations and their replacement by the corrupt values of the adult world'.

Yet, although Nicholas comes to see and understand what goes on he remains personally insulated from much of what is suspect. Throughout the novel he avoids the worst features of ambition, the jockeying, arrogance and boring earnestness; he steers clear of bogus political commitment which, in this work, means almost all political commitment; and – breathtaking, this – he stays faithful to his wife. Ambition, political excess and adultery are three principal frailties covered in *ADTTMOT*, with the first two treated as desperately seedy matters, evil or fatuous or a combination, and likely to produce those doctrinaire figures who, as Arthur Mizener points out in *The Sense of Life in the Modern Novel* (Boston, 1964) 'are men so egotistical as to be incapable of enough human experience to engage their feelings'. The third, adultery, is rampant, recurrent, pervasive. In this work Powell has gone a fair way towards creating that most difficult of qualities to render bearable in fiction, goodness. The beginnings appear in *AQOU*; and – remarkably – the success will be maintained over twelve volumes. Nicholas is too clear-sighted, human and humane to interest himself in career progress to the point where natural feelings and understanding are subjugated; too sane, balanced and agnostic to be taken in by political modes; and, in a set where infidelity is standard, too steady, considerate and – risking a piety – too honourable for womanising.

I cannot say that this adherence to virtue of so many sorts will always be managed with complete skill. Now and then it is hard to swallow Nicholas's inflexible political temperateness and unwavering post-marital purity. There can seem, too, a degree of passivity about his goodness – a matter of not dropping into the Pit rather than of mounting up to heaven – which makes one think more of gaps in his personality than strengths. All the same, on the platform of innocence and enlightened isolationism established for Nicholas in *AQOU*, Powell will present to us in the series a character whose control, acuteness, consistency, sensitivity, tolerance and wit are immensely attractive and far more often credible than not. Sentimentality does get a look in, but only that. This is as fine a portrait of the upright man in a dark, flippant grab-all world as we are likely to meet in modern fiction.

I have spoken of balance and control and I would like to clarify them a little by a few examples. In *AQOU* those who make the heaviest weather of life get the briskest mockery. We see Widmerpool striving to improve his games status with solitary, hopeless training runs, the kind of self-punishing effort which will kill him in *HSH*. Le Bas, Nicholas's housemaster in *AQOU*, laboriously and ridiculously seeks first to destroy Nicholas's story that it was Uncle Giles, not himself or Stringham, who had smoked in their room; then painstakingly to dismantle Templer's excuse that his late return to school was caused by weaknesses in the train service, not his own misbehaviour. In contrast to these, Nicholas almost never gets into a sweat, not in *AQOU* or later. Now certainly this easy-going coolness is a traditional public school mannerism (though missing, apparently, in some pupils and members of the staff): a cliché indeed. Nicholas's contempt for the sort of push and plod represented by Widmerpool – not just in roadwork but also in the gravity with which immediately after leaving school he maps his career – derives from admiration for an elegant casualness possible only to the well-off insider. And although much of *ADTTMOT* ostensibly shows Nicholas to be wrong in his judgement of Widmerpool (*AQOU* refers to Nicholas's 'crude' and 'inadequate' view) the tone of the books, in fact, always upholds such privileged opinions. We are to regard Nicholas as pretty good and Widmerpool as pretty unspeakable long before he is revealed as a monster.

But Nicholas's sanity goes much further than old-school-tie sang-froid: it is genuine poise, not pose, a sense of proportion achieved more from intelligence, artistic sensibility and good-heartedness than from the blasé instincts of a clique, though he has some of those. This sense of proportion will keep him intact when other members of his group fall disastrously. Throughout the *Music of Time* it will save him from excess and from emotional aridity.

Interestingly, in *AQOU* Nicholas does drop his poise once and, under pressure, steps not too happily out of character. After school and before university he goes to learn French with the Leroys, friends of his father, at La Grenadière, a house in Touraine. It is here that Widmerpool, also a guest, reproaches Nicholas for having no properly serious career plans. Nicholas finds himself attracted to Suzette, a niece of the Leroys, but does little about this until, near the end of his stay in France, he decides that he should adopt some sort of attitude to life, Widmerpool's remarks having helped unsettle him. He plans to make a love declaration to Suzette on his day of departure and, in this admittedly imperfect fashion, achieve an advance from his 'state of chronic inaction', a phrase which some might wish to use against Jenkins over the whole of *ADTTMOT*. In a magnificent comic scene he gets things wrong, though, a little after the style of Mr Moddle in *Martin Chuzzlewit* who, in his excitement, 'kissed Miss Pecksniff's snuffers, in the passage, when she went upstairs to bed: meaning to have kissed her hand but missing it.' Nicholas makes a larger mistake. He delivers the avowal prepared for Suzette to another woman. A Madame Dubuisson has borrowed Suzette's straw hat and, seeing her from behind, Nicholas uses it to make the wrong identification. Having once begun his steamy declaration he feels compelled to go on, although immediately aware that he has blundered, and tells Madame Dubuisson that she has brought romance to his stay. Although only recently married she accepts this statement with aplomb, and asks Nicholas to send her a picture of Buckingham Palace. Not often in the books is he on the receiving end of the irony. Here, it is used to underline an appealing clumsiness, which comes from innocence; but also to indicate that Nicholas has his own pace and style and would be better off sticking to them.

It is, of course, the ambiguous advance of Nicholas – an impression of lingering childhood seen against signs of emergence as an adult – which makes *AQOU* seem at the same time symmetrical yet about to move into an enormous future: important attributes in a book which must be able to stand alone as well as provide the start to a sequence. (Incidentally, the *TLS* reviewer apparently did not know the kind of work Powell had in mind but pointed to a clue that 'seems to promise a sequel'.) This first volume illustrates well the high skill with which Powell can give a book remarkable solidity of structure – a sense of entity and completeness – while suggesting that all has not been said.

To take first the aids to solidity: I have mentioned already the circular movement involving Nicholas and Giles. This taste for strongly patterned repetition is also seen elsewhere in *AQOU*. At school, near the beginning, Nicholas and his friends are variously inconvenienced by Le Bas, not just about alleged smoking and lateness. Then, not far from the book's end, Le Bas calls on Nicholas at his university rooms. Although Nicholas reflects that, until this reappearance, Le Bas had passed completely from his mind, they soon begin to reminisce about school and a fragment of the old atmosphere is recreated; Nicholas thinks about a celebrated practical joke played on Le Bas by Stringham. For a moment it is as if there has been no development, another circle, another topping and tailing, with Le Bas exercising his school habit of climbing on to the fender.

Immediately afterwards, though, Nicholas meets Stringham – on the occasion when Stringham tells him he must break an appointment. Nicholas mentions the encounter with Le Bas. Stringham can only just recall him and the famous practical joke. 'I began to realise that considerable changes had been taking place', Nicholas reflects. Without being mechanical or obsessed with point counter-point, *AQOU* gains a powerful sense of cohesion through these echoes; plus a sense of development, since the echoes cannot recreate the past, cannot even be heard by someone like Stringham.

A similar tendency towards paired episodes balancing each other, amending each other, shows in Nicholas's visits to the Stringham and Templer homes. Placed strategically close to each other, these sections enable Powell to exercise one of his chief accomplishments, the portrayal of English social distinction, and particularly those fine but crucial differences between levels of the upper class. Nobody would quarrel with V. S. Pritchett's words in the *NS&N* review of *ABM* (28 June 1952): 'Mr. Powell's social curiosity has been his growing point.' Stringham's home near Berkeley Square has about it the feel of 'old money', of some lineage, since Stringham's mother, now Mrs Foxe, was once married to Lord Warrington. At the Templers' on the other hand business is the thing. Their house is new and they are *nouveaux*. Significantly, a comic sequence set at the

Templers' centres on what seems likely to be a deeply unsuccessful business project involving one of Templer Senior's colleagues, Sunny Farebrother: a machine for turning white collars so they can be used twice which, in practice, mashes them.

Powell's success in establishing this sense of well-organised unity allows him to include simultaneously some elements of the long-distance, multi-book novel, the *roman fleuve*. One of the most obvious examples happens to be in the character of Sunny Farebrother. Although he may be important to the complex picture of social backgrounds required by Powell, one might feel that Farebrother is developed here to a degree quite out of proportion to his usefulness, his immediate usefulness, that is. He will return. On a smaller scale, the same must be said about Miss Weedon, whom Nicholas meets at the Foxes'. Similarly, Nicholas's relationship with Jean Templer never reaches beyond a warm thought or two in *AQOU*: this chimes well enough with Nicholas's indeterminate sexual development, but also signals a fuller relationship later.

In other words, *AQOU* is put together with such architectural finesse that apparently tentative, imperfectly resolved matters can be comfortably accommodated and cause the reader no unease. We can see functioning within the comparatively small scope of the single volume Powell's theory of pattern and system in life, while sensing at the same time that these tendencies will show themselves over the full sequence.

A Buyer's Market

It would be nearly true to say of this book that when Nicholas is not at a party he is at a dance. Socialising has him in thrall. Sizeable risks are involved for Powell: that the volume will seem a gossip column *augmenté*, preoccupied with drones and boulevardiers and treating them with at least some respect; and that he will curtail the activities of his characters to what is feasible during evening pleasure-mongering at various levels of English society, and not all that various. One does, I think, feel uncomfortable on finishing this book: life seems to have been reduced to lubricated chit-chat and unepic crises of manners. Style can touch its most self-indulgent: facetiousness out on the town. In his *NS&N* review (28 June 1952) V. S. Pritchett praised the scene where Barbara Goring covers Widmerpool in sugar for the 'brutal thoroughness' of the prose; but this is a standard technique of waggery.

Those who write about manners do tend to work a very confined area: thus Jane Austen could find next to no space for the huge contemporary wars. Like Jane Austen Powell confines himself rigorously to what he knows and except, as it happens, in the war novels, this will largely exclude life below the level of the upper middle class. Largely but not entirely: throughout *ADTTMOT* the arts give Nicholas a link with people of indeterminate class; Mr Deacon in this volume, for instance, and via him Gypsy Jones (designated middle-class by Barnby, it is true, her father being a schoolmaster); there is Quiggin; elsewhere we meet Trapnel, the novelist, son of a jockey, and several musicians of unknown background. In *HSH* we will move further still, but into the world of dropouts where class loses much relevance. Powell knows the upper classes because he has lived among them; creativity and its hangers-on because he has been engaged in it; soldiering because he has been engaged in that. Combined, these make up his literary patch. He knows at first hand about marriage and the family, too, but has apparently taken a decision based on tact, or on a writer's scepticism about the chance of getting these things on to paper properly, to ration such material. He knows also about work and we can find a fair amount to do with business, publishing, journalism and the City in *ADTTMOT*. But although work can be fascinating in a novel, parties are inclined to be even more fascinating and so get precedence. One does not need to go all the way with the Marxist demand for 'relevance' in the arts – mocked frequently, effectively and justifiably in the novel through figures like Tokenhouse and Guggenbühl – to regret now and then that the sequence gives little sense of lives being carried on somewhere by people to whom the words 'dinner party' would be a puzzle. Anthony Burgess asks in *The Novel Now* (London, 1967): 'Can the author really justify the vastness of the plan in the face of such smallness of scope?'

Yet, while *ABM* certainly gives an idea of why that question can be asked, it also provides a kind of answer: not a wholly satisfactory kind, but substantial. Powell's point, of course, is that this footloose and well-heeled class live under threat, and deserve to. After all, in *ABM* a party at the house of Mrs Andriadis, friend of Stringham and, by repute, once mistress of royalty, is devastated by Mr Deacon and his subversive newspapers, *War Never Pays!* He and his companion, Gypsy Jones, bring with them the powerful smell of social unrest. Mrs Andriadis, we may take it, in view of her name, reputation and Cockney accent, is herself not out of the top drawer; her parties, though fun, are a bit mixed. After a dinner at the Walpole-Wilsons' and a ball at the Huntercombes', which occupy most of the first long chapter of *ABM*, her gathering represents a comedown. Gypsy and Mr Deacon speed the slide. About to leave in a huff after a row with Max Pilgrim, the entertainer, Mr Deacon drops his bundle of newspapers, which are carried and spread by a draught through the hall of Mrs Andriadis's house, 'even up to the threshold of the room beyond'. There follows a burst of 'wild, African laughter' from a watching Negro who, until this, has been a pinnacle of dignity. Infuriated by the mess and the noise Mrs Andriadis orders Deacon out. I know – from correspondence – that Powell is not always happy with symbolic interpretations of his work; but when bolshy literature is battering at the doors of Hill Street and black laughter explodes in the hall some overtones have to be heard.

What one has in *ABM*, and elsewhere in *ADTTMOT*, is a small group of characters who do represent some part of that larger, rougher, poorer world outside. They are certainly not the man or woman, in the street. Quiggin may come from a proletarian home (disputed by Brightman, a don), but is soon a formidable literary figure. Gypsy lives deep in politics and will go deeper and grow more important as the series develops. Individual, even freakish, characters they represent at the same time some force, some movement, some historical process, to take a Marxist term. Exactly which aspects of Leftism are portrayed might be hard to define, but we can say that these people are anti-upper-class and populist, at least in theory, at most in theory for some of them. In other words, the outside world has a foot in the door and has begun shoving. We may not be able to see its face too clearly but we can feel the pressure, even in such a good-time-Charlie book as *ABM*. We are to sense that lined up behind rococo leaders like Quiggin and Gypsy are those classes we see little of in *ADTTMOT*; lined up, it is true, as an idea, rather than as people, notion not nation. That could be how someone of Nicholas' background would regard the working class, perhaps: short of definition except when servants, troops or clownish labourers. We might wish that he could see more clearly and journey further and more often off the socialite map. Powell would then have been in strange country, though, and the books could have become inaccurate and dull.

On this map the social gatherings of *ABM* – and of *AQOU* – are code tints to indicate important shadings of class; they mark out most of the territory to be covered in the series. Distinguished titles, diplomats, and a guardee figure in the opening gatherings; then we move to Mrs Andriadis's rented house where cosmopolitanism has set in; we transfer briefly to a house-party at the country home of the Walpole-Wilsons, Hinton Hoo, before a visit to that supremely bourgeois figure, Sir Magnus Donners at Stourwater (we have met him already at the Hill Street party), though he is said to have gone 'to some quite decent school' and his father may have been knighted 'for what that's worth'. Near the end, in a distinct social drop, comes the death of Mr Deacon, who falls while on his way to complain about the lavatories at the Bronze Monkey, a disreputable night-club closed down shortly afterwards by the police, where he had been holding his birthday party. Now and then in *ABM* one feels that the title of John Wain's novel, *Hurry On Down*, might have served, although here it is the background, not the hero, which slips. A small dinner party at Widmerpool's mother's closes the book and restores decorum if not éclat.

ABM says clearly enough that society is shaky and that the agents of disruption are already well placed. The endless dining out and parties signify decadence, as parties do in *AM*. One thinks of Archie Gilbert, who appears at the Walpole-Wilson dinner party. His life seemed 'irrevocably concentrated on "debutante dances" ' and he conducted such a tirelessly social existence that he was 'unthinkable in everyday clothes'. Yet something happens – something small and not important, to do with a taxi fare – which makes Nicholas wonder suddenly whether in fact Archie 'danced his life away through the ball-rooms of London in the unshakable conviction that the whole thing was a sham.' It is an affectionate portrait, and a satirical one, and the final observation by Nicholas makes sure we see it in the way Powell wants. As in *AM* we face the difficulty, though, that novelists can depict a deficiency or fault over-thoroughly. In growing impatient with these seekers after diversion we respond as *ABM* intends, but perhaps we respond more than it intends. We might feel that too much goes into knocking down this puff-ball edifice.

For the most part, then, social standards drift downwards in this volume, a fairly simple movement. Nicholas's development here is also fairly simple, in contrast to the tentativeness of *AQOU*. Sexually it starts with an unsatisfactory, idealised love for Barbara Goring, shifts to an unresolved renewal of connection with Jean Templer, and culminates – a purple word in the subfusc circumstances – in sex with Gypsy: disappointing as the act turns out for Nicholas, it does justify his belief that life had now begun in earnest. No circular construction here. Nicholas is on his way, and the way seems likely to be another slide, 'careering uncontrollably down the slippery avenues of eternity': not quite the same as the dance image, with its sense of measure and order.

Few central figures in fiction can have spent as much of their early life as Nicholas does looking upon clean pairs of heels. Templer, Stringham and now Barnby, the womanising artist, make his sexual efforts seem juvenile; intelligent people are beginning to esteem Widmerpool's business ability, although Nicholas found him 'almost too grotesque to take seriously' at school; and now Quiggin and Mark Members, contemporaries of Nicholas at university, have begun to make literary careers for themselves, leading Nicholas to reflect wistfully about their success. The standard expectations of fiction, though, probably cause the reader to wonder whether, in these various races, Nicholas might be the tortoise who wins by staying power. (I have to guess here, since it is impossible to recall first feelings on reading *ABM*, before knowledge of the sequels.) Powell seems to be building for Nicholas that unexciting but estimable quality of steadiness: he may not get the girls too easily when young, but his final choice will be lasting; Widmerpool will come terrible croppers; and, of the talented literary pair, Quiggin at least will never quite live up to his promise (manuscripts are burned by him, we hear, for not reaching his rigorous standards) and ultimately tumbles as low as the boardroom. Powell interests himself deeply in dud potential: Bill Truscott's abilities seemed to guarantee whatever career he wanted, but success somehow never quite turns up; even Members apparently fails to land his expected first-class degree.

Against this flashy competition Nicholas offers durability. Taken over the whole of *ADTTMOT* his qualities provide the deepest comment of all on the world of gloss, inconsistency and inconstancy. They are not scintillating attributes and, with their emphasis on plod and discretion, might even look a little square. They work, though. They are quietly solid. And, most important, they do not corrupt, and do not poison feelings and natural responses.

But plod, as applied to Nicholas, is a different commodity from that shown by Widmerpool in these opening books, though Widmerpool is certainly a believer in effort. At our first sight of him in *AQOU* he is 'hobbling unevenly, though with determination' on his training run; and in *ABM* he once more comes trailing clouds of gaucherie and earnestness while settling into a career. To a degree he and Nicholas are comparable in that neither is quite at home in the social group he inhabits: it is the differing reasons which are crucial. In Widmerpool's case it is awkwardness, ugliness (Rosie Manasch calls him 'the Frog Footman') and a not too brilliant lineage: his father sold liquid manure. Widmerpool compensates for handicaps by hard work and gravity. Nicholas, on the other hand, is set apart by his intelligence, wit and insight, though we also get the impression that his family are nothing like as rich as many of the people he associates with. Nicholas has charm and casualness where Widmerpool is painstaking, is, in Nicholas's words an 'embodiment of thankless labour and unsatisfied ambition'. In these early books this is Widmerpool's prime fault; not simply to work hard but to be spotted working hard: a flaw only of manners, really, and, as Nicholas comes to realise, not necessarily a failing at all in adult life, though poor form at school. (One thinks of Cyril Connolly's description of candle-lit study under the bedclothes at Eton in *Enemies of Promise* (London, 1938)).

Although we see the corrections to Nicholas's estimate of Widmerpool, we feel from the way he is guyed that Powell allows considerable weight to Nicholas's instinctive social grace and unexceptionable, though also unspectacular, family. In short, snobbery colours the contrast between Nicholas and Widmerpool at this stage. Widmerpool gets it in the neck for being pushing; Nicholas has no need to strive, not simply on account of being an insider, but because his chosen field, novel writing, requires no social self-assertiveness. In *ABM* that career is not under way and he reflects on how he took it for granted that pleasure should assume precedence over work. Explicitly these early books will censure him for this attitude. Implicitly, and emphatically, they will endorse his casualness by portraying Widmerpool's ostentatious and aggressive devotion to advancement as comically vulgar. They are, of course. In the later books, though, we will see Widmerpool's lack of polish transformed into something else: poor manners become evil morals. The best comedy of manners does deepen in this way. But in one sense it is a worrying equation which makes social ineptitude and lowish family signify latent delinquency. My own ultimate reservation about the drawing of Widmerpool – in so many ways superb – arises I think from something akin to my unhappiness over *ABM*: Powell's wish to satirise society while at the same time appearing drawn to it, and inclined to endorse some of its basic values, perhaps unconsciously. Bad form, it is suggested, means bad fibre. In a *NS&N* review of 28 May 1955 Richard Lister wondered whether Powell was 'aware that the world he describes is as nasty as it is'. This notice was for *TAW*, but the question applies here. Nicholas has both social flair and moral depth. One accepts this characterisation and also accepts that natural reliable goodness will do well at any level. What remains troublesome is the thesis that an inability to win popularity at Eton, as revealed in Widmerpool, could point to an adult life of sexual perversion, disregard for human life, political opportunism and a final collapse into lunatic self-abasement.

The Acceptance World

Overtones sound louder still in *TAW* and the political symbolism
grows quite emphatic. Even here, though, one can see why Powell
might feel impatient with such a reading. There is a portrait of Peter
Templer in this volume which it would be crass to regard only as
'standing for' something, or representing some contemporary type.
When complexity lights up a character – as it does so vividly for
Templer at the Ritz – we have a person, not a proposition. As one
of the most expert creators of upper-class males writing in this
century Powell must find it baffling to see the amount of critical
space given to the social and political background of his books – *mea
culpa* – when, against the job of getting blood and feelings into a
figment, such documentary matter provides small difficulty. Criticism
finds it easier to spot themes, ideas, values in a novel than those
apparently simple but in fact bewilderingly elusive qualities which
make a character stand up out of the printer's ink; (and, come to
that, those which make effective narrative). Forster has something
about this in *Aspects Of The Novel*; he suspects the commentator
who, instead of concentrating on what the author has written, 'would
rather relate a book to the history of its time, to events in the life of
the author, to the events it describes, above all to some tendency.'
In Powell's work there are many moments when questions of class,
milieu, society seem of only incidental importance, or none. It is
this which makes him a novelist worth talking about, not merely
his recording of a period. Possibly to argue this point from the portrait of Templer is slightly unfair since Nicholas tells us that
Templer, like Uncle Giles, resisted classification at any social level
in case 'mobility of action' were restricted. There are, though, any
number of comparably brilliant pieces of characterisation where the
class label might be more firmly fixed, and where it looks equally
subordinate to individuality and human vigour.

Templer, then is a contradictory, coherent mixture of charm, melancholy, business energy and well-suppressed intellect; although class-conscious he lacks social ambition; both bohemianism and smartness offend him. An admirable lavishness attends such character construction, a fine extravagance which may be special to the *roman fleuve*. In this kind of multi-volume work there need be no immediate relation between character and narrative; no requirement exists that everything should visibly contribute to the line and structure of one book. When line and structure have to be maintained over twelve volumes we cannot know at any particular point what might finally turn out important. Powell's most successful people have a fulness not altogether taken up in behaviour. These figures live not so much within one pair of covers – though they do that – but are tangible enough, and have the psychological luggage, to make the trip from volume to volume. Possibly this very success makes for problems in later books: newly created characters, like Murtlock, Tokenhouse, Glober, no matter how vivid by customary single-volume standards, can look rather pale and slight. To return to Templer in *TAW*: obviously ideological generalisations can be made from the portrait. They are far from his essence.

All the same, *TAW* is a very political book, one of the most briskly and effectively satiric about the Left. We are bound to see some of the characters as butts rather than developed personalities. Powell, like many other novelists, writes about two kinds of characters. There are those whose drifting, up-and-down, complicated lives may seem to us conceivable for real people: Templer is one, Nicholas, particularly in this book, another. Against such figures are those who carry more representative status than genuine individuality: who do, in fact, 'stand for' something. A good deal of the political attack here is pointed at St John Clarke, an ageing, once popular bad novelist, and at J. G. Quiggin, the Left Wing critic. St John Clarke, although previously very much a salon figure, avid for upper-class acceptance, turns Marxist. As symptom – or part cause – he dismisses his secretary Mark Members and engages Quiggin instead. The bitterness and bitchiness between Members and Quiggin over this change are given with delightful edge: Members huffily recounting to Nicholas how 'St J.' had shifted suddenly from advocacy of the 'ivory tower' to concern for 'the European Situation'. Members bemoans the emergence in St John Clarke's vocabulary of the word 'bourgeois' as an overall term of abuse, eventually applied by him even to Cézanne. Powell allots St John Clarke his symbolic role specifically enough, in fact: 'Looking back afterwards, the dismissal of Members might almost be regarded as a landmark in the general disintegration of society in its traditional form.' (Participles are handled without pedantry in *ADTTMOT*.) According to Alan Brownjohn's profile of Powell in *The New Review*, September 1974, Powell now regrets the conservatism in this paragraph; but since the theme is so strong implicitly, such second thoughts can only be to do with spelling it out. In Nicholas's view, recklessness of the kind shown by St John Clarke 'illustrates the mixture of self-assurance and ennui' which brought about social collapse.

Quiggin, too, portends. His arrival at the Ritz in leather coat and grey sweater, followed later by the defection to him of Templer's wife, Mona, clearly carry an ideological implication or two. Revolution has marched into the haunts of the rich, touched the hearts of the pampered. True, it does take something from these moments of parable that Quiggin should be so brazenly charlatan: Powell is too skilled and civilised to confront us with a plain 'message' and, in any case, has another allegorical purpose for the character of Quiggin.

Or, to come to the point about him and St John Clarke, should the word be caricature? Quiggin is, by some accounts, at least, the talented working-class boy who has been driven, part by upbringing (a question of, as it were), part by fashion, part by intellectual conviction, to Marxism. At the same time, he is on the make: a sort of political Zouch. These two elements make up the sum of his personality, and we wait to see which side will triumph. covetousness or idealism, knowing pretty well the way things will go. As caricatures often do, he flashes with vitality and the scenes which include him here are among the funniest and liveliest in the book: the sudden collapse of his scepticism during Mrs Erdleigh's séance at the Templers' house; the blurted materialism, when he demands to know whether they are very rich before accepting an invitation there. All the same, he stands at a comparatively simple level of creation, as does St John Clarke, whose ruling passion, like that of Pope's Wharton, is 'lust of praise' and of acceptance: if society is all the thing he will turn there, and, if Leftism, he will turn there.

TAW works because it can contain this range of variously constructed people, and can move easily between them: an effect of well-ordered richness. It makes possible the beautiful sequence with which *TAW* nears its close. Stringham, a figure of considerable subtlety, gets put to bed by Widmerpool, essentially much slimmer in characterisation, despite the load he carries in the books: basically he is

ugly, unscrupulous ambition. This episode in *TAW* gleams with significance, of course, and repeats the theme of disintegration already
encountered in the St John Clarke–Quiggin–Members relationship:
for 'Widmerpool to restrict Stringham's movements . . . suggested a
whole social upheaval: a positively cosmic change in life's system.'
Verve, poignancy and humour attend this sequence, though, as well as
theme.

As to life, it crackles more vigorously in *TAW* than in either of the
previous volumes, thanks largely to the skilled mixing of modes. The
book's vitality certainly comes in part from the sense of comic, important social conflict created by these caricature figures. Perhaps
more, though, it is a matter of the elaborate development given to
Nicholas in this book. His love scenes with Jean have passion, humour
and pain. The account of his feelings on learning that Jean has slept
with the despised Jimmy Stripling is ferociously powerful. Has a better picture been given not just of love's alternating joy and despair –
routine in novels – but of the devastating way closeness in an affair
can change abruptly to distance; and of how supposed understanding
of the loved one may be revealed as enormous ignorance? On occasions in *ADTTMOT* the prose seems deliberately fashioned to put
wraps over emotion: hide the colouring, blur the outlines. Even during the Nicholas–Jean scenes here we meet lengthy general theorising
about love, as well as a wantonly unromantic image comparing some
features of an affair to difficulties of command in the army. At the
same time, though, the prose somehow manages to keep a hold on
the specific anguish and frailty of this relationship, and carry the
vehemence of Nicholas's feelings.

He has other feelings beside the sexual. We are bound to notice a
tone of censure and regret in his analysis of the St John Clarke–
Quiggin–Members situation. Nicholas's attitude to what he regards
as St John Clarke's dereliction of social responsibility seems to typify
the opposing views of privilege seen in the novel: Nicholas prizes
an ordered and affluent social position but, of course, indicates here
and in the earlier books that he sees society's decadence. He knows
it is not only St John Clarke who is guilty of self-assurance and ennui.
There is what Nicholas soon recognises as his own, and Eton's,
stupidly complacent sense of superiority over Widmerpool: wear a
quaint overcoat and become an enduring joke. And, as to ennui, can
it be seen in that contempt for the whole circus possibly shown by
Gilbert in *ABM;* and in the reluctance of Templer and Stringham to
take a conventional place in society? It is part of Nicholas's reason-

able and lifelike complexity that he wants the substance of the old order, but wishes it were a bit better.

We would be naïve to pretend, though, that Nicholas's attitude can be treated simply as convincingly unreconciled aspects of character. Where does Nicholas stop and Powell start? A novelist is not his narrator but I think we have to accept that an overlap exists. It is impossible to enjoy Powell fully, of course, without accepting that an endorsement of privilege exists in his novels; not as much as might appear at first, but some. Here and there this produces poor fiction, recognisably poor, regardless of one's political views. It is evasive levity that there should be hardly an expression of genuine Leftist views in the books, only a clutch of entertaining, phony, grasping, unstable figures, many of them at caricature level. One sees what Mizener means in *The Sense of Life in the Modern Novel* when he speaks of Powell as being 'in every respect undistorted by doctrine'. In Britain, however, political doctrine tends to be a matter of the left. Powell, while free of this, has his share of what stands in its place on the other side of politics: a belief that those who wish to change society are probably self-seekers and possibly crooked. This is not doctrinaire but deeper. Through the obnoxious poet and university lecturer, Malcolm Crowding, in *TK* Powell will take a swing at the search for 'social significance' in fiction, by which we assume he means the whole working-class, committed, progressive paraphernalia; only too deadly, agreed. An endorsement – even a satirical and tentative endorsement – of high life is also socially significant, though.

We may recognise these worrying aspects of *ADTTMOT* without reacting as if they signified that the whole novel rested on crumbling foundations, to borrow a cliché from *TAW*. These are books about well-placed people, the kind who existed and still exist, though their situation is probably shakier still by now. Fiction may look at them, is entitled to like some of them, or some aspects of some of them. Many – like Templer – have a life outside category and that is what counts.

At Lady Molly's

A balancing process, a sort of counterpoint, operates in the development of Widmerpool: as his will and ability push him forward in a career his life of the feelings declines. It is not just that materialism makes him heartless, a routine literary sermon. He retains some emotions and desires but grows more and more inept at finding an outlet for them. We do ask ourselves whether Widmerpool is callous, but also whether he is competent. In *ALM* he has become a reasonably respected City figure yet views the sexual side of his approaching marriage with worried naïveté, and has, in any case, palpably chosen the wrong woman: Nicholas remarks on the incongruity almost at once, but Widmerpool seems unaware. Then, as he moves to greater business and political eminence in later books, he will link himself with Pamela Flitton, a woman sure to bring him monumental anguish; sure, in fact, to remain beyond his comprehension. We have already seen his forlorn worship of Barbara Goring, ending in humiliation by sugar; and in *ABM* there is a bizarre – abortive – liaison with Gypsy. Of course, most men have trouble with their sex lives in *ADTTMOT*. None suffers on Widmerpool's scale, though. None seems so catastrophically lost when dealing with women. There is a sense in which he is not natural. Determination has ousted impulse, outlawed amiability and warmth. Determination can get a man engaged or married, but not ensure harmony, nor even a timely performance in bed.

How far we should generalise from this about Powell's views on the man of will I am not sure. Quiggin, too, is a man of the will and can also fall short on finer feelings; yet although 'not particularly adept with girls' he clearly has sexual magnetism. Still, it is hard to avoid seeing in Widmerpool a suggestion that 'the severe rule of ambition' and the attendant qualities of egotism, ruthlessness, solemnity and narrowness of outlook cause serious emotional trouble. That these failings of the soul and heart should be complemented in

Widmerpool's case by sexual deficiencies and extreme plainness perhaps loads the argument: his feelings have to keep afloat despite a couple of tidy-sized millstones, both of which have their relevance in *ALM*. But we also learn here, from Widmerpool's poignantly uncomfortable relationship with the racy widow, Mildred Haycock, that the man who has eyes in the back of his head when it comes to business intrigue can hardly see his nose before his face in matters of love. A luncheon at Widmerpool's club when he seeks advice from Nicholas on whether it would be proper to sleep with Mildred before marriage is deeply funny; and, if we feel anything for Widmerpool, which I think we do, somehow, powerfully sad. Full of provisos and circumlocutions, his statement to Nicholas about a weekend he might risk with Mildred sounds like a complex business arrangement and causes him alternating gloom and embarrassed giggling. Yet in discussing Mildred he is talking about what we might call a tireless sleeper around. Before the end of this book the engagement will be dead, Widmerpool having failed the bed test. In *TK* Pamela will publicise his further sexual eccentricities.

We are meant to make some comparison between Widmerpool's sombre difficulties and Nicholas's own uneven but normal emotional life. He, too, takes a fiancée in *ALM*, Isobel Tolland; and there are a number of other parallels in the early love experiences of him and Widmerpool: both want Barbara and fail to get her, and both are unsatisfactorily involved with Gypsy, in their various ways. It is the man of will against whatever we take Nicholas to be: man of imagination, perhaps; man of feelings; man of no will, possibly, or little. Nicholas has his problems with women until serenity sets in at the first meeting with Isobel in *ALM*, when he knows at once that he will marry her. But even when love is at its most unrewarding for Nicholas – in the garden at La Grenadière, or during some encounters with Jean – we do not feel, as we do constantly with Widmerpool, that he has no business at all in matters of the emotions, that he is out of his league. Nicholas will reproach himself for regarding Widmerpool as 'almost in a vacuum as far as the emotion of love was concerned' and for experiencing surprise when he shows signs of sexual interest: freakish appearance and manner, Nicholas reminds himself, do not preclude a regard for women. Correct, naturally. The implication of what happens in *ALM*, though, and in other volumes, is that Nicholas's first, instinctive judgement was fair enough. Widmerpool will try and try again in love but will never have much to show for it beyond wounds. Towards the end of *ALM* General Conyers tells Nicholas how Widmerpool left Dogdene, the Sleaford seat, after a fiasco in Mildred's room during the night. Widmerpool was downstairs and ready to depart before Conyers arrived for an early breakfast. 'Fellow looked like death. Shaking like a jelly and the colour of wax', says Conyers. Widmerpool claimed that there had been a telephone call summoning him, and he left for London; the butler reported that the only telephone call had been outgoing, from Widmerpool. These are the actions and appearance of a man panicking when out of his element, unable to come anywhere near coping with a woman, particularly a socially and sexually assured woman who had 'slept with every old-timer between Cannes and St Tropez', according to Chips Lovell. As Mizener puts it in *The Sense of Life in the Modern Novel*, 'This disaster is the revealing climax of all the triumphs of prestige Widmerpool has won at the cost of failing as a human being.' There must be a better word than climax.

In friendship Widmerpool will have no rosier luck. Isolation starts at school and continues, except for Nicholas's faithfulness; and that is not entirely credible, having more to do with narrational demands than likelihood. In personal relationships, then, Widmerpool is nowhere. With Nicholas, on the other hand, they are generally a matter of supreme ease, culminating in the kind of moment known to heyday Hollywood romantic drama and to the lyricist of 'Some Enchanted Evening', when a new face is encountered in a room and immediately becomes the object of requited love.

Powell is not all that far from *Howards End* and Forster's look at the opposed worlds of the Schlegels and Wilcoxes: culture, sensitivity and a regard for feelings against business drive and hardness. In *ALM* we begin to see this opposition clearly. Like the Wilcox men Widmerpool is philistine, having been heard by Nicholas to praise spontaneously only one painting in his life – and that a bad one – compared with Nicholas's own wide-ranging appreciation and love of art; Widmerpool is also clearly out of his depth when conversation turns to books and shows no real interest in music, though we do see him singing ardently in chapel just before leaving school in *AQOU*.

Forster would like the two sides to join and has 'only connect' as the epigraph of *Howards End*. There is a proselytizing deftness about this which leaves one unconvinced. Powell's approach is more complex. A modest, likeable narrator speaks wistfully about the career progress of a bumptious, grotesque, titanically off-putting character, and the reader's response is sympathy for the narrator and endorsement of the values he stands for. When he bemoans his own seeming aimlessness and lack of dynamism we generously correct – 'only correct' might do as an epigraph for *ALM* – and feel certain, rightly, that we are probably watching someone store credit for himself in future volumes. There is a token recognition that business must be run and countries governed, but we are to gather, even before Widmerpool is revealed as not just awkward but evil, that those who take on such jobs are essentially inferior – though on the face of it superior – to others who look for less, and more, in life. Reflecting, Nicholas puts the matter quite sharply in *ALM*. He had been asked by Mrs Conyers whether Widmerpool was 'nice', and dodged the question. Later, he decides that 'Widmerpool could hardly be described as "nice". Energetic: able: successful . . . but "nice" he had never been and showed little sign of becoming.' When in *CCR* we hear from Lovell that Widmerpool believes Nicholas to be 'a drifter with the stream' we are inclined to favour drifting if it is the opposite of what Widmerpool does. At no matter which point we take *ADTTMOT* Nicholas is, of course, found to be better, nicer, than Widmerpool. The man of feelings, creativity and infinitely tentative will is more in tune with life than those interested in power and status. It follows that the man of feelings should have no real wish to connect; occasional flukey meetings will do, and formal expressions of envy.

As I have suggested elsewhere some romanticism touches this attitude, particularly when our man of feelings is identified with the boy who can get on well with his public school contemporaries. Margaret Schlegel had a good argument: those who travel on trains should not look down on those who made the railway. The point about Widmerpool, though, is that his will to succeed takes him beyond what is acceptable conduct, by any standard; on a minor level it leads to the absurd intrigues of his business and army careers and to his general pushiness; more seriously it results in irresponsibility with the lives of others – to put it no worse – and to disreputable political behaviour. Do we infer, then, that all men of will are in danger of such excesses? This could be to force on Widmerpool the kind of representative function which deprives a character of individuality. Even so, we must take it that Powell wants to say something about the diminution of a man's life through the intemperate search for power, and we cannot help but see some general implications in that. We are able, I would say, to accept the thesis, while wondering at the same time whether life's large practicalities would get effective handling if left to Nicholas. The point, though, is that nobody seems to be looking after these practicalities with much skill: the world of the series and the world of fact bears signs of disintegration, after all. Who is to say that Nicholas's standards do not count? Not *ADTTMOT*. In its oblique but unmistakable fashion the novel insists that Nicholas has the answer. Powell is not concerned with that theoretically sensible give-and-take understanding which Forster thought attractive. True, it is unlikely that the values of the sensitive, balanced man of imagination and feeling will in reality exert notable power in our world. We should regret it. Gently, and with good humour, the novel puts its values forward through a self-critical narrator who is inclined sometimes to speak against them; they look admirable, just the same, and Powell means them to.

Possibly some would argue that it is not Widmerpool's lack of feelings which finish his chances with Mildred in *ALM* but lack of lineage. Are there class overtones? Is Widmerpool's disgrace in the noble setting of Dogdene a parable about the defective social upstart failing to make it with an established family? Is Zouch one of Widmerpool's forebears as well as one of Quiggin's? After all, Mildred was the Honourable Mildred Blaides, daughter of Lord Vowchurch, who was a friend of Edward VII. In an almost literal sense we could be talking about a failure of breeding on Widmerpool's part. If that were so, though, how would we explain the Jeavonses? Ted Jeavons, Lady Molly's husband, an amiable, generally admirable figure, has married into upper classes – his term for it – with success, as well as having spent a satisfactory leave with Mildred in 1917; yet his background is no more distinguished than Widmerpool's. It depends, as it should in a novel, on the people.

Casanova's Chinese Restaurant

Crossing the road by the bombed-out public house on the corner and pondering the mystery which dominates vistas framed by a ruined door, I felt for some reason glad the place had not yet been rebuilt. A direct hit had excised even the ground floor, so that the basement was revealed as a sunken garden, or site of archaeological excavation long abandoned, where great sprays of willow herb and ragwort flowered through cracked paving stones; only a few broken milk bottles and a laceless boot recalling contemporary life. In the midst of this sombre grotto five or six fractured steps had withstood the explosion and formed a projecting island of masonry on the summit of which rose the door. Walls on both sides were sunk away, but along its lintel, in niggling copybook handwriting, could still be distinguished the word *Ladies*. Beyond, on the far side of the twin pillars and crossbar, nothing whatever remained of the promised retreat, the threshold falling steeply to an abyss of rubble; a triumphal arch erected laboriously by dwarfs, or the gateway of some unknown, forbidden domain, the lair of sorcerers.

Rhythmic and patterned, this opening to CCR has been written with fierce attention to smoothness of flow. Yet its distinction comes mainly from the sharp pull, customary in ADTTMOT, between the resonant and the banal, the poetic and the farcical, incantation and deflation. 'Vistas framed by a ruined door' gets its let-down in the same sentence through the near slang terseness of 'the place'. The romantic 'sunken garden' with its 'great sprays of willow herb and ragwort' also contains broken bottles and an old boot. Any lingering aura of stricken grandeur about the ruined door is disposed of near the end by the revelation that it had led to a ladies' lavatory, the lowliness of this function being caught in the deliberately over-stretched – one might almost say dribbling – phrase, 'niggling copy-

F

book handwriting'. That 'forbidden domain' and the 'lair of sorcerers' which between them close the paragraph on a sonorous note do so ironically, of course: through this gateway to some unknown domain women once went to spend a penny. The passage is a highly accomplished exercise in mock-heroic (though one could wish for a less routine symbol of modern flotsam than the old boot, and for a marginally less jocose description of the lavatory than 'that promised retreat'). As with the best of its genre the success of this paragraph lies in that control which enables Powell to avoid knocking the heroic right into the ground with the mockery. One gets the jokes all right but also feels the dignified regret for time lost and for destruction: despair before 'the abyss of rubble'. Beauty of form holds up against the humour, which is a constituent of the beauty.

All the opening sequence of *CCR* is made to this fashion. Looking at the wrecked Mortimer, Nicholas finds his nostalgia suddenly assisted by the exquisite singing of a crippled woman, last heard years before when Nicholas was with Moreland, the composer. Despite what we know of the ruined doorway by now, Powell can frame her in it and make us accept that she seemed to glide by 'some occult power' and was 'about to sail effortlessly through its enchanted portal'. Here we have prose getting it both ways: aggrandisement of the doorway, reduction, aggrandisement again. The skill is phenomenal. And this last aggrandisement is to be reduced yet again. The woman's song, although sweetly performed, is corny — 'Pale Hands I Loved' — and, in those recollected days, its words were pedantically, even tiresomely, queried by Moreland. Further, while the sight and sound recall Moreland's announcement of his intention to marry, it was also an afternoon when they bought an undrinkable (even by Moreland) bottle of 'tawny wine (port flavour)'. That obnoxiousness is as much a part of the tang of this sequence as the sort of haunting, double-stage reminiscence which we also meet at the start of *AQOU* and *ABM*: the narrator looking back to the bombed pub from a time when it has been unpleasantly rebuilt and carried from these ruins into a past pre-dating the end of *ABM*.

Brilliantly put together as this opening may be, *CCR* seems to me overall one of the less successful volumes of *ADTTMOT*. Qualities which make the opening so effective — its skirting of immediacy, the wish to deflate each moment as much as establish it — can at book length produce inertia. A notable shortage of activity slows the first half of *CCR*: much talk of what people are doing, little sight of them actually at it. One comes to feel like an invalid who has tales of interesting events brought to him at second or third hand, and not always by riveting messengers. About some of these incidents – Erridge's expedition to Spain, for instance – we are told several times, as characters break the news to each other and discuss implications. Reactions vary, it is true, and we learn a lot about people in this way. That does not altogether compensate for narrative sluggishness, though. We are up against a condition of Powell's story-telling method: simply, Nicholas cannot be everywhere so he is – and we are – heavily dependent on what seem at times laborious, rather slabby reports. Coupled with this is a tendency here to supply painstaking dossiers on people's backgrounds, some of it in the guise of conversation, but really more like recited notes by a policeman giving character evidence in the box: details on Matilda Wilson are a case in point.

This volume is attempting a considerable change of ground: into the down-at-heel realm of professional musicians and critics, though without completely losing the society and business world of the previous books. Powell has not managed the mix too well. Although most of the scenes with Moreland and his musical cronies have real life to them, the Tolland gathering at Hyde Park Gate is dull and statuesque: seems only a formal device to remind us that things are not all creativity, poverty, squalor and concerts, and to do a presentation job on Nicholas's new in-laws.

(Some might argue that Moreland's episodes are especially vivid because the character of the composer is based on that of Constant Lambert, a friend of Powell. What he says in a Memoir in Richard Shead's *Constant Lambert* (Simon Publications, 1973) is significant, both to the particular case of Moreland and the general question of characters' real-life origins. Briefly, he denies any depth of resemblance and states that Moreland, like the Narrator of *ADTTMOT*, springs from 'mixed origins'. The same sort of point is made in *Proust as a Soldier*, Powell's contribution to *Marcel Proust 1871– 1922, A Centenary Volume*, edited by Peter Quennell (London, 1971): the 'comparisons and contrasts' of fictional characters with real people are 'beside the point, almost frivolous' because in good novel writing 'a new figure emerges; one that lives entirely on its own', even if there are many resemblances to an actual original.)

In much the same way as the Tollands are introduced, Widmerpool pops up in a nursing home for no more apparent purpose than to show his face in the story again, and arrange a luncheon with Nicholas, from which next to nothing comes either. The many-sided-

ness of Powell's scheme seems occasionally to have baffled him in
CCR. To convince us that we are in the presence of drama the prose
will turn to devices which might have been borrowed from the pages
of St John Clarke himself; Nicholas is surprised by an event at a
party: 'This was nothing less than the arrival of Stringham. I could
hardly believe my eyes.' In his diary for 4 January 1961, Evelyn
Waugh, looking back over 1960, the year CCR came out, wrote that
it had been a bad one for 'the old steeplechasers – Elizabeth Bowen,
John Betjeman, Leslie Hartley down and out of the race; Nancy
Mitford and Tony Powell just clinging in the saddle' (*Observer
Magazine*, 13 May 1973).

  Nor is it only a matter of what I suppose could be called superficial technique. More than most others this volume suffers from a
lack of proportion; it arises from an omission I have mentioned
elsewhere. The book is largely about marriage, and less formal but
established sexual relationships. Numerous liaisons are set off against
each other: Moreland and Matilda; Moreland and Priscilla; Priscilla
and Lovell; Maclintick and Audrey; Erridge and Mona; Mrs Foxe
and Chandler; Mrs Foxe and Buster; Edward and Mrs Simpson
crowning the theme. Most of these relationships are under stress;
few seem happy. Out of sight, though, Nicholas's marriage to Isobel
proceeds, we understand, with dazzling serenity. Together, they step
deftly over the wreckage of other unions and calmly round the sadness of a miscarriage. In the nursing home Isobel says: ' "I shalln't
be sorry to come home." ' Nicholas replies: ' "I shalln't be sorry to
have you home again.' " We must read thoughts that lie too deep
for expression by the upper classes in that magnificently inarticulate
exchange, a return to the method of AM. Just the same, one has a
strong sense in this book that something is missing; that we are
deprived of as much as we get about love, sex and marriage.
Normality and contentment are difficult to accommodate in an entertaining novel; causes of break-ups more tricky to show than the
actual break. There is a gossipy quality to this book. The *roman
fleuve* has begun to babble for a while. True, Nicholas explains to
the reader why it is impossible for an existing marriage to be
adequately described by one of the participants. 'To think at all
objectively about one's own marriage is impossible.' Think sub-
jectively, then. In *Tradition and Dream* Walter Allen says of Isobel's
miscarriage: 'It is the index of Powell's control over us that we never
begin to wonder about Jenkins's feelings about his wife at this time.'
In fact, at that stage in the book I wonder about nothing else and

feel deprived at being offered 'No comment' by a novelist, Powell or Jenkins.

Powell's intentions are fairly clear; one may recognise them without being won over. Views on marriage and the instances of it contained in CCR are realistically various and irreconcilable, deliberately so. It would be absurd to advance a settled standpoint on marriage, and the book is certainly never in danger of doing so. There are good marriages and bad in CCR; more bad than good, and this would accord with the facts of real life, especially for the kind of social terrain Powell is crossing: the upper classes and bohemia. He may have decided that to depict Nicholas's marriage at any length would load the case: proclaim a standard and so simplify what needs to be shown as eternally complex. As it is, the romantic implications of the Abdication, which is frequently mentioned in this volume, have to be taken alongside the pain and tragedy of Maclintick's home life with Audrey. On top, marriage, which may come between a king and his duty, is also – according to Moreland – an 'entity' which can come between the very husband and wife. Other more conventional paradoxes are shown. Audrey is a shrew, yet also her husband's ideal. The two sides of such worship are contained in Moreland's reminder that Petrarch's Laura was a member of the de Sade family and so, he implies, could have taken pleasure in giving pain to a doting lover. Every good aspect of love and marriage is countered by a tough rebuttal in CCR. Moreland's early excitement over Matilda will, in the course of the book, turn to sourness and infidelity (unconsummated) with Priscilla. Again, there may be frank, easily understood sexual liaisons like Barnby's with the waitress here; but we have, too, Mrs Foxe's strange obsession with Chandler. Marriage dominates thoughts and conversations yet, in Matilda's word, is unlikely to be 'fun'. Although Nicholas queries this – not, as far as we can make out, from personal experience – it does seem the nearest one gets to a generalisation on marriage: few of the unions we see in CCR or throughout the series display that quality. This would appear reasonably close to the circumstances of real life, at no matter what social level.

The contradictions in marriage, between marriages and in characters' estimates of it are not, then, resolved; an indecisiveness which is honest but scarcely avoidable. The book would, in fact, have provided a sensible, frank and full account of modern marriage if we did not suspect almost continuously that the one made in heaven was being kept up Powell's sleeve.

Lacking something in depth and in movement CCR might provide arguments for those who hold that Powell's main role is as social historian. Social demarcations are certainly portrayed most subtly here. Two incidents gleam with reflections on class. In the first, Maclintick speaks a doggedly ungrateful, in fact, rude, farewell to Mrs Foxe after a party in her house to celebrate performance of Moreland's symphony. Mrs Foxe remains wholly affable, insisting that Maclintick must come again. Ultimately he agrees that he probably will. At the same party Audrey Maclintick meets Stringham, now under Miss Weedon's care because of alcoholism. He finds Audrey *outrée* in both behaviour and dress – a Bo-Peep costume as he calls it. For much of the evening he rags her, but with such style that she takes it as pleasant teasing. In both instances the Maclinticks are being managed, dealt with by superiors, one feels. All the charm and assurance are on one side: Stringham can even exercise it when tight.

How much do we generalise from these confrontations? How hard is Powell pushing the class point? Perhaps it is significant that when the rich have their troubles – Stringham's alcoholism, for instance – these too can be managed, dealt with, because resources are to hand: Miss Weedon. Whereas the prolonged, bitter difficulties of the Maclintick household can only come to a miserable end. For the established, money, poise, breeding keep tragedy within bounds, just as they provide Mrs Foxe with inflexible politeness and Stringham with a flair for banter, though nothing can diminish the horribly well-portrayed tragedy of his present situation. Artists like Moreland – like Nicholas, for that matter – can cross class demarcations easily enough and are at home anywhere. For others – including third-raters like St John Clark and artisans like Maclintick – social classifications remain an irritant and a fact.

All this has been put together with consummate sensitivity to social nuance. Features on the landscape of class distinction could not be better mapped. Simply, one asks for more signs of life from this fascinating region.

The Kindly Ones

Giles dies and, among belongings at the seaside 'private hotel' where he had been staying, Nicholas finds his uncle's army commission. Not too seriously he measures the realities of Giles's life against the ringing officer qualities listed in this royal document. As many of us would, he comes out of this pretty badly. Since Nicholas finds also his uncle's copy of an eastern love guide, *The Perfumed Garden*, with its suggestions of furtive readings and/or sexual ambitions not quite right for his years and manner, our impression of him at this valedictory point is not high. (The enema gear unearthed by Nicholas does not do much for our memory of Giles either.) Nowhere in the *Music of Time* has he commanded great admiration.

He is an excellently drawn figure, more caricature than character, brilliantly individual. We must regard him as being never really up to standard as a person, but we cannot leave it there. As a querulous, eternally disgruntled voice he provides a good corrective to Nicholas's bland irony. Jenkins – both as a retrospective and contemporary figure – may satirise the world; but his stronger note is of acceptance. Giles brings welcome and apposite suspicion; fundamental, bracing disrespect. At times – as I suggest in the chapter on narration – he becomes virtually a second story-teller, introducing a note of belligerent, well-informed worldliness unavailable to Nicholas, particularly when young, of course.

We do not take the views we get from Giles as word for word reliable, nor even every other word; but we do not dismiss them, either, especially as some are shown to be accurate (on Conyers' womanising, for instance). Despite his grouchiness we have some sympathy for Giles, as one tends to for all those who are implacably agnostic about the system, particularly in novels. Giles's aggression is comic – delightfully comic – yet lacking neither sense nor a washed-out dignity.

At the same time, we are made to feel that Giles's failure to fit in, to behave in a fashion bringing credit to family and class, is bad: that review in the hotel, skittish or not, is the last word on him, after all. *TKO* suggests that, although a creditable spikiness of disposition might have made it hard for Giles to accept authority, his aggressive independence and contempt for established power were out of proportion to his abilities. Non-conformity can be the stuff of which great men are made. In Giles it looks more like an inability to organise himself and accept those compromises which would fit his status and resources. His attitude to those who have got on is funny twice: first for its debunking malice; but also for its fervid and artless devotion to the creed of sour grapes. Giles decided that what he had failed to get could be got only by means unacceptable to his rigorous code; standards which he could not reach had to be obnoxious. A comparison with Widmerpool can be made: both are guyed for being outside the social norms, even though these norms may be continually guyed themselves by Nicholas (or Powell). Unlike Widmerpool, though, whose social ambitions remain frank and energetic at least until *TK* and *HSH*, Giles is one of those dropouts who have found it beyond them to drop in at the level demanded by self-esteem. If he cannot win, the game must be wrong. If Giles used today's idiom he would refer to the life he affects to despise as 'the rat race'.

At first sight then Giles looks a two-way bet by Powell: Giles can excite some sympathy through his hostility to the set order of things, the rat race being real and odious as well as an excuse for not competing; and we can laugh at him for so doggedly and transparently trying to make incompetence sound a consuming virtue. Powell may equip Giles with the occasional sharp criticism of people and institutions. On the whole, though, he is shifty and opportunist, is so ardently a scrounger that we look behind all his stated attitudes for selfishness. He is 'a bit of a radical' not because he wants to change society but as an impotent, irritable retaliation for what society has done to him: another of Powell's suggestions that middle- or upper-class protesters cannot be sincere. This radical admired Hitler (as, let us recall, did other radicals like Lloyd George). What *TKO* – and *ADTTMOT* generally – seems to be saying is that life, as ordered and organised, has many dire flaws, which may be consistently satirised; but that such a disintegrating system is still better than the ramshackle escapism, self-pity and niggling envy of Giles. It is becoming almost necessary to call up the word ambivalent, so let us move on.

In *TVOB* we will hear a good deal about the philosophy of Alfred de Vigny, the French romantic poet, mainly about the military man's life. Looking at the evaluation of Giles, and of St John Clarke earlier, one wonders whether Vigny's thought contains a deeper application to the books. He has his moments of stoicism. At the end of *La Mort du Loup* he makes the dying wolf recommend a life in which one carries out energetically a 'long and heavy task' in 'la voie où le sort a voulu t'appeler' ('in the sphere to which Fate has called you'). Against both St John Clarke and Giles the point is explicitly made that they have turned their backs on allotted duties: Giles's are actually laid down in the words of the commission; St John Clarke's are only implied, though his irresponsibility in flirting with Marxism is powerfully spelled out. Powell's argument, two-pronged, not two-faced, is that society may be a poor thing, but that those who dodge out of their proper position in it are both a sign and cause of further disintegration. A tough doctrine. Some will hear echoes of the corporate state, where everyone has his place and may not shift from it; or of the famous 'scale of being', that fixed, hierarchical order of the Middle Ages. Certainly we must identify here something about the duties which accompany privilege: even the very limited *noblesse* of Giles and St John Clarke brought obligations which they neglected or ditched. As a result, collapse advanced by geometric progression and the good elements of the old order were put at risk with the admittedly bad; put at risk when, in Powell's view, only flagrantly bogus replacements were on offer. Above all a brilliantly lively, comic figure, Giles also represents a subtle, cogent, conservative view of social decline.

Giles dies just before the Russio–German non-aggression pact of August 1939; war is much less than a month away. We have met him previously, near the start of *TKO*, as news of Sarajevo breaks, and even before that there had been much talk of war. *TKO* is another of the books where pattern comes over very strongly. It is not simply a matter of putting alongside each other three chapters tracing the approach of two wars; though, to achieve this, Powell will boldly take the opening of *TKO* back to the earliest period of *ADTTMOT*, when Nicholas was about nine or ten and still being educated at home. On top of this, the 'private hotel' where Giles dies, the Bellevue, becomes a remarkable assembly point for many of *TKO*'s – of *ADTTMOT*'s – people and themes. The Bellevue is kept by Albert Creech, cook at Nicholas's parents' house near Aldershot in 1914. For Giles to patronise the Bellevue is natural enough, Albert's reputation in the kitchen being high. In addition, though,

Dr Trelawney, the mystic-crank, likewise seen near Stonehurst, the Jenkins house, in 1914, also appears; has to be persuaded to release himself from the bathroom by Nicholas, who uses a cult catch-phrase he first heard as a child. Mrs Erdleigh, a fortune-teller, whom it was once thought Giles would marry, also turns up (announcing in one of the book's funniest lines that Lady Warminster was memorably grateful 'when I revealed to her that Tuesday was the best day for the operation of revenge'). Mrs Erdleigh now lives in the town (where Moreland once conducted the orchestra) and has a connection with Dr Trelawney. At dinner after examination of Giles's belongings Nicholas meets Bob Duport, former husband of Jean Templer, who gives Nicholas unpleasant information about her love affair with Jimmy Brent, first encountered by Nicholas during that phenomenally significant jaunt in Templer's Vauxhall when Nicholas was an undergraduate.

What is Powell's purpose? Is the Bellevue reunion credible? As to purpose, we can find certain superficial, technical answers first. The *roman fleuve* takes some controlling; and what the Bellevue does is establish a unifying centre for *TKO* and also draw to it elements from other books of the sequence, Duport and Mrs Erdleigh not having appeared earlier in *TKO*. In addition, the 'private hotel' exercises its bellevue in two directions, backwards through memory, forward to hostilities through intelligent guessing and Dr Trelawney's vision of 'the sword of Mithras': we are being prepared for the first of the war novels. Quite simply, too, we experience entertaining shocks as characters pop up again, a familiar device in *ADTTMOT*. (As it happens, Widmerpool does not appear at the Bellevue – though he has a bearing on Duport's presence – but comparable with the surprise entrances of *TKO* is the recurrent announcement throughout the books, 'It was Widmerpool', as he comes un-expectedly through a door or turns to face Nicholas. Widmerpool's advent or emergence in this fashion will often constitute the dramatic peak of a chapter, and a long chapter, at that.)

Powell is interested also, of course, in presenting through the Bellevue suggestions about recurrence, coincidence, the cyclic nature of the dance. One does not look for meaning in the specific details: why, say, it should be Duport who is staying there, or Trelawney. It is almost sufficient that time has asserted its flair for pattern again; that people are met, names mentioned, memories stirred in a way which proclaim's life's interlocking nature. On top, we may notice that the meeting with Duport reveals how the past as much as the present can be savaged by events. Nicholas dwells on the retrospective pain caused by Duport's disclosure that Jean slept with Brent; an interesting, and touching, extension of the thesis that the past can return in some form. Also, we may be allowed to speculate that the presence of Mrs Erdleigh and Dr Trelawney, both claimants to other-worldly insights, may indicate that there are more things in heaven and earth than mere likelihood.

This brings us to the matter of credibility. In his *New Review* profile of Powell, Alan Brownjohn discusses the improbabilities of the Bellevue gathering and 'the air of remoteness from reality' of the hotel itself. Brownjohn sees *ADTTMOT* generally as 'a huge comic fantasy, its plot and characters seen in their totality being absurdly larger and odder, much less real, than the Life they have been assumed to represent so meticulously'. Assumed, one has to say, by Powell himself. During an interview with W. J. Weatherby in the July 1961 issue of *The Twentieth Century* he claims to be 'a naturalistic writer . . . that is to say [aiming] never to describe anything that could not have happened in everyday life'.

That is categorical enough. Just the same I think this is an instance where we trust the tale, not the teller. Brownjohn is surely right to suggest that at least parts of the novel rest on assumptions which are not realistic or credible in any straight, simple use of that word. No matter how often we are told about it, and see it referred to as commonly acknowledged fact, few of us encounter in real life the kind and quantity of coincidences which attend Nicholas throughout the sequence, and which attend other characters. Do many of us actually know one or more symbolic figures – of the type that Widmerpool is to Nicholas – 'round whom the past and future have a way of assembling', as *ABM* puts it? For most people life is not a bit like a dance and there is no music of time, little pattern. Perhaps special conditions affect the sort of upper-class groups Powell deals with, who intermarry, inter-deal, and who are pushed together by wealth, schooling and London. One cannot, all the same, take a confluence like that in the Bellevue as within the limits of tolerable likelihood, any more than we can believe in, say, the manner that both Jean Templer's South American husband and her daughter, Polly, are separately brought into accidental contact with Nicholas later on in the *Music of Time*.

Jenkins tells us there is a pattern to life and, because we have all known coincidences and may have experienced what we regard as key moments, we find ourselves some way towards accepting the suggestion, though the scale on which Powell works out these trends is beyond anything we have seen or heard about in actuality. What Powell seems to have done is take the shaping duty of a novelist very frankly for what it is – a required artifice – and provide a new expression of it: patterned coincidence; infinite links across time, place and even class; and amended re-runs of the past.

For good reasons such shaping is probably at its most ostentatious in *TKO*: juxtaposition of the two pre-war periods; the placing in the Bellevue of four people who were at or around Stonehurst before the First War (Nicholas, Giles, Albert and Trelawney). Through this repetition the book wants to say something about duty, its inescapable, recurrent, possibly patterned demands; particularly duty in war and, even more particularly, as duty bears on Nicholas. In Chapter 1 he watched his father and Bracey go to fight in France. Now, Nicholas's father seeks to join up once more and Nicholas himself will pull strings to get in. Obligation to fight for country – or, more accurately, the privilege of fighting – is often a theme in the books (even the odious Brent intrigues to enlist) as much as in Waugh. Giles's commission tabulates these obligations and, seeming as they do, to imply wider duties than those of soldiering, link the responsibilities of caste and class with those of patriotism. Although not a new point of view, it is put here with such subtlety that the feudal, aristocratic elements do not become offensive. War is the main test of a man's awareness of his role. There are others, subordinate, like those on which Giles and St John Clarke fail. Such tests will come and come again. The sound man will face up, like the dying wolf.

The Valley of Bones

Powell's subject here is war and the trivia of war: sonorous title, downbeat matter. Soldiers get killed in *TVOB*, some far off, one at hand, but the chief concern is with Mess practical jokes, exercises, drinking, womanising, petty intrigue. Emphatic moments come not from passage of arms but from a unit commander's discovery that his girl friend has been simultaneously carrying on with one of his corporals; from a drunken officer's scuffle – kiss? – with a Mess waiter; from Nicholas's discovery of Widmerpool in a position of power. In one fine comic scene a general demonstrates that, as well as his expected concern for the larger matters of strategy and logistics, he holds obsessive views on the value of porridge as a military breakfast. We do not see the enemy, but someone steals the unit's butter and the general's tin hat. The nearest approach to fighting are the small-scale battles for career advantage between officers; and the rivalry of C. of E. and R.C. padres to seem unholier than thou, as a *Punch* cartoon once put such competitive denials of the cloth. If any one part of *ADTTMOT* makes one doubt whether we should attribute the humour to fantasy it is *TVOB*. Beautifully low-profile comedy, it attempts nothing beyond the wholly credible. It is the period of phoney war treated with the most delicate understanding of banality, bathos, aimlessness. There is an extraordinarily authentic feel for a time which so lacked definition that it could have easily have been obscured by barracks minutiae.

Here and there, in fact, the deflation does reach the point of flatness. Powell has spotted the danger and to spike our guns, along with the book's, brings in a discussion based on Alfred de Vigny about the worthwhile role of dullness in an officer's career. We are being informed that there is significance to a book – as to a soldier's life – even when it appears to be marking time. We may feel, just the same, that the philosophising, as well as David Pennistone, the character who takes part in it with Nicholas, are makeweights, a little painstakingly and blatantly introduced.

I do not think the purpose here is ironic though, of course, the overall purpose of the book certainly is. We witness continual contrasts between news of large – and disastrous – military operations (the fall of Norway, the retreat in France) and the comically footling preoccupations of an army still far from the fighting and from readiness. This volume offers its corrective to that rhetoric about the Sword of Mithras in *TKO*, and to the implied patriotism and noble feelings which impelled Nicholas and others towards enlistment. What continues to interest Powell in the war novels – all of them, not simply *TVOB* – is human personality rather than great events. War, even war, will make little serious impact on Nicholas's character. He holds up as always; so do the Tolland family hold up: they are seen here in displaced but formidable array, and the losses they suffer do not detract too much from that impression of continuing strength. When war bears in on someone too forcibly, changes him, pushes him to excess – like Gwatkin – we see failure. As ever, Powell is keen to show that men and women should act out their natural selves, with sense and balance, not succumb to frenzy for a belief, for an organisation – not even an approved organisation like the army – nor for the most admirable ideals, like patriotism.

Irony goes further still. This volume opens with that Powell mannerism, the narrator looking back on the narrator looking back. The example in *TVOB* is among the most effective: one gets very powerfully the feeling that the books are part of a developing story whose dimensions run in all directions. Nicholas is stationed in a Welsh coastal town. He tells us that he stayed there once before – 'long, long ago, in another existence' – when wishing to look over country where his family had lived a century earlier. Young antecedents had set out from here as officers in the Marines or East India Company, many dying overseas. This history of service, he now feels, imposed a pattern on him 'the fulfilment of which was in some ways a relief'. His thoughts go deeper yet into the past: to Celtic forebears who might have reigned in South Wales; to ancient days whose imprint now was part history, part folklore, part legend.

The note, then, is one of some resonance, some dignity; an invocation of times 'at once measurably historical, yet at the same time mythically heroic'. Against these noble sounds from the grand past, the rich Welsh names and echoes of fine deeds, we listen now to the voice of browned-off soldiering in the early 1940s, talk of improperly folded blankets, urine buckets and a cap badge out of position. Was this what time's 'required pattern' had lined up for Nicholas? It is as if one of the chief themes of *ADTTMOT* – repetition, the cycle – were being cut down to size. The Music of Time becomes, for a moment, almost squeaky, by intent. Such touches are useful, bracing. Here and there in the novel Nicholas's reflections on the movements of time are dazingly trite. In *ALM*, for instance, he discovers that time may change relationships; but does have the grace to brand these thoughts 'rather banal'. He might have offered a similar apology in *TSA* for deciding in heavy-going prose that friendships could be ended by change of circumstances. The time-death musings prompted in *TVOB* when Robert Tolland is killed in France are not so much banal as woozily mystical. Did Robert arrange for his own death, the narrator asks, by refusing a commission so as to 'fulfil a destiny that required him to fall in France'? Or, possibly, it was the persistent bad luck of Flavia, with whom he was having a love affair, which had reached out for him. But, then again, 'Robert could even have died to escape her.' (The War Office very much regrets to inform you that Corporal Robert Tolland was killed during operations in France owing to his liaison with a Mrs Flavia Wisebite.) Fatalism, the subconscious, superstition are dropped into the pot and given a stir in a manner which suggests the cook may temporarily be suffering from convictions of infallibility. It is consoling, when faced with such weird speculations, to know that from time to time Powell will take a puncturing approach to one of the novel's own most insistent ideas. Recurrence can mean bathos.

It is likewise consoling to see, in the person of Gwatkin, soldiering examined with an eye to anything but the spiritual and mysterious. Gwatkin holds *TVOB* together. Free from any trace of caricature, he is drawn with unfailing compassion, accuracy, irony and comic invention. A vastly fallible, often posturing, unit commander, he could easily have been lampooned in the style of war novels composed around sensitive heroes like Nicholas. Such simplifications are rare here, or in *TSA* or *TMP*. Powell, son of an army officer, is alert to the genuine difficulties and virtues of soldiering, as well as to its absurdities.

Gwatkin's fall comes because he has not learned what de Vigny said about the vital part of dull routine in a soldier's life, and the artificial role of army authority: there is 'as little room for uncontrolled fervour as for sullen indifference'. Nicholas sees the first of these as natural to Gwatkin; the second to a waster in the ranks,

Sayce. They come together in Gwatkin's office when he tries to move Sayce from his grim habits through an appeal to loyalty and better nature. Neither understands the other. Vigny, endorsed by Powell, is making an appeal for compromise, temperateness. Gwatkin's manic emphasis on security brings disaster when he fails to tell even his own officers important code-words. Concerned to an obsessive degree with the need for sexual purity in a soldier he then slides into inefficiency through an affair with a flighty local girl. Fixations have robbed him of ordinary sensible judgement. Kedward, who takes over from him, although devoted to his fiancée, and inclined to show and kiss her picture without much prompting, is more controlled: while Gwatkin, in Nicholas's view, wishes to 'cut a dashing military figure against a backcloth of Meissonier-like imagery of plume and breast-plate', Kedward does not 'deal in dreams'; his marriage is to wait until he makes it to captain.

All this would square with the general feeling in *ADTTMOT* against undue commitment. We ought to notice, though, that the reader does not like Kedward as much as Gwatkin. Kedward is cold and self-centred, not noticing Gwatkin's distress when deposed; and Powell always tends to regard these qualities with rather more suspicion than he gives to fanaticism. Whatever moral Gwatkin may carry, and however justified we may regard his displacement – even, perhaps, finding it bleakly amusing – he remains a wonderfully sympathetic figure, created with thorough appreciation of complexity in human nature and a subtle understanding of the contradictions in personality: the weaknesses where a man looks least vulnerable, the practicalities fighting against theory, attempted worldliness riven by *naïveté*. Small-scale and convincing, Gwatkin's tumble is in the recognisable pattern of classical tragedy: a good man off balance, trying to be what he is not.

With Gwatkin Powell steps successfully outside the limited social group he has allowed himself in all his previous books: the upper classes and bohemia. War enables him to write about people lacking money and status as something other than grotesques. Gwatkin is an officer, it is true, and worked in a bank, so he is some way off the social floor. Non-commissioned officers and men in the ranks are treated with similar care and sympathy, though, notably Sergeant Pendry. These three war volumes bring an additional maturity to Powell's work, a new scope. I do not say that he has altogether caught the tone of ordinary troops, most of them here ex-miners, though the good nature, mocking humour and obliqueness are dead right.

As to the quaint, back-to-front dialogue it avoids the worst elements of look-you English invented for *How Green was my Fair Country* novels, without getting very near to actual valleys talk. Not even Kedward, an officer with a peacetime background like Gwatkins', speaks quite as he should. Of a new Mess-mate, the superbly drawn Bithel, Kedward reports 'he played rugger for Wales once.' Rugger is an English word and would probably not be used even by a South Walian exposed to the anglicising influence of banks. 'He played for Wales once' would be more like it: only if it were some other game would there be need to specify. Possibly I quibble as a South Walian: this first step out into a rougher world than we have so far visited with Powell is confidently done. One can, I think, see why Powell might respond to the atmosphere of this unit. The sense of a very cohesive – though temporarily transposed – community recalls at its different level the kind of inter-linked society we meet in the earlier books: after all, as a civilian, Gwatkin had wanted to marry the sister of another officer in the unit; Sergeant Pendry's domestic troubles are familiar to some of the men; it is even possible – though only possible – that Gwatkin links military society with high society, Gwatkin having been Lord Aberavon's family name.

A short glimpse of that high society is given in *TVOB*, with names and information rather heaped on, as Powell does some infilling; trying to keep as many factors from earlier in *ADTTMOT* solidly in our minds. The *TLS* (5 March 1964) reasonably found this interpolation ill-managed, confused after the strength of the military scenes. What must interest us about this upper-class group, though, is the sameness of its ways among the pressures of war. Like the soldiers, these relations and friends of Nicholas have also been transposed: some have joined up themselves and a reunion takes place at the former country vicarage which his sister-in-law Frederica has taken for the duration. Despite such changes, the steady, intricate pace of the dance continues; as ever, partners switch, but all come from the same sort of world. Umfraville and Frederica are to marry. Robert Tolland and Flavia Wisebite (Stringham) are having an affair. Mrs Foxe, we hear, has gone off with Chandler. These shifts tell of stability. In only one way is that stability really disturbed. Nicholas goes to Frederica's house in the car of Odo Stevens, a subaltern he meets on a training course. Stevens sold imitation jewellery before the war and did some provincial journalism. In other words, he is neither upper-class nor bohemian, though he will turn literary later. Frederica invites him in and, as the *TLS* noted, Powell points the difference in class by dialogue alone. Another of Nicholas's sisters-in-law, Priscilla, whose husband is away with the Marines, falls for Stevens. During *TSA* this encounter develops into a flagrant affair and Lovell, Priscilla's husband, will speak of Stevens and reproach Nicholas for 'having introduced him into the family'. Unsettling of class demarcations is emphasised in *TVOB* by having Robert Tolland, an n.c.o., address Stevens as 'sir', and by making Stevens grandly tell him to be informal off duty. Yet one feels that Stevens is a minor incursion. It is not social reshaping which seems most noticeable at Frederica's but the continuance and durability of the Tollands and their set. In his review of *ADTTMOT* in *The Times* of 6 September 1975, to mark publication of *HSH*, Michael Ratcliffe noted that a 'pervading theme' in Powell was 'that the more the surface of English life changes the more it stays, astonishingly, the same'. The Tolland community, like the Welsh valley community represented by the troops, looks entirely able to survive the disruptions of war, particularly since those disruptions will only rarely get on to the page in serious and active form.

The Soldier's Art

We meet one of Powell's most frank uses of coincidence here. A bomb kills Chips Lovell at the Madrid, a London café. Nicholas sets out immediately to tell Lovell's estranged wife, Priscilla, who is staying at the Jeavonses' house. He finds that the house has been hit in the same raid and Priscilla also killed.

Little reflection follows. Jenkins has nothing to say about pattern or time; only a reference to Dr Trelawney's warning of 'the slayer of Osiris and his grievous tribute of blood', an allusion virtually facetious in view of the language and of what Dr Trelawney is. We are left to make more or less what we like of this stark chance.

Does it work? I do not want to take on that grim conundrum of how far fiction may imitate the unlikelihoods of real life. There are, though, instances where the very largeness of fictional coincidence can aid credibility; as if the reader assumes that the author would not take such a risk unless it were – to stretch a term – true. Especially may this be so in a volume where the general tone otherwise is low-key plausibility. The novelist earns our confidence and we may then feel prepared to see him blue some of this on one piece of spectacular invention. Powell works like that here. The death of either Priscilla or Lovell alone at this point in the narrative might have looked arbitrary. Instead, we have what is obviously a daring but carefully calculated item of plot. Boldness carries it.

But I have not yet given the full range of coincidence in these synchronised deaths. Priscilla had arrived at the Café Royal with her new escort, Odo Stevens. Unexpectedly they met Nicholas, Audrey Maclintick and Moreland there, Lovell himself having just left. Stevens insisted they all dine together. After a while Priscilla grew upset; she claimed a headache, but we remain unsure. She left early, alone, and was therefore at the Jeavonses' in time to be killed.

The point would seem to be that although life had pushed Lovell and Priscilla sadly apart, a terrible chance – series of chances – gave them some sort of reunion finally; made the heartache of their relationship, and Lovell's hopes of patching it up, suddenly trivial and irrelevant. It is, though, a fiercely dark irony, not the sentimentalising formula of 'In death they were not divided' which 'unites' Maggie and her brother at the end of *The Mill on the Floss*. Incessant talk about the war ostensibly touches off Priscilla's agitation. In view of what comes later, though, are we to take it that she sensed something had happened to Lovell? Was she somehow drawn to where the next bombs would be? Possibly we are seeing a more thorough working out of the kind of speculation offered on Robert Tolland's death in *TVOB*. There the off-hand, undeveloped presentation made such notions look wild. Here, too, there is still a strain on credibility, upon down-to-earth rationality. Can we swallow that someone may sense the death of a loved one, a previously loved one? On top, what do we make of a suggestion that some force might, unknown to her, draw a wife to where she will follow her husband into death?

Spelled out this sounds unhinged, an early sight of the strange transcendentalism which will figure in *HSH*. Fantasy? As we have seen, Powell himself might not care for this explanation, claiming in 'Taken from Life' (notable title), the *Twentieth Century* interview, that he aims at naturalism. The point about the coincidences in *TSA*, and elsewhere, is that they rarely strike the reader, even on a second or third trip through, as being wholly beyond the feasible. If we accept that Priscilla has been upset by hearing from Nicholas that Lovell is back in London the rest of the evening's events could – just about – follow. Powell is not generalising from these incidents: not suggesting that all who marry and drift away from each other are likely to be killed simultaneously by a tidy-minded Fate; nor that all women subconsciously feel their husband's death if they are apart, and involuntarily move towards matching it. If there is a generalisation it is one we have met before: that life can now and then produce fearfully balanced, related shocks. In serious fiction such surprises will be tolerable, effective, if they are not frequent; and if they are not obviously intended to give the novelist a leg-up over some plot difficulty, in the style of, say, Dickens or Forster. We cannot say either against *TSA*. What we do say is, Yes, this is at the limits of painful, symmetrical coincidence, but it could be, and particularly in war. Now and then life does hand out the old one-two.

We can see what Powell wants from these linked shocks. *TSA* continues the piffling, amusing, army intrigues first encountered in

TVOB: for perhaps three-quarters of *TSA* war has once again been reduced to barracks scheming about promotion and postings; career, not military, tactics. Powell needed a large and brusque reversal to show that this was not everything. He found it in a sudden darkening of the narrative, a double darkening, which brings the worrying implication that reason might not understand everything about the way life and people operate. It is interesting to notice how news of the Madrid bomb breaks. Frequently in *TSA* it is suggested that war is play-acting: when Nicholas buys a greatcoat the outfitter assumes it to be for a stage production, as if 'the soldier's art' were histrionics. We spot the theme again when Max Pilgrim, an entertainer whose act at the Madrid was interrupted by the bomb, reports to Nicholas that the café is finished. Does he mean his engagement or the season, asks Nicholas. Then Pilgrim describes the reality: wreckage and deaths. This bomb and its partner smash the surface, assert the tragedy of war, apply a formidable corrective to the nonsense and fret of the Mess.

In its way the appearance of Stringham as a Mess waiter in this book does much the same, perhaps going further. On the face of it his position could scarcely be more humiliating: forced to put up with the crude ill-temper of Biggs and Soper, two low-caste officers; posted eventually to the Mobile Laundry under the drunken liar, Bithel. And yet one feels not simply sympathy for Stringham but a suspicion that he may be right to eschew the Officers' Mess, except as a paid hand. In particular, we compare him with Widmerpool. Stringham, the reformed alcoholic, in one of the army's least glorious trades, unsmart and sick-looking, none the less comes over as preferable to the questing, infinitely formidable, infinitely trivial and scheming, commissioned Widmerpool. Power corrupts and the abnegation of power and status brings a strange, down-at-heel dignity. One hears echoes of 'leave all that thou hath'; or of Lear on the heath.

Of course, it is at points like this in *ADTTMOT* that one realises how immovably set are the novel's ratings of people; fixed, some of them, from *AQOU*, a kind of predestination. Superficially time has brought enormous changes in the situations of Stringham and Widmerpool. Stringham, who at school possessed a natural, social and material ascendancy over Widmerpool, now finds himself deeply subordinate. Powell stresses the extent of Stringham's fall by having the oafish Biggs mock his 'la-di-da voice' and question him derisively about the Ritz; Stringham adding to the effect by recalling a meal with the Duke of Connaught and the Bridgnorths. Yet, although Stringham has in one sense been degraded hugely by time's dance, in another, the more important, he has not moved at all. Regardless of the pips on Biggs's shoulder and the crown on Widmerpool's Stringham still radiates superiority. He does not need officer qualities; by nature or breeding he has something better. He lives above the insults and can view his position as a joke – 'I never dreamed I possessed such potentialities' – or put it out of his mind by reading Browning. True, he is not completely resigned and knows it: he will not go out to dinner with Nicholas for fear it might remind him of what life was like previously, 'spoil the rhythm'. But, immediately afterwards, in his melancholic, precise way he makes the claim which Powell is portraying in him: that he has achieved a kind of freedom: '. . . what I'm doing is what I've chosen to do. Even what I want to do, if it comes to that.' One certainly sees him as more happily placed than Widmerpool; perhaps than Nicholas, too. He makes the Officers' Mess look a comedown. We recall that below decks naval officers were known as pigs, long before the term was turned on the police. One recalls, also, Alastair Digby-Vane-Trumpington in *Put Out More Flags* who, when asked 'Don't you want to be a —— officer?' replies 'Not —— likely.' He and Stringham remind us that other values exist. Although one may – should – feel some unease that judgements about people based on public school acceptability are so consistently endorsed throughout life and a World War, there is an obvious sense in which Stringham's army career denies that background. He has emerged from almost everything he was taught, whether at home or school. All the assumptions about privilege and leadership have gone: what's bred in the bone can come out in the wash. Stringham stands apart from all packaged ethics, bowed but nothing like broken, by choice one of the mob, but wholly individual. This is more than Fiona Cutt's modish, and temporary, denial of her upbringing in *HSH*.

Out of these contrasts between surface and reality, trivia and real worth, which dictate the structure of *TSA*, Powell will develop an idea central to *ADTTMOT*. It, too, concerns Stringham, but Widmerpool more. Until now Widmerpool has been shown as a comical, ambitious social misfit, able to get on, and get on very well, through plod and his single-mindedness. He has lacked style, but not much more than that (though there is the report of treachery as a schoolboy in *AQOU*). During these later books, and starting with his decision in *TSA* to transfer Stringham to the Mobile Laundry, Widmerpool becomes something worse than pompous and ungainly; we move from awkwardness to malevolence.

Widmerpool feels uneasy at having Stringham in the Mess and arranges the transfer, though aware the Laundry may be shipped overseas, probably to the Far East. Stringham will die there. The moral questions involved are not especially easy to deal with. It would be pushing contingency very hard to blame Widmerpool for Stringham's death in a Japanese prisoner of war camp, which we learn about in *TK*. Jenkins is, though, outraged in *TSA* by Widmerpool's disregard for what might happen to Stringham because of the posting. Nicholas presents it as a grossly selfish abuse of power. One might object, I suppose, that mobile laundries have to be staffed and if it had not been Stringham it would have been somebody else. Is Nicholas suggesting that the old boy network should be employed to keep schoolmates out of the front line, even schoolmates who treated one with contempt?

Yet what Widmerpool does here is not simply fail to look after Stringham. He goes out of his way to have him shipped abroad, apparently to make his own situation more comfortable; in fact, since Widmerpool is himself posted shortly afterwards, even this self-interest proves irrelevant. Powell is showing how someone obsessed with advancement can develop from being a solemnly pushing bore – someone who offends against the surface regulations of life – to a ruthless, even vindictive, schemer. On the whole he makes of this in these later books of the sequence a credible, impressive case. Perhaps there is some slide into melodrama during *TK*; and it continues to stick in the throat that a schoolboy diagnosed as not quite right by a favoured group of cronies should duly turn out a frenetic villain. But the charting of Widmerpool's journey from those days when he sought self-improvement through solitary training runs to the time when he is ready to walk over or kick out of sight all who menace, embarrass or oppose him is so carefully set down that we are, I think, convinced. Widmerpool has willed himself into evil. He is that figure, traditionally harried by English literature, the overreacher. And it is in *TSA*, a book constantly occupied with showing the relationship between surface and depth, that we see his consistent selfishness and insensitivity turn into more than social ineptitude. 'He'll grow out of that rather unfortunate manner, of course', says Truscott in *ABM*. Instead, he grows into rottenness.

The Military Philosophers

By the end of this volume we can see that Powell has devised a special kind of war novel; the term, in fact, looks a bit gaudy for these three books: they have few affinities with *War and Peace* or *The Naked and the Dead*. They do cover the period and there are air raids; people discuss major battles and, out of sight, characters get killed. The books do not involve us in the feel of total war, though. True, in *TMP* we enter a larger world than that of the previous two volumes. When Nicholas crosses the Channel and meets members of his old unit, including Kedward, we are not too far from the actual fighting. And his liaison duties with the exiled officers takes us outside that very limited realm of bickering and jockeying which comprised most of the war in *TVOB* and *TSA*. Yet we do not quite reach the front line. There is a sense in which Nicholas's dealings with the foreign officers are simply the previous Mess rivalries internationalised.

In the chapter on style I have said something about the way action is treated or, rather, is generally skirted, in *ADTTMOT*, and cited the arrival of Nicholas and his party of foreign officers in France. If we look at how the writing is fashioned as the visitors cross into the Netherlands and approach the battle we can see more of Powell's intention. 'Armour was moving in a leisurely manner across this dull flat country, designed by Nature for a battle-field, over which armies had immemorially campaigned.' We are witnessing one of the war's most crucial and dramatic periods – the advance into Germany – yet the obvious aim is to dampen excitement, put a halter on pace: one feels that primarily in 'leisurely', 'dull', 'flat', of course. What is achieved becomes clearer if we substitute 'slowly' for 'in a leisurely manner'. There might then be some ominousness, some impression of dogged menace. Instead, Powell picks the easy-going word; one which needs a long-winded clause – one might say a leisurely, flat and dull clause – to operate adverbially: 'in a leisurely manner.' Then follows the fanciful 'designed by Nature for a battlefield', in case we have taken too solid and thrilling an image from even the abstraction 'armour' – doing duty for exactitudes like 'tanks' or 'armoured cars'. Finally: 'over which armies had immemorially campaigned.' This is war and we are faced with belligerent literacy: Tennyson is for ever in 'immemorial'; and, to switch poems, the labial play of 'armies had immemorially campaigned' unfurls like one of those hanging waves around the Lotos shore.

It is the age-old context of the fighting which interests Powell, not immediacy of present conflict. This is a re-enactment, to be not briskly and excitingly reported, but given a feel of timelessness and pattern through the rhythms of special prose. One suspects Powell might not be up to much as a war correspondent. A little later we are taken even further back. The troops of Nicholas's former unit, we hear, will 'move eastwards towards the urnfields of their Bronze Age home.' That is, these Celts are returning to the burial grounds of their ancestors in the sixth and seventh centuries B.C.. The cyclic note could hardly be stronger. Then at Tactical Headquarters the Field-Marshal (Montgomery, cursorily disguised: a brilliant portrait) gives the foreign officers and Nicholas a briefing with maps of the current situation. Nicholas, though, treats it as an exposition of the past: for him the place-names are significant not for their current importance but for what they suggest of history and literature. Zutphen recalls Sidney, who brings to mind de Vigny again. Maastricht was referred to by a Restoration poet. Rochester? Did the original D'Artagnan fall at Maastricht? Then Nicholas ponders Marlborough, is led on to remember remarks of Pamela to Odo, and ends with some general mulling on sex and war. Any urgency, any contemporary interest in the Field-Marshal's lecture, are kept from us.

TMP is probably more allusive, less concerned with the immediate, the obvious, the concrete than any other of Powell's books; and it is a calculated break from the normal requirements of this gentre that he should have chosen a 'war novel' to exercise such freedom. The digression about Proust at Cabourg is of a piece with the references to Sidney and Rochester; they all embody a determination to assert the liberty of the narrator's mind and the supremacy of what he thinks and feels over what he sees: a rejection of the tyranny of plot, locale, even incident. It is the emotions which count.

Similar rejections have been made by other novelists in this century. Joyce and Woolf gave the impulse. Nicholas's reactions to the Field-Marshal's address come as near to stream of consciousness writing as makes no difference. We meet more towards the end of *TMP*: it is the Victory Day Service at St Paul's, and Nicholas's mind strays again. Monuments set him thinking of their originals, then of Stendhal and Barham. Later, the words of the hymn and of the reading from Isaiah send him roaming further yet, into areas which have no connection with what started the day-dream going; his mental journeys now are more random than those at Tactical H.Q. Momentarily, for instance, we are with Borrit, the fruit and vegetable merchant, reminiscing about a Spanish honeymoon couple. And then, as the Service continues, come more literary reflections: about Blake, Cowley, Pope, Poe, followed by a memory of Jean. Certainly Nicholas directs an occasional thought towards the day's great symbolism. That is not the main preoccupation, though, nor anything like. The Service simply offers a prompt to Nicholas's unspoken soliloquy. Deflation could not be more emphatic; it is prose snubbing the big event, making its flight from pomp, circumstance and aura to what Nicholas regards as the worthwhile: a man's personality and memories; literature; friendship, feelings, love. He takes us with him.

But it would not do to represent *TMP* as an exercise in interior monologue. After all, at the Victory Service occurs a twist of storytelling which has affinities with a much older tradition of novel writing. Nicholas is asked to take charge of a South American officer, Colonel Flores, for the Service. Afterwards, walking away, he meets this officer again. Flores says he has a car parked some distance off and Nicholas accompanies him to it. The Colonel's wife and daughter are waiting there. His wife turns out to be Jean (née Templer) and the daughter, Polly Duport. Thus, another of those take-it-or-leave-it coincidences which Powell so much likes; a risk, at least at the limits of credibility, and perhaps over the edge. It is certainly not the sort of coup to interest an author concerned only with the free drift of characters' minds.

But somehow these modes go together very well in *TMP*. They each presume that Martin Seymour-Smith called in the *Spectator* review of *TSA* (16 September 1966) Powell's 'plotlessness'. First, the digressions, the mind-wandering, are acceptable because no narrative pace has been established, no atmospherics of grandeur, tension, excitement. We tend to ask not so much 'What happened next?' as 'What will Jenkins think of next?' Should he think, for instance, of Cowley – that is fair enough, as long as he can make it gripping. We are not rushing to a story climax, nor anxious to know the present fate of this or that character. As to the matter of gripping his reader, Powell does sometimes slacken his hold. The Cowley aside lacks magic and might be thought ostentatiously bookish (but Nicholas is a bit). For the most part, Nicholas does keep our attention. What it amounts to is that we are prepared to dawdle for a while along these by-ways because the books have been carefully built without narrative highways.

Then, turning to the second feature, the coincidences, I think they become acceptable here, as elsewhere in *ADTTMOT*, through their disarming purposelessness. This is not a novelist amassing unlikelihoods during the last instalments in order to tidy up matters pitched in for a thrill earlier. Nothing much comes of Nicholas's meeting with Jean: coincidence without intent. She and Nicholas meet, they talk, they part again. In those circumstances the reader does not protest, feels no unease; such meaningless chances do occur. It is the strength of Powell's novel that the form allows a marvellously rich mix of techniques by excluding one: narrative drive.

This may sound like an attempt to turn a lack into an asset, like praising someone with no dress sense for the range of garments worn. I do not think so. Narrative drive would not do. A narrator viewing retrospectively finds himself in a position where he will not be unduly impressed by single incidents, even incidents as big as the pursuit and defeat of the German army or the Victory Service. Nothing stands alone. Occasions regarded at the moment as epic may be given a mention then allocated their spot in the general scheme of things, that scheme having started in what we might call time immemorial. Chapters like these show the larger aspects of what Powell wants to say about time and the dance. It is not only a matter of people bobbing in and out of each other's lives, to a kind of rhythm. There exist, too, these links through history; pattern and recurrence on the grandest scale. It is not blindingly original to declare for pattern in history: how else to justify the study? What Powell gives is the sense of connections, large and small-scale, which establish themselves across time and distance, but especially time, and which make emphatic definition of passing events disproportionate; they are, after all, reruns of similar previous occurrences; Montgomery now, Marlborough then.

Incident is distanced. Frequently in these three war books – in fact, frequently throughout all of Powell's novels – we seem to be deliberately put in a position where we are hearing an account of action through a witness other than the narrator. We are at a remove, rather than seeing it direct. One might exaggerate and say that in Powell's novels action is what goes on somewhere else. We do see Bithel drunk or Widmerpool under the sugar shaker. Other matters, though – some of them important – will come through hearsay: in *TSA* we learn about the death of Chips, Priscilla and Molly Jeavons through Max Pilgrim and Eleanor Walpole-Wilson; Nicholas was out in *TKO* when Billson appeared naked; a good part of the most eventful material in *TK* is recounted after the events by Pamela, Moreland and Stevens, just as in *V* the shooting is related to Lushington, not seen by him; the main war activities take place far away. To a degree these are simply drawbacks of the narrative method. The story-teller cannot be everywhere: Nicholas is unable to be on location for Templer's doomed adventure and death, and for Stringham's suffering; in *V* the 'eye's' eyes must sometimes close in sleep. But there is more to it. Frequently action gets deliberately filtered. Powell seems almost as interested in the style of recounting as in the event: one feels this during Pilgrim's description of the Madrid bomb and during Moreland's and Stevens's differing versions of the Glober-Pamela-Polly imbroglio in *TK*. Powell regards incident as bare, dull and quickly over. Of course, one can say of all serious novelists that they concern themselves with the effects of incident on character, rather than with mere description of events. Few relegate action as ruthlessly as Powell, though. Always he aims to give first place to perspective, not drama. One has to say that this can produce prose which wallows, its sails limp. That never lasts long. Powell is always able to whistle up a wind.

Books Do Furnish a Room

There is a very interesting single word of dialogue in *BDFAR*. Jenkins and his brother-in-law, Roddy Cutts, the Conservative M.P., go back with Widmerpool to his flat from the House of Commons. During this visit Widmerpool will discover that Pamela has left him. As they enter, unaware that anything is wrong, Widmerpool glances around the room and notices that a picture is not in place. In mock irritation he says that Pamela frequently rearranges the pictures, and is particularly prone to move a drawing by an Italian whose name Widmerpool admits he can never recall. This picture, the one missing, was left to Pamela by her uncle, Charles Stringham, says Widmerpool. Someone suggests, correctly, the artist's name: 'Modigliani'.

This word is the entire line of dialogue and we are not told who spoke it: on the face of things, either Nicholas or Cutts could be responsible. Of the two, it is Cutts who has recently been identified as a speaker; by convention we would assume an unattributed line to be his. We all feel, though, that it is Jenkins who names the artist. Some readers may remember, of course, that Jenkins saw this drawing in Stringham's room during the drunk scene near the end of *TAW*. But not everyone who picks up *BDFAR* will have read *TAW*; and, to put it mildly, not everyone who has will recall the passing reference to the Modigliani: a twelve-volume *roman fleuve* bears some matters off to be lost and forgotten in the deep. (Auberon Waugh's *Spectator* review of *BDFAR* on 20 February 1971 alleged incomprehensibility because so much knowledge of earlier volumes was needed.)

Even without the pointer from *TAW*, though, a reader who has formed as much as an approximate idea of how Nicholas stands to Widmerpool will recognise why this line would come most probably from Jenkins. First, it is important that Widmerpool should be left behind by Nicholas on a matter of this sort. Widmerpool is philistine, we already know. Supremely able to organise his mind and will to cope with objects which may help his career, he cannot be bothered to give an artist elementary respect, and light-heartedly admits it. By this single word, Widmerpool the career-monger (by now Parliamentary Private Secretary to a Cabinet Minister) gets put in his place in a larger, more worthwhile system of values. The reader feels it, even if Widmerpool does not.

There is more. The picture came from Stringham and carries the suggestion that he, like Nicholas, was more enlightened than Widmerpool, even though apparently defeated by life; one hears an echo of *TSA*. Nicholas's one-word reply lines him up with Stringham's values, rather than with Widmerpool's, though it is true we could hardly be in much doubt on that. The picture has an emotional, even a sexual, significance. It was a bequest. Nicholas holds Widmerpool at least partly responsible for Stringham's death; and Widmerpool has now taken Pamela, who had been close – she suggests exceptionally close – to Stringham. To treat the picture as casually as Widmerpool does is to trample the affection between Pamela and Stringham and to make a little deeper the injuries which Widmerpool has already done him and his memory. We are entitled to feel reproach reaching to contempt in Nicholas's reply, along with some sadness; and the effect is intensified later when we find that Pamela has gone and, of all her belongings, took only the drawing and photographs of herself. Stringham, Pamela and Nicholas are shown to possess, or to have possessed, qualities wholly lacking in Widmerpool, qualities which this book prizes beyond anything else, which, indeed, all the books prize; genuine affections, sensitivity, love of the arts. Such a view spelled out could fall into romanticism and sanctimoniousness. Powell here accomplishes all he wishes with economy, and more or less imperceptibly wins the reader's accord. In *HSH* the Modigliani's symbolic function will be rather less subtly handled.

Pamela, we find in *BDFAR*, has gone to live with X. Trapnel, a very talented but indigent novelist. What draws her from the comfort and prestige of Widmerpool's life to a scruffy flat north of the Maida Vale canal? We are clearly to take this as a further declaration, more developed, in favour of the feelings, imagination, soul, against the mechanistic egotism of Widmerpool. This theme sounds throughout *BDFAR*.

With the Pamela-Trapnel affair Powell is in tricky country. To a degree we are being asked to admire the genius in his garret against the rich, powerful and pushing, a dog-eared romantic position. Trapnel has about him several standard qualities of the artist-hero in fiction: poor, he is none the less beguilingly spendthrift; sexually, he has formidable powers of attraction; and he talks with verve about the principles of his craft. Although the general run of things in the books is away from message and theme, Powell does seem intent on saying rather a good deal about men of imagination and artists in *BDFAR*; and, despite the terseness of the Modigliani episode, will say some of it with symbolism which becomes a little florid, a little unbalancing to the narrative. Keats is in a number of *ADTTMOT*'s artists: they carry a touch of doom and die young. Barnby is killed in the war. Maclintick commits suicide. Moreland will die in *TK* and shows signs of serious illness before. Trapnel is defeated, drops into hack-work and obscurity for about ten years and will also die, the circumstances more colourful than for Moreland. Maclintick and Trapnel are destroyed by women. It is true that Moreland and Barnby have a breezy aptitude for taking care of themselves, and especially Barnby; it would be wrong to suggest that a grim conspiracy exists to persecute the man of imagination and, or, creativity, or even ignore him: Moreland is made quite a fuss of socially; he and Barnby get commissions from Sir Magnus. With the death of Moreland in *TK*, though, one does feel, I think, that artistically gifted people are deeply vulnerable; it is the third-raters like St John Clarke and Deacon who reach old age (and, it must be said, Jenkins, though that is a condition of the narrative method). Deacon will also get a revival of his popularity in *HSH*.

This uniformity becomes worrying. So does Pamela's bearing on the subject in *BDFAR*. We have heard from Mrs Erdleigh in *TMP* of Pamela's supposed links with disaster and death. In *BDFAR* and *TK* her personality hardens grimly as we watch: some part of the Burton melancholy, which Nicholas is researching, crystallises in her. She becomes a malign vandal power which razes Trapnel's talent and morale. Audrey Maclintick, who brings about her husband's suicide, is obviously comparable, but does not go far beyond a tireless irritability and belligerent dissatisfaction. Pamela is far more. The Furies drive her. She makes a fiercely comprehensive attempt to annul Trapnel's flair: she both resents his work and thinks endlessly about it, implacably highlighting faults. And, as parts of the same operation, she will cast out Trapnel's major work, *Profiles in String*, and cast out Trapnel himself, a rejection from which he does not recover.

There are moments here when, in the attempt to project this sombre allegory about the artist, Powell's plotting grows uncertain, the overtones intrusive: one might believe that Pamela would throw

Trapnel's manuscript into the canal, but it is too palpably set up when Jenkins, Bagshaw and Trapnel find it floating there, on the way back from a night's drinking, despite all the explanations of how she might have schemed in that way. In fact, there is about the whole last quarter of *BDFAR* an over-coloured quality to the story-telling; one feels that the coincidences turn up not to represent the drifting, recurrent patterns of life, but to make a sensational and emphatically 'meaningful' read: Widmerpool's arrival at the Maida Vale flat while Nicholas is there with Trapnel and Pamela; the sword-play; the manuscript incident; then the astonishingly fortuitous meeting with Widmerpool again, while Pamela pursues her acquaintanceship with a schoolboy. The *TLS* review (19 February 1971) referred to a 're-alistic untidiness' as contrasted with the patterns of repetition in earlier volumes. The manipulation of plot towards the end of *BDFAR* makes this a generous judgement.

Powell is not to be held, though, altogether inside a thesis on the artist. After all, Pamela does leave Trapnel and return to Widmerpool. She has her own life and will break out from the tidy stockade required by symbolism. Although there is intensity in the relationship between her and Trapnel we see little happiness: he can do not much more for her than Widmerpool, and before the end she is with her schoolboy, while Trapnel sinks into misery. Both he and Widmerpool have been reduced by Pamela, in fact; they are comparably desolate when *BDFAR* closes. At this point, they seem to represent nothing, are men made unhappy by the same woman, that is all. All? It is a mark of sureness of touch in Powell; of a wish to portray the likely behaviour of people, rather than push themes too hard. For the same sort of reason, labels like 'man of will' and 'man of imagination' have their usefulness but tend to look inadequate now and then during these episodes; to lack precision. Who can say that Trapnel lacks will? He may sport some externals of the bohemian – beard, ornamental walking-stick, an affection for pubs and pub talk, the girls and his debts – yet is anything but slipshod about work: as Nicholas points out, a writer, good or bad, must be capable of organisation and, in his way, has considerable drive, perhaps as much as Widmerpool. Now and then, Powell will seem ready to push characters inside the confines of easily-understood generalisations. Their vitality will not allow them to stay long, though.

Temporary Kings

Reviewers of *TK* – and to a less extent *BDFAR* – commented on a darkening of tone as the sequence approached its end. As noticeable as this, though, is the move towards more emphatic plotting, already mentioned in the examination of *BDFAR*: towards violent confrontation and startling incident; towards, in fact, a kind of melodrama, often sombre. Examples from *TK* may be quickly given: Widmerpool is accused of spying and only just avoids going to jail; Pamela's French lover dies while she is in bed with him; she accuses Widmerpool, aloud and in public, of being a voyeur and of having watched her with the Frenchman; Glober strikes Widmerpool during a street row; Pamela – once again publicly and aloud – tells Polly Duport, protégée of Glober, daughter of Jean, about his habit of collecting pubic hair from women he has just possessed; Glober makes love to Mopsy Pontner on the dinner table, breaking liqueur glasses; Pamela is encountered naked in Bagshaw's house. In most books of *ADTTMOT* it would be hard to select narrational peaks. There are startling events, of course, but the method of presenting them seemed almost invariably chosen to lower excitement, lessen shock. In *TK* Powell appears much more concerned to net what most novelists want from careful plotting: impact, surprise, tension. It is true that some of these startling events, too, reach us indirectly: for instance, the account of Pamela's behaviour to Polly is given to Nicholas by Moreland and Odo Stevens; Glober's encounter with Mopsy is a very distant and roundabout flashback. But the general approach is much more straightforward, the story-telling considerably brisker, in *TK* than most of what has gone before. There are times here when we could be reading a conventionally plotted single volume novel. Powell might have been seeking a more popular market, creating a story able to stand pretty well on its own, reasonably self-contained. John Bayley in his *TLS* review of *HSH* (12 September 1975) found the plots of this book and *TK* 'particularly gripping, almost as

G

if the increasing popularity of the series had led its author to experiment, in his own inimitable fashion, with the commonest and indeed most hackneyed kind of modern fictional topic: dark goings-on, something nasty in the woodshed.' The suggestion here that Powell has turned to parody is interesting, but not the whole of the matter.

The diminishing requirements to suggest a distanced, leisurely viewpoint as we move towards the present makes sharp plotting more feasible; Powell may also have decided to make sure that his novel finishes strongly, vigorous with fresh invention and pace: the group of new, excitingly drawn figures like Glober, Gwinnett and Tokenhouse would also help. Clearly, though, most of the spectacular plotting is needed to accommodate Pamela. By the time we reach *TK* she has developed into a creature of such bizarre force that the narrative cannot allow her moments of self-effacement or passivity. If she is in a room we are kept aware of it. Extravagant individuality has become the very least that we expect from her; a detonation the norm. That circling, ruminative prose of the earlier books could not have coped with her.

Why, then, has she been drawn in this way? As I point out in discussion on other aspects of her life, she is exceptional to the books not simply in being so consistently and anarchically dynamic but in a far more basic matter; no other woman reaches anything like this level of character complexity. Most young women in the novel exist so that men may switch partners. Jean Templer could be regarded as more, but not much more. Gypsy and Audrey Maclintick are certainly no male playthings, but neither ever acquires the kind of dimensions that would enable her to control a prolonged scene; the same goes for Isobel. In his *NS&N* review of *TAW* (28 May 1955) Richard Lister said Powell's was 'exclusively a man's world', and thought it a correct representation of this social group. Perhaps. One does feel now and then, though, that Pamela has been created to compensate; as if, by way of making up for earlier part-drawn women we were now given a woman and a half, who needs a plot and a half, at least by the standards of what we have been used to.

She cannot, of course, take on a role as typical womanhood. Pamela has been growing with such monstrous inevitability since *TMP* that we accept her excesses as entirely right for her; she is a marvellous, basically sympathetic figure. But the blaze of her individuality consumes any chance that she might present a standard female viewpoint. Her links with normality seem so frail that, although she may fascinate and convince us, we do not feel ourselves to be watching a character made in the same fashion as Nicholas or Widmerpool or Umfraville but one designed, with great success, to startle everyone, especially the reader. There are still no women in ADTTMOT who behave in a style comparable with the men's: that is, who discuss, plan, intrigue, joke, speak about art, politics, literature, music and money. My feeling is that while Pamela remains substantially credible Powell does work her hard in TK, and her amassed exploits give the book a sensational quality. We have moved from the understated to the overwrought. Although TK's many remarkable events are treated with Powell's customary assurance and tact, in bulk they seem garish, touched with purple. One can just about believe the episode of voyeurism followed by the public upbraiding of Widmerpool. What gets hard to understand, though, is why he and Pamela stay together, she being uninterested in him or his status. They are together, perhaps, because as a pair they make, in both senses, memorable scenes: a good reason, but not good enough.

I would not want to suggest that Pamela exists only to make up for an earlier lack of positive women. She has her role as the irrepressible, crushing distraction which hinders the real artist; a crucial role given the theme of this book and of BDFAR. It may be significant that she is defeated in TK by Russell Gwinnett, a scholar hoping to write the life of Trapnel. Pamela meets him in Venice and is obviously attracted. Gwinnett, though, can handle her, is as tough as she is. She may grab his testicles in the basilica of St Mark's, but that will be as close as she comes to the castrating attack she made on Trapnel's personality. Gwinnett is an American, one of whose ancestors signed the Declaration of Independence, a point repeatedly made. Perhaps we are permitted to sense an implication or two here. Does Gwinnett embody a secure, formidable culture, some ancestry, some frank spirit of the new country? He is certainly not the Jamesian innocent in Europe; has no links with Cortney of V. Possibly, though, the main point about him is that he is not an artist: Pamela may give him trouble but he does not disintegrate like Trapnel; instead, he goes off and happily takes a job as a water-skiing coach in Spain. Pamela will be the one to grow distraught and die. Talent – perhaps genius – has a fragility which the sombre powers of Pamela find easy enough to smash. Gwinnett is made of more banal and more durable stuff, and may be better bred (Trapnel's father was a jockey). Gwinnett can stand up to this enemy of promise, Pamela, because he has no promise; Trapnel, though, is routed. One does not question the likelihood.

Together, then, *BDFAR* and *TK* say a great deal about creativity, literature and art. Much of this material is light-hearted; yet – even leaving aside the unambiguous pessimism of Trapnel's fall – we must detect some anxiety. Committed literature and painting have already been satirised in St John Clarke and Isbister. *BDFAR* and *TK* sharpen the attack, noticeably through some splendidly dismaying titles for articles in the magazine *Fission*, and for books handled by the Quiggin & Craggs company. There is *Affirmative Action and Negative Values* by Widmerpool and *Integral Foundations of a Fresh Approach to Art for the Masses*, by Len Pugsley. A novel is offered called *The Pistons of our Locomotives Sing the Songs of our Workers*, which Quiggin perceptively decides may be cumbersome; it is reduced to *Engine Melody* and the book earns the critical comment 'muted beauty'. Vernon Gainsborough, formerly Werner Guggenbühl, publishes *Bronstein: Marxist or Mystagogue?*, granted a favourable notice along with seven books on like subjects in a *TLS* major article. (Even when not lampooning heavy political works, Powell has delightful fun in devising genre titles: Trapnel's works *Camel Ride to the Tomb* and *Dogs Have No Uncles* bring a promising flavour of enigma and wilful oddity, almost in the class of *Books Do Furnish a Room*; Ada Leintwardine's three works *I Stopped at a Chemist*, *Bedsores* and *The Bitch Pack Meets on Wednesday* put her in a literary group which, if one does not quite recognise it, one can imagine.) Politics reach the titles of paintings, too. In *TK* we meet Tokenhouse, who has turned to art in his retirement and paints as a means of combating social injustice: one work is called *Three Priests Rigging a Miracle*.

In keeping with the political tone throughout *ADTTMOT* it is, of course, Leftist commitment which excites Powell's amusement and dread: one need not look in his debunking guide to post-war literary fashion for, say, the Tory, Roman Catholic ideology worked by Evelyn Waugh. Some title such as *The Candles in the Revisited Chapel Illumine Memorials to Gallant and Wellborn Recusant Families* might have given a useful completeness to the scene.

Powell knows his enemy. In *TK* he shows an attempt at politically-inspired prevention of literature – if we may stretch that Orwellian phrase to cover military memoirs – by Gypsy Jones, now a figure of sinister Marxist power, and a force in the Quiggin & Craggs firm. She has the manuscript copies of Odo Stevens's book, *Sad Majors*, 'liquidated' because it reflected badly on the Communist party. But although Stevens has become an unlikable figure in these later books, he is not altogether a fool and has hung on to a spare copy of the book. This appears later from another publisher and gets lucratively serialised. Writing and private enterprise will not be easily put down, we gather.

Powell does not hammer these political points; the blows are glancing. Dulness seems to bother him just as much. One of St John Clarke's ill-written novels is favoured by a film company instead of a life of Trapnel; and Sillery's disappointingly flat diaries produce a good critical reception all the same. What we learn from BDFAR and TK is that the bogus and ungifted may have their successes while the real artist sinks. Pope looked at the same phenomenon, as he did at Dulness. HSH restores some optimism, by hinting that Trapnel will be remembered; though, as if to counter that, Deacon's unprepossessing works grow popular.

There are, in fact, constant reservations. Odo triumphs. More important, merit does earn some recognition in TK. Gwinnett's regard for Trapnel rates higher in the reader's mind, naturally, than the success of St John Clarke's or Sillery's work; particularly since Nicholas also thinks very well of Trapnel as an artist. Although at the end of TK Gwinnett has suspended work on the critical biography of Trapnel we feel that this book will be completed. (It is and wins a prize). Nicholas is too self-effacing to say much about his own work, but I think that the reader deduces here and in HSH that his quiet, steady effort, uncorrupted, we take it, by political intent, is the way to produce genuine literature. I do not want to make the mistake of identifying Powell and Jenkins but, by the time he wrote TK, Powell may have felt confident that ADTTMOT could demonstrate through distinction of style, personal vision and stamina how lasting worth might be achieved. Oddly, TK itself indicates some wavering of those qualities, some move towards flashier plotting. It is the whole work though – the *Music of Time* – which comfortably proves Powell's point.

Art endures: is that the theme of TK? If so, we may see some glow of hope in a volume whose incident, humour and sex are often shadowed: Moreland dies; Pamela, Gwinnett and Glober are all death-obsessed and two of them will be dead before the end; love is poisoned; kingship is temporary. What will last? Is it significant that the book closes with a vintage car drive? Those handsome old vehicles might represent man-made artefacts which, as it were, keep going: comparatively up-to-date versions of Keats's Urn or Yeats's Golden Bird. But this is symbolism, so we had better tread gingerly.

Hearing Secret Harmonies

We leave Widmerpool as we first met him, out on a run; vain, grotesque effort the chief quality now as then. During those clumsy jogs in *AQOU* he was trying for an athletic competence that would never come, though as an exercise of will his dogged sorties showed the kind of toughness that would help him later. Complicated ironies tie his final ludicrous, tragic sprint in *HSH* with our sight of him as a schoolboy hopelessly training in *AQOU*. Now, he is elderly, sick, naked, a dropout who has dropped as far as he could. Under orders, Widmerpool is running with a group from the commune who, with his permission, have moved into his house, and who seem to provide all he now seeks in life. That could be more than mysticism, though. Delavacquerie, businessman, poet, critic, thinks Widmerpool spotted 'immense power possibilities in the cult'. This might be the sort of withdrawal from conventional politics meant to precede a coup come-back. Widmerpool as Hitler or de Gaulle? That ambition is presented as absurd. Often in the books Widmerpool achieves an aura of real menace, but never in *HSH*. Throughout this volume he appears mad, disintegrating, pitifully worked over by time. Collapse and death come as he strives for supremacy in self-abnegation, that spiritual pride known to the Church; 'self-indulgence not self-mortification' as Dorothea Brooke describes it in *Middlemarch*. Widmerpool will not slow down, on this run meant to reduce the ego. 'I'm leading, I'm leading now,' he cries, just before falling. Nobody, Widmerpool would say, can subjugate the will with as efficient and determined a will as I. That foolish, comic persistence of *AQOU* lingers.

After *HSH* there can be no doubt that *ADTTMOT* is primarily about Widmerpool. Simply, he is the only character of any sizeable previous development left alive. There had seemed – to me, I mean – a chance that as the period of the novel approached the present the retrospective and contemporary Nicholases might coalesce, as images can in trick photography, and become a rather more positive force; though, of course, he is elderly by the time we reach this volume, not altogether in shape to emerge as a vivacious hero. If anything, he is less personally involved in *HSH* than during any of the previous books. His reporting duties have grown weighty. One is aware of ends being dutifully tied: Bragadin dead; Gypsy dead; Shuckerly dead; Guggenbühl in a teaching job; Polly to remarry. Even if there were ever the intention, space is not available in this book to allow Nicholas to stretch his personality, and one should have realised it. The same goes for Isobel, though the book's first line of speech is delivered by her, and she is presented as if an established character. Umfraville and Flavia Wisebite (Stringham) do make beguiling appearances, and Matilda and Quiggin more than that.

The chief secret harmonies, though, are those sounded now and earlier in Widmerpool's life. Time leaves him with his yearning for eminence still powerful. In *HSH* there is, it is true, the anti-order speech, to countermand that famous career-monger's outpouring in *TAW*; there is the renunciation of Donners and his values (representing 'in his public life all that I most abhor'); there is the quaint alliance with Quiggin's student daughters; or an attempted alliance, at any rate, since they bring the super-anarchy of a stink bomb even to this anti-order declaration. There is, too, Widmerpool's lavishly contrite performance before Sir Bertram Akworth; the Akworth whose expulsion from school he caused by intercepting and disclosing to La Bas the homosexual note written to Templer. All truck, then, with the world's apparatus of authority, prestige and morals have gone ('so called right and wrong being illusory concepts', he tells Nicholas). He becomes a university chancellor, but one more sold on the student disregard for such office than they are themselves, and he resigns it fairly soon.

What has happened is that the intemperate ambition and drive which took Widmerpool through ten books and part of the eleventh (he finishes *TK* with clear indications of break-up) have changed to an intemperate rejection of all that made the world go round. This, though, is not a book about those standard ways of the world. We are meant to hear secret harmonies, not the open if subtle rhythms of the dance. This is a volume which says that perhaps Mrs Erdleigh, Dr Trelawney and the new figure, Scorpio Murtlock, have something. Is it this something which Widmerpool wants – the special, transcendental harmony preached by Murtlock's followers; or is the search for a power-base, as Delavacquerie maintains? Either way, in keeping with all we know about Widmerpool he insists that when dropping out his must be the biggest splash. He does not come up.

We are to make of Widmerpool at the end of *HSH* what we have made of him all through: he is a fool, knave and bore. He sought treasure on earth for the wrong reasons and now gives it up for the wrong reasons. So much in Powell is contradicted, half-contradicted, left in doubt that it would be foolish to enunciate with any pretence at certainly what the whole novel is 'about'. In a general way I have attempted something of that in the Introduction, perhaps, but with due tentativeness, I hope. Looking at Widmerpool in *HSH* I think one can say that his course through these books demonstrates that an absence of style, moderation, sense and imagination, coupled with devotion to will, egotism and materialistic push, will result in at least fatuousness, possibly disaster, probably evil; 'so called right and wrong' not being illusory concepts at all. The world has beaten Widmerpool and driven him towards bizarre supernature because the natural is too much for him; just as Giles, in a less flamboyant way, was driven towards contempt for ambition because his ambitions always came unstuck.

Having said that much, though, we must then go on to recall that life has defeated others, too: Templer, Trapnel, Pamela, possibly Stringham. We do not find a thesis here that the decent or talented or imaginative or emotionally questing shall inherit the earth. As a matter of fact, though, the meek do seem to do pretty well, if we may use that word about someone as tough in outlook, though not in action, as Nicholas. He stays faithful, sticks at his work, does not go wild on any creed. (Possibly it also helped to marry well.)

Matters are nowhere clear-cut. Although Widmerpool's conversion and subsequent behaviour may look phony, the book's title does seem to be an affirmation more than an irony. We are meant to take it, I think, that there are secret harmonies, beyond the more obvious beat of the music of time. This volume appears to give at least a nod towards that 'cranky' quality which Nicholas told us in *TMP* he found uncongenial in Blake; reason and reasonableness are at least a little under question in *HSH*. Murtlock is freakish but very formidable, far more sinister than either Mrs Erdleigh or Dr Trelawney. Despite the abominable sexual rites and general turn to oddballism and mumbo-jumbo, a worried respect for some of what he stands for has to be felt here and there. Perhaps all he stands for is charisma. Perhaps. Powell's attitude is not fully defined, and one would not expect it to be. Murtlock has a power, no doubt of that, yet it is frail. Although it can see off a challenge from Widmerpool, see off Widmerpool himself, it is not strong enough to hold either Fiona Cutts or Barnabas Henderson. What is more, Murtlock stands, finally, in opposition to that most consistently purveyed symbol of good in *ADTTMOT*, the Modigliani drawing, originally Stringham's, then Pamela's under Stringham's will, then Widmerpool's when she in turn dies. At the end of *HSH*, Bithel, still a drunk and now ancient, manages to save the drawing from a ritual bonfire of Widmerpool's possessions proposed by Murtlock. It is brought to Henderson, now running an art gallery, who may keep it, may sell it. Powell might conceivably have had Nicholas himself make an offer for it, and so commemorate or preserve, or in a sense, revive his connection with Stringham; a proclamation that friendship, style, art and love (Pamela's for Stringham, several times hinted at) will survive. That would have been strident. Proclamations are not Powell's manner. No, the Modigliani has to be saved by a character who has never been more than a wreck, Bithel, and who is now pretty near submerged – 'the nearest run thing you ever saw'. The Modigliani rests with someone who may regard it only as means to an easy profit. Another reservation is needed, too. We should not assume that good art alone will somehow keep alive. That might seem implied in the recovery of the drawing and in the success of Gwinnett's Trapnel biography, which ought to guarantee the dead novelist more recognition. But dubious work may not do too badly either. It is a delightful irony that Deacon's paintings – so often and so convincingly presented throughout the books as large-scale rubbish – should receive a revival of prestige. Henderson is as excited about 'discovering' Deacon as he is about the Modigliani. Likewise, Duport, never shown as much of a man of taste, finds that he has presciently collected Victorian marine painters, now elements in a seller's market and able to provide for his crippled old age.

Nevertheless, the Modigliani does tell us something. There is optimism in the fact that it has remained intact, only 'a little crumpled'. At this point, Murtlock has come to represent a philistine, destructive cultism; there is impressive power, but evilly impressive: we are, of course, put in mind of the Nazi burning of the books. Is this the future? Have the hopes of Leftism – always given a rough time in the novel, but at least granted a lot of space – now expired: Widmerpool dead, Gypsy, too, Quiggin bourgeois, even prissy, Guggenbühl a backslider from Trotskyism? Might Scorp Murtlock and his troops step into the gap, then? True, the Right goes on healthily enough. Sebastian Cutts has his morning-coat wedding and joins the Akworth family to the Cutts–Tolland dynasty. When the commune team invade this ceremony it is they, not the togged-up guests, who seem preposterous and of no lasting meaning. By now, the Cutts's daughter, Fiona, has left Murtlock's gang and made a kind of return to conventionality (though her marriage to Gwinnett, star of the cult orgies, is something less than an assertion that a nice upbringing is sure to bring out the best in a girl, finally) *HSH* proposes that, with the Left having failed, and established families offering only tolerance and blandness, a Murtlock might have little trouble getting somewhere. The idea is not new and is advanced with many reservations; with nothing as vulgarly precise or noisy as a warning. Yet I think it is one of the strong feelings we bring away from *HSH*, and from the whole novel.

And Nicholas? At the end he is working peaceably in his garden and, one assumes, continuing his writing (we hear of 'all those books' he has produced), without too much worry; without in this volume even very much irony. Quarry developments are afoot near his home and these stir a brief token movement of self-assertion in him, the rural conservation thing, but nothing frenetic. If we look to Nicholas to tell us anything at the end of this sequence it is this: keep calm, keep steady, keep individual – that above all. Hear the secret harmonies if you can; listen to the music of time and observe the dancers. That will do. Otherwise, we should cultivate our garden.

Further Reading

Walter Allen, *Tradition and Dream* (Dent, 1964)

Bernard Bergonzi, *Anthony Powell: Writers and their Work 144* (Longman, Green for the British Council and the National Book League, 1962)

Bernard Bergonzi, *The Situation of the Novel* (Macmillan, 1970)

Bernard Bergonzi (ed.), *The Twentieth Century: Sphere History of Literature in the English Language* (Sphere, 1970)

Anthony Burgess, *The Novel Now* (Faber, 1967)

Arthur Mizener, *The Sense of Life in the Modern Novel* (Boston University Press, 1964)

Robert K. Morris, *The Novels of Anthony Powell* (University of Pittsburgh Press, 1968)

John Russell, *Anthony Powell, A Quintet, Sextet and War* (Indiana University Press, 1970)

Martin Seymour-Smith, *Guide to Modern World Literature* (Wolfe, 1973)

Evelyn Waugh, *Diaries* (*Observer Magazine*, 25 March–13 May 1973)

Index